Child Maltreatment

Contemporary Issues in Research and Policy

Volume 8

Series Editors

Jill E. Korbin, Ph.D., Professor of Anthropology, Associate Dean, College of Arts and Sciences, Director, Schubert Center for Child Studies, Crawford Hall, 7th Floor, 10900 Euclid Avenue, Cleveland, OH 44106-7068, USA
jill.korbin@case.edu

Richard D. Krugman, MD, Distinguished Professor of Pediatrics, University of Colorado School of Medicine, 13123 E 16th Avenue Box B-390, Aurora, CO 80045, USA
richard.krugman@ucdenver.edu

This series provides a high-quality, cutting edge, and comprehensive source offering the current best knowledge on child maltreatment from multidisciplinary and multicultural perspectives. It consists of a core handbook that is followed by two or three edited volumes of original contributions per year. The core handbook will present a comprehensive view of the field. Each chapter will summarize current knowledge and suggest future directions in a specific area. It will also highlight controversial and contested issues in that area, thus moving the field forward. The handbook will be updated every five years. The edited volumes will focus on critical issues in the field from basic biology and neuroscience to practice and policy. Both the handbook and edited volumes will involve creative thinking about moving the field forward and will not be a recitation of past research. Both will also take multidisciplinary, multicultural and mixed methods approaches.

More information about this series at http://www.springer.com/series/8863

Lisa Merkel-Holguin • John D. Fluke
Richard D. Krugman
Editors

National Systems of Child Protection

Understanding the International Variability and Context for Developing Policy and Practice

Springer

Editors
Lisa Merkel-Holguin
University of Colorado School of Medicine
Aurora, CO, USA

John D. Fluke
University of Colorado School of Medicine
Aurora, CO, USA

Richard D. Krugman
University of Colorado School of Medicine
Aurora, CO, USA

ISSN 2211-9701 ISSN 2211-971X (electronic)
Child Maltreatment
ISBN 978-3-030-06644-4 ISBN 978-3-319-93348-1 (eBook)
https://doi.org/10.1007/978-3-319-93348-1

Softcover re-print of the Hardcover 1st edition 2019

Printed on acid-free paper

This Springer imprint is published by the registered company Springer International Publishing AG part of Springer Nature.
The registered company address is: Gewerbestrasse 11, 6330 Cham, Switzerland

Foreword: International Child Protection Systems

It was the best of times, it was the worst of times, it was the age of wisdom, it was the age of foolishness, it was the epoch of belief, it was the epoch of incredulity... [1]

The opening lines of the *Tale of Two Cities* by Charles Dickens seem an apt description for the state of children and child protection around the world. Child abuse and neglect are not recent inventions of humans; there is ample evidence for a long history of harm inflicted on children by their caregivers.[2] It is not a problem confined to one country, one people, or one continent.[3] Parental age and family income are intimately tied to rates of abusive punishment[4] and the highest rates of death and injury may be occurring in low- and middle-income countries.[5] Despite many thousands of years of human history, it has only been just since the 1800s that there were widespread organized efforts to prevent the harm of child labor and the organization of a medical specialty addressing the care of children occurred.[6] The rapid escalation in knowledge, service delivery systems, and public attention to child abuse around the globe since the seminal work by C. Henry Kempe and his colleagues[7] had been remarkable. Dr. Kempe himself led the organization of efforts to organize health and social service professionals in many countries to protect

---

[1] Dickens, C. *A tale of two cities*. 1859.

[2] Ten Bensel RW, Rheinberger MM, Radbill SX. Children in the world of violence: the roots of maltreatment. In Helfer M, Kempe R, Krugman R. *The battered child (5th ed)* Chicago: U Chicago Press 1997.

[3] Dubowitz H. Bornes N, Tummala P. (Eds.) *World Perspectives on child abuse.* (12the Edition) Denver: International Society for the Prevention of Child Abuse and Neglect, 2016.

[4] Runyan DK, Wattam C, Ikeda R, Hassan F, Ramiro L. Child abuse and neglect by parents and other caretakers. In Krug E, Dahlberg L, Mercy J, Zwi A, Lozano R. (eds) *World report on violence and health*. Geneva: World Health Organization. 2002.

[5] Krug E et al. (Eds) (2002). *World Report on Violence and Health.* Geneva, World Health Organization.

[6] DeMause L. *The history of childhood.* Philadelphia: Psychohistory Press 1974.

[7] Kempe CH, Silverman F, Steele B, Drouegmueller W, Silver H. *The battered child syndrome.* JAMA. 1962; 181:17–24.

children and championed an approach that involved reporting the children and organizing services for victim children (https://www.ispcan.org/who-we-are/history/).

Cultural and social factors in different countries shape how children are fed, disciplined, employed, educated, and raised. Culture is a society's "negotiable and negotiated template" guiding daily life.[8] These same factors shape a society's conceptualization of what children need and how they can be best be served by government and private child welfare agencies, community-based organizations, and the courts. The organization of services and public/governmental response in different countries on how to organize the response to and protection of abused and neglected children is the topic of this book. A lot has been accomplished in a remarkably short period of human history. Despite the recent dramatic documentation and call for action by the UN Secretary-General's *Report on Children and Violence*,[9] the historical record and data on child maltreatment epidemiology suggest that the world's children are safer in their own homes now than at any previous time in human history.[2,10] Systems of care have been established and interventions for the children and their families have been organized. In this volume we get to see how that was done in nine countries. These chapters will help us see how humans have reduced the burden of child abuse and neglect by overcoming foolishness, addressing beliefs, bypassing incredulity, and organizing coherent responses.

The Kempe Center
Aurora, CO, USA

Desmond K. Runyan

---

[8] Estroff SE, Henderson GE. "Social and cultural contributions to health, difference, and equality." In Henerderon G, Estroff S, Churchill L, King N, Oberlander J, Strauss R. *The Social Medicine Reader*, Volume 2 (2nd Edition) Durham NC: Duke University Press 2005.

[9] Pinheiro PS. *World report in violence against children.* Geneva : UNICEF 2006.

[10] Pinker S. *Enlightenment now.* New York: Penguin Random House 2018.

Preface

While the abuse and neglect of children has been observed in our societies for thousands of years, the effort to address it on national scales has only evolved over the past hundred years or so. Governments and a wide variety of nongovernmental organizations have been looking after the welfare of children for some time, but a focus specifically with the issue of the abuse and neglect of children is more recent.

Much of the literature on child abuse and neglect cites the work of C. Henry Kempe and his colleagues with their landmark paper, "The Battered Child Syndrome."[1] In fact, that paper and the work done by Henry and his colleagues in Denver in the decade following publication of that paper have led the child welfare field to develop multidisciplinary approaches to the treatment and prevention of the various forms of child abuse and neglect, evolving beyond problem recognition. It was clear to Kempe and the Denver team from the beginning that a multidisciplinary approach was necessary to accurately and comprehensively recognize an abused or neglected child. The disciplines, at a minimum, included professionals from medicine, social work, adult and child psychiatry and psychology, law enforcement, child welfare, and lawyers and judges in the civil and criminal courts. Getting all these professions to recognize that child abuse existed and that they had a role to play in protecting the child and treating the family was a huge task. Getting those same professions to work together on treatment and later prevention was even more daunting.

Many books have been written on the multidisciplinary approach, and there are dozens of different multidisciplinary teams that have specialized roles in hospitals, agencies, and communities.[2] In our years of observation, the closer the team works directly with the individual parent/caregiver, and extended family, the more effectively do those teams practice. In our experience, some health, mental health, child welfare, law enforcement, and court systems in county, regional, or provincial areas

[1] Kempe, C. H., et al. (1962). The battered-child syndrome. Journal of the American medical Association 181:17–24.

[2] The new child protection team handbook: Edited by Donald C. Bross, Richard D. Krugman, Marilyn R. Lenherr, Donna A. Rosenberg, and Barton D. Schmitt. Garland, New York, 1988.

collaborate well. However, in many others, these different systems do not work well together and may have quite different assumptions and policy frameworks for how the abuse and neglect of the child should be addressed. This lack of a cohesive process of agreeing on what the child protection policy should be at a community or jurisdictional level is a problem.

In the 1970s, many professionals came to Denver to learn how the Kempe teams did their work. They took these lessons back to their states and countries and began the conversations with their governments as to how best to address child maltreatment within their own societies. Now, decades later, child protection efforts are going on in most countries of the world, but none is identical to any other. In addition, the developmental paths of child protection systems have been quite varied and have been uniquely affected by local and national events, oftentimes shaped by the most egregious child maltreatment fatality cases that receive the attention of special commissions or the media. It seemed worthwhile to us that given the heterogeneity of approaches to child protection internationally, and the reality that none of these systems have comprehensive datasets to demonstrate their effectiveness on many child and family outcomes, inviting contributions from nine countries from four continents might offer useful information for those practitioners and policy makers overseeing child protection in their own country.

As one reads the chapters in this volume, there are a number of lessons that can be drawn, and a number of questions that professionals would want to know the answers to that cannot be answered anywhere. Among the similarities are that child welfare professionals have the responsibility for being "on point" or "on call" for cases of child abuse and neglect that are reported to whatever hotline or agency is appointed by the government to respond. In some countries, depending on an assessment of the severity of the information provided to the hotline, law enforcement may have a modest role or a large one during the initial phase of intervention. Some, but not all countries, have mandatory reporting laws or guidelines for professionals who work with children to report suspected cases. Countries vary widely as to whether the child protection agency is an arm of the national, provincial, state, county, or local municipality. In some places (e.g., the Netherlands) there has been a devolution from national government to regional centers to municipalities over a 30-year period. At the same time, other places (e.g., Australia) are moving toward centralizing services. These nation-specific approaches to child protection have evolved out of the prevailing culture and history of the population of the country.

In addition to geographically different approaches, there are also clearly culturally different approaches. Child abuse and neglect is viewed in some places as a symptom or warning sign of a family struggling with providing a safety and stable environment for their children. Across many countries, the reasons families are reported often relate to issues of poverty, substance misuse, domestic violence, and untreated mental health concerns. The governmental response to the presenting concerns is to try to decrease the safety and risk factors that may be affecting the parent/caregiver's ability to parent their children, without governmental oversight. Child abuse and neglect may also be viewed as an attack on the integrity of the child's right to normal growth and development, and the governmental approach is designed to achieve permanency for those children within their kinship network, through other foster care providers or via adoption. In reality, individual cases are not so neatly divided, and thus the approach (at least as conceptualized by Kempe and his team in the last century) has to be unique to the particular needs of the child and family being served.

Over the past two decades, there has been increasing recognition that adverse childhood experiences including child abuse and neglect, particularly in infancy and early childhood, significantly increase the likelihood of serious health and mental health conditions for the adolescent. If one accepts child abuse and neglect as being a unique problem, it suggests that without having a repository for accruing outcome data, the approach taken at a given time by a given agency acting on behalf of a given family may or may not be successful. As each of the chapters in this book reveal, the countries described have at best only begun to measure the quality of the services provided or the outcomes for the children and families served. Most have process measures, but none really knows whether the children and families they have been involved with are better or worse off months or years after the agency intervention. Further, in nearly all of the countries described, it is clear that much of child protection policy at a national level is driven by scandal, adverse events (usually a child death), or by budgetary constraints. That leaves the frontline workers, who for the most part do their best to work with difficult families with limited resources, in a very precarious situation that appears to demand an unrealistic standard of care.

One hopes that by the time the next look at International Child Protection systems happens, there will be an evolution everywhere to begin to recognize (as the Health Care System in the USA recognized in 1999) that "To Err is Human."[3]

Aurora, CA, USA

Lisa Merkel-Holguin
John D. Fluke
Richard D. Krugman

[3] To err is human: building a safer health system. Linda T Kohn; Janet Corrigan; Molla S Donaldson; Institute of Medicine (U.S.). Committee on Quality of Health Care in America. Washington, D.C.: National Academy Press 2000.

Contents

Contributors

Asher Ben-Arieh The Haruv Institute and the Paul Baerwald School of Social Work and Social Welfare, The Hebrew University of Jerusalem, Jerusalem, Israel

Nina Biehal University of York, York, UK

Flora Bolter Observatoire national de la protection de l'enfance (ONPE), Paris, France

Helen Bouma University of Groningen, Groningen, The Netherlands

Kenneth Burns University College Cork, Cork, Ireland

Tonino Esposito School of Social Work, University of Montreal, Montreal, QC, Canada

Barbara Fallon Factor-Inwentash Faculty of Social Work, University of Toronto, Toronto, ON, Canada

John D. Fluke Kempe Center for the Prevention and Treatment of Child Abuse and Neglect, Department of Pediatrics, University of Colorado School of Medicine, Aurora, CO, USA

Ruth Gottfried The David Yellin Academic College of Education, Jerusalem, Israel

Hans Grietens University of Groningen, Groningen, The Netherlands

Andreas Jud Child and Adolescent Psychiatry/Psychotherapy, University of Ulm, Ulm, Germany

School of Social Work, Lucerne University of Applied Sciences and Arts, Lucerne, Switzerland

Heinz Kindler German Youth Institute, Munich, Germany

Erik J. Knorth University of Groningen, Groningen, The Netherlands

Richard D. Krugman Kempe Center for the Prevention and Treatment of Child Abuse and Neglect, Department of Pediatrics, University of Colorado School of Medicine, Aurora, CO, USA

René Knüsel Observatory on Child Maltreatment, University of Lausanne, Lausanne, Switzerland

Bong Joo Lee Department of Social Welfare, Seoul National University, Seoul, South Korea

Mónica López López University of Groningen, Groningen, The Netherlands

Caroline McGregor National University of Ireland, Galway, Ireland

Lisa Merkel-Holguin Kempe Center for the Prevention and Treatment of Child Abuse and Neglect, Department of Pediatrics, University of Colorado School of Medicine, Aurora, CO, USA

Laura Sophia Miehlbradt German Youth Institute, Munich, Germany

Jennifer Nutton School of Social Work, McGill University, Montreal, QC, Canada

R. Kim Oates University of Sydney, Sydney, NSW, Australia

Valerie Rosser School of Social Work, McGill University, Montreal, QC, Canada

Eric van Santen German Youth Institute, Munich, Germany

Gilles Séraphin University of Paris, Nanterre, France

Nico Trocmé School of Social Work, McGill University, Montreal, QC, Canada

Susanne Witte German Youth Institute, Munich, Germany

Chapter 1
Introduction

John D. Fluke and Lisa Merkel-Holguin

The complex evolution of child welfare systems described for each country can be considered a reflection of their respective histories, economic development, and culture. While we focus in this introduction on the primary systems of protections embedded in social services, the addition of various law enforcement and judicial authorities creates a more complex layer for this picture that is detailed in each chapter.

1.1 System Organization

While it is difficult and complicated to generalize about the country level organizational approaches that are in use, it is possible to group each country into broad descriptive categories. For the countries included in this book the categories and the associated countries are shown in Table 1.1.

Organizational approaches for child protection approaches extend to several domains. These include: (1) laws or legal frameworks that set the source of authority for the system; (2) the specification of operational policy; (3) the resources and staff needed to provide services; (4) the ongoing physical and technology infrastructure needed to support, monitor, and evaluate the system's operations; and (5) managing interactions with other related governmental and non-governmental systems that have overlapping responsibilities. Thus, we would urge the reader to be cautious in applying the definitions we offer below:

J. D. Fluke (✉) · L. Merkel-Holguin
Kempe Center for the Prevention and Treatment of Child Abuse and Neglect, Department of Pediatrics, University of Colorado School of Medicine, Aurora, CO, USA
e-mail: john.fluke@ucdenver.edu; Lisa.merkel-holguin@ucdenver.edu

L. Merkel-Holguin et al. (eds.), *National Systems of Child Protection*, Child Maltreatment 8, https://doi.org/10.1007/978-3-319-93348-1_1

Table 1.1 Countries included by type of child protection system organization

	Centralized	Localized	Hybrid: Nationally centralized functions with localized services	Hybrid: Federal with centralization of provincial/state services	Hybrid: Federal with mixed centralization of provincial/state services or devolved to sub-jurisdictions
Australia				x	
Canada					x
England		x			
France			x		
Germany		x			
Ireland	x				
Israel		x			
Netherlands			x		
Republic of Korea			x		
Switzerland		x			

1.1.1 Category Definitions

Centralized: The domains of the organizational approach are the responsibility and are provided by a national governmental body.

Localized: While the laws or legal frameworks are often national, local sub-jurisdictions are responsible for all other organizational functions.

Hybrid: These are somewhat more complex organizational approaches that blend responsibility for organizational domains. For example, services may be provided by local social service authorities for lower risk referrals to child protection, but escalated situations involving greater risk and the potential of out of home placements may be the responsibility of a national entity.

1.1.2 Country Specific Organizational Approaches

Among chapters included in this volume Ireland is the sole nationally centralized organizational system represented. This is a recent development in as much as Ireland's Child and Family Agency (TUSLA) was created in early 2014 with authority for child protection services. There are other examples of countries with centralized systems, New Zealand for one. However, such systems, responsible for all aspects of child protection at a national level, may be rare.

In this volume the four countries representing localized systems are England, Germany, Israel, and Switzerland. In England while there is national oversight provided through law and policy as well as infrastructure such as information systems, the primary staffing, training, and funding, and all primary protective and judicial services are operationalized through local authorities. For Germany basic child protection functions are operationalized through 563 Jugendamt, although as the authors of that chapter point out, the system itself is much more complex. Nonetheless, the German approach appears to rely on local capacity for services to the extent possible. Similarly, in Israel there are 270 local social service departments supervised by the Service for Children and Youth within the Israeli Ministry of Labor, Social Affairs and Social Services, the central government authority for child welfare. The Service for Children and Youth is responsible for policymaking, interventions, credentialing, and other infrastructure. Finally, locally-based Child Protection Authorities (CPA) typically at the cantonal level in Switzerland are responsible, based on national legislation, for protecting children through their ability to deputize a social service professional to oversee services. However, the local services agency may or may not be specialized to address child protection.

The last category, hybrid systems, are represented by six of the twelve countries in this volume. Of these, four fit into the sub-category nationally centralized functions with localized services. While French law creates the framework for the policies that the 100 local departments follow to provide most services for families whose children are at risk, under circumstances where children are at great risk, the national operated court system intervenes. This is similar to the system in the Netherlands, where services are most often provided to families by local agencies operated by municipalities. However, for the cases that may require more intrusive interventions, the national Child Care and Protection Board in the Netherlands is the authority responsible for overseeing interventions such as out-of-home placement. Finally, in South Korea, there is a strong national authority that oversees many of the most severe cases with a focus on punitive actions with respect to perpetrators, but for less severe situations services are often provided by private non-governmental agencies. The remaining two countries, Australia and Canada are characterized by federalized services where States (Australia), Provinces (Canada), or Territories (Australia and Canada) are the primary authorities that provide oversight for child protection and where the national role is quite limited. In these two countries, the range of systems includes centralized systems operated at the State or Provincial level to localized systems where local agencies are responsible for all aspects of the services and where the provincial or state government provides policy oversight. Australia appears to be moving toward a nationally centralized system where the national government is assuming more authority for aspects of the system.

Several countries have undergone recent shifts in their overall approach to organizing their systems; notably Australia, Ireland, Netherlands, and South Korea. With the exception of the Netherlands, most of these shifts have been in the direction of centralizing more authority for various, if not all functions, at the national level. At this point is not possible to evaluate whether these shifts will result in improvements in the capacity to protect children and, more importantly, improvements in the outcomes for children and families. Given a relatively nascent global understanding of the effects of child protection policy at national levels, it may be some decades before we are in a position to compare the evidence regarding the relative effectiveness of policy across countries.

1.2 Orientation of Child Protection Systems

Perhaps related to the different organizational approaches to child protection, the philosophical orientation of child protection systems across countries also seems to vary considerably. On a continuum of child safety to family support (Gilbert 2012), among the countries described, this orientation impacts the nature and array of services. Such services include the assessment and investigation processes, the type and level of services available to children and/or parents and/or other family members, the involvement of children and families in decision making about their own lives, the availability of preventive and early intervention services, and how systems approach the placement of children when they can no longer live safely with their parents, caregivers or guardians.

In this collection, South Korea may be the best example of a child safety oriented system with a retributive orientation to punishing perpetrators who are most likely parents. As such, the author describes a lack of emphasis and sufficient resources for family preservation and family reunification services. Canada and England also are more closely aligned with a child safety framework with some, but internally varied, emphasis on family support. This is borne out in the low rates of placement of children in formal kinship care in England, although the rates are rising given the greater stability of such placements. Israel also focuses on services to the child, not the family system, which impacts the likelihood of reunification. While there is a recommendation that the Israeli child protection systems increase the voice and involvement of the child and family, a recent evaluation showed this to be a rare occurrence. Moving toward family support, Ireland and Germany are illustrative. Ireland has an increased emphasis on prevention, early intervention and family support, and has adopted various practice models and approaches that embody that emphasis. Germany's child protection system has a current emphasis on family support measures, and is conceptualized as a system to provide supports to, and collaborate with, families.

1.3 Workforce

While organizational approaches and orientations direct and guide the operations of child protection systems, it is the child protection and child welfare workforce who implements the associated practices, policies and regulations. Ireland's stable child protection workforce, with high retention rates, may be worthy of additional study, given the burgeoning rates of turnover in child welfare systems internationally that can cripple operations and servicing of children and families. A number of factors may contribute to Ireland's success in workforce retention, including the professionalization of the role, excellent benefits, and that the workforce views the child protection and welfare role as meaningful and stimulating, with high levels of autonomy and peer support. Another interesting development in Ireland is the establishment of Meitheal, a preventive service to decrease the likelihood that families are referred to child protection and welfare services. Relationship with the family, and not the discipline of the lead practitioner, serves as the basis for matching families with service providers. England has a renewed focus on skilled social work with families, which is hampered by what is described as excessive bureaucracy and centralized systems that decrease professionals' use of judgment. Germany and Switzerland also stress the professional discretion of social workers in decision making, and there is some effort to ensure that the social work profession is viewed as necessary and important. South Korea and Israel documented high caseloads as a growing concern that impact the child protection worker's ability to perform their job functions. Other challenges include concerns over the safety of child protection workers and the insufficient public resources that challenge even the most proficient workers to meet families' needs.

1.4 Challenges Ahead

Child protection and child welfare systems are complex entities that have committed professionals working for the safety, permanency and well-being of children and, in some countries cases, the well-being of their families. Societal phenomena, including increases in the rates of substance misuse, domestic violence, homelessness, and minimally treated mental health concerns, coupled with some governments' decreased emphasis on family poverty programs, family support services and early intervention programs, makes the work of child protection systems and their professionals, even more complicated but necessary. Emerging issues of sex trafficking and children in migration is even further confounding child protection systems. The convergence of these factors is creating a growing demand for child protection services.

Reference

Gilbert, N. (2012). A comparative study of child welfare systems: Abstract orientations and concrete results. *Children and Youth Services Review, 34*(3), 532–536. https://doi.org/10.1016/j.childyouth.2011.10.014.

Chapter 2
Child Protection Systems in Australia

Kim Oates

2.1 Introduction

In Australia, as in other countries, we know that most child abuse is never reported, only coming to light during population or community retrospective surveys. These types of studies in Australia show that 5%–9% of the population was physically abused during childhood (Australian Bureau of Statistics, 2006). For child sexual abuse, including non-penetrative forms, the prevalence is 12% for males and 23% for females (Najman et al. 2005). Neglect and emotional abuse are estimated to occur in 12% and 11% of Australian children, respectively (Child Family Community Australia 2013). These are massive public health problems (Oates 2014).

2.1.1 *Some Relevant Facts About Australia*

In terms of land area, Australia is the 6th largest nation and the world's largest island. However, its population is relatively sparse with a population of just under 25 million, 2.5% being indigenous and one quarter comprising migrants from over 200 countries. It has a high growth, low inflation economy and has been recession-free for 25 years.

In 1901, the Commonwealth of Australia was established, comprising six states and two territories. Child protection was a state responsibility, meaning that each state and territory has its own response to child protection. This has resulted in lack of uniformity of legislation so that services in each state need to be considered separately.

K. Oates (✉)
University of Sydney, Sydney, NSW, Australia
e-mail: kim.oates@sydney.edu.au

L. Merkel-Holguin et al. (eds.), *National Systems of Child Protection*,
Child Maltreatment 8, https://doi.org/10.1007/978-3-319-93348-1_2

Australia adopted the British Westminster model as the basis of government. Additionally, the relationships between the national and state governments are similar to that of the United States with states having control of some areas, such as education and child welfare and the national government controlling areas such as defence and welfare payments.

The GDP per capita is $US 45 K compared with an OECD average of $US37K. However the gap between rich and poor is widening, not as wide as in the UK or the USA, but inequality has now crept over the OECD average. Australia has universal health coverage, with 2015 health expenditure at 8.9% of GDP, the OECD average being similar.

2.1.2 Childhood in Colonial Australia: Early Services to Protect Children

For over 50,000 years Australia was populated by its indigenous population, the original owners of the land. Things changed in 1788 when the First Fleet arrived from England to establish a British penal colony. It comprised 11 ships carrying 759 male and female convicts and their marine guards. This followed the American War of Independence, resulting in Britain no longer being able to send its convicts to America. Britain chose Australia as the replacement penal colony. Canada had refused to accept convicts at that time.

Australia's first European children comprised the 22 born on the long voyage from England as well as some child convicts, the youngest being an 11-year old chimney sweep who had been imprisoned in England when he was eight.

Life was difficult for all of the new arrivals, particularly the children. The climate was harsh, farming was difficult compared with England, the marines and convicts had few farming skills and the lack of understanding of the culture of the aboriginal population often led to conflict. Exposure of the Aboriginal people to new diseases decimated their population, including their children.

There was no concept of children's services or children's right in the new colony. The first priority was survival.

The children of convicts were regarded as the responsibility of the British government, but the number of children was small and little official attention was paid to their plight. As the colony grew, children without parents or guardians were put into orphanages, or into asylums along with destitute adults. Some were even put in prison, sentenced for being vagrants.

The first child welfare legislation, introduced in the 1850s was designed to remove children from these environments. As a means of achieving this, the child would be charged by a magistrate with being neglected and then committed to an institution, such as a reform school until they the age of 18. The concept was not one of protecting children from harm; rather it was to protect the state from the danger thought to be posed by destitute children. These children were thought to require control, rather than care.

By the late 1880s, influenced by the child rescue movement in Britain, the focus became protection of children from neglectful parents or guardians. Societies for the Prevention of Cruelty to Children were established in the 1890s. They were modelled on the British NSPCC (National Society for the Prevention of Cruelty to Children) with emphasis on reporting and investigating neglect and abuse.

2.2 Early Australian Literature on Child Protection

There has always been child abuse in Australia, based on retrospectives surveys and the confidence older victims were given to speak of their past as the topic ceased to be a taboo. However, it was not until the 1960s that recognition and awareness developed.

Not long after "The Battered-Child Syndrome" was published (Kempe et al. 1962), similar publications came from Australia. In 1965, Wurfel and Maxwell published their findings of 26 cases of child abuse seen at the Adelaide Children's hospital. The next year, a report was published on the medical and police records of children and babies admitted over a 20-month period to a transit centre to accommodate children where there had been family or foster care breakdown. Two hundred and eighty nine cases of neglect were described, with the babies having poor health and delayed development (Bialestock 1966). The Birrell brothers, one a police surgeon and the other a paediatrician, documented a series of maltreated children, seen in the state of Victoria, who had presented with unexplained fractures and other non-accidental injuries (Birrell and Birrell 1966, 1968). Failure to thrive where there was no organic cause was documented in 1971, showing a profile in these infants and their families dominated by both emotional and material deprivation (Oates and Yu 1971).

These early papers, led to media and public attention, resulting in pressure on state governments to become aware of this problem and to commit to greater responsibility to prevent abuse and neglect.

2.2.1 Mandatory Reporting

In the 1970s, following the influence of the USA, and concerted lobbying by a small number of pediatricians, mandatory reporting laws were introduced in most states of Australia. However, they are far from uniform and were phased in over 40 years, starting with the state of South Australia in 1969, followed by the other states; Tasmania in 1974, New South Wales (NSW) 1977, Queensland 1980, Victoria 1993, and the most recent, Western Australia in 2009. Of the two territories, the Australian

Capital Territory introduced legislation in 1997 while the Northern Territory introduced mandatory notification in 2007.

However, this summary of dates does not explain the evolving process in legislative development nor does it indicate the significant differences between the States and Territories (Mathews 2014).

Over the years the relevant legislative Acts have been revised, with addition of new mandatory reporters, harsher penalties in some cases and the addition of sexual abuse, particularly in those states that were early to introduce legislation at a time when sexual abuse of children was barely recognised.

What the different laws have in common is confidentiality and immunity from legal liability as long as the report is made in good faith. Also in common is that reporting is obligatory, rather than discretionary. In all state and territory legislation the mandated reporter is obliged to report if concerned "on reasonable grounds" that the child has been abused or is at significant risk of abuse. As well as the four classical types of abuse (physical, sexual, emotional and abuse), Tasmania, NSW and the Northern Territory also require exposure of children to domestic violence to be reported.

Although the groups required to report differ between the states and territories, they generally now include members of four occupations who work regularly with children; teachers, doctors, police and nurses. Some states include dentists. Only South Australia includes members of the clergy, although this does not apply to suspicions about abuse revealed in the confessional. Other states have added to the groups required to report as the extent of abuse became better known e.g. in NSW teachers were only added once the extent of sexual abuse became known.

As well as mandated reporters, any citizen may make a report and as long as it is in good faith, the reporter is protected under the same legislation as mandated reporters. Only the Northern Territory has made all citizens mandated reporters.

As ordinary citizens make a large proportion of all reports they need to be aware through media and other sources of their responsibility.

In Australia, mandatory reporting is regarded as a strategy that measures and acknowledges the prevalence and seriousness of abuse, reinforces the moral responsibility of community members to report concerns and helps create a culture that will not tolerate abuse of children. It can also be used to provide services as once mandatory reporting is introduced, services must be provided to respond to those reports. It can facilitate early detection of abuse, or risk of abuse, that may not otherwise have been noticed.

As long as the introduction of mandatory reporting is accompanied by training (not always the case in the Australian states that led the way in mandatory reporting), it has the effect of making professionals more aware of child abuse and creates conditions to enable them to report.

Perhaps most importantly, mandatory reporting has sent a clear signal from governments that child abuse is a serious matter that governments need to be involved by creating a culture that will not tolerate abuse or neglect of children and that all community members have a moral duty to report suspected cases.

Of course there is no universal agreement in Australia or internationally about the benefits and the harms of mandatory reporting. However, as has been found in other countries, there has been a concern that the large number of reports that follow legislation can result in services being overwhelmed and not having sufficient staff to respond. (Child Family Community Australia 2016). At times this has led to changing definitions of what has to be reported to achieve lower reported numbers in the hope that the system will cope. Quite apart from the questionable nature of such initiatives, this makes it difficult to accurately compare reporting figures over time.

Because child protection is a child and family welfare, or a police, responsibility and because police and welfare are state agencies, Australia does not have uniform legislation. This may make it difficult for exchange of information about offenders who move between states. If they are known offenders and are on a state's register, this information may not be immediately available to authorities in a different state.

As well as the state and territory laws, there is a Commonwealth, national reporting requirement that mandates personnel from the Family Court of Australia to report suspected abuse. This includes federal magistrates, family consultants, family dispute resolution practitioners or arbitrators and lawyers independently representing children's interests. The legislation states that when in the course of performing their duties or exercising their powers, they have reasonable grounds for suspecting that a child has been abused or is at risk of being abused, the person must, as soon as practicable, notify a child welfare authority.

To look at the impact of mandatory reporting of child sexual abuse legislated in Western Australia, Mathews et al. (2016) analysed data about numbers of cases reported and outcomes of reports for a period before 2006–2008 and after 2009–2012, mandatory reporting having been legislated in 2009. Perhaps not surprisingly, they found that the number of reports by the three mandated reporter groups (police, doctors and school personnel) increased almost fourfold. More importantly, the number of reports that were investigated increased by a factor of three and the number of officially substantiated reports doubled. The authors found that in the first 2 years following the legislation, the proportion of reports investigated declined, suggesting that the size of the increase in reports had not been anticipated. However, the proportion investigated subsequently increased to the pre-legislation proportion, suggested that the system had adapted and responded to the increased numbers. Currently, 46% of 304,097 of notifications in 2013–2014 were investigated, less than the 57% in 2009–2010 when total notifications were lower at 286,437. The decision as to whether or not to investigate is generally made by an experienced case worker, based on information received, with cases suggesting concern or risk of physical harm or sexual assault going to a full investigation. Less concerning cases are often referred to community agencies, usually from the voluntary sector. This screening process is an imperfect one with potential to miss serious cases based on inadequate information.

While there continues to be some concern in Australia that mandatory reporting overburdens an already busy system, a study by Segal (2015) found that in relation to identified cases, Australian mandatory reporting laws do not produce excessive rates of reports and investigations. It is the view of this chapter's author that, without the introduction of mandatory reporting, we would have much smaller child welfare services and many children would have gone unprotected. The experience documented in the above study from Western Australia is similar to the anecdotal evidence from all other states; mandatory reporting legislation is introduced, a surge occurs in reports and in response to that surge, services to educate the public and investigate reports are increased. For example, when mandatory reporting was introduced in NSW in 1997, extra staff were employed and training courses in recognition and management became more widespread. This in itself could be regarded a compelling argument for mandatory reporting.

2.3 National Reporting Figures

2.3.1 Background

Since 1990, the Australian Institute of Health and Welfare has compiled annual national figures for child protection reports. As definitions of what constitutes abuse and neglect vary across the different states and territories, and may be changed over time, it has been difficult to obtain consistent, comparable figures. Consequently, a Child Protection national Minimum Data Set (CPNMDS) has been developed. Since 2013 the CPNMDS has replaced aggregated data from the states and territories allowing better data analysis. However, Queensland and NSW still supply aggregate data. For example, NSW has a two-stage investigation response where only the more serious cases lead to a recorded substantiation. Despite this structure, data collection overall is of much better quality than previously, giving a more accurate picture of child abuse reports in Australia. When interpreting the national figures, it should be noted that there are different legislation, policies and procedures in each state and territory, as well as variations in mandatory reporting requirements and substantiation thresholds. Thus national data, while of more use than previously still need to be interpreted with caution. In addition, not all children included in these statistics will have been maltreated as child protection authorities are required to intervene if a child has been, or is currently at risk of being harmed, meaning that a proportion of the statistics will include children who have not been harmed but who are at risk of harm (Child Family Community Australia 2015a).

2.3.2 National Reporting Figures 2013–2014

The most recent national figures indicate that during 2013–14 there were 304,097 notifications (a rate of 37.8 notifications per 1000 children). This represents an 11.4% increase in notifications compared with the previous year. As a result of these notifications (where the same child or family may have been notified by more than one source) 198,966 Australian children suspected of being harmed or at risk of harm from abuse and/or neglect. Finalised investigations occurred in 137, 585 cases (69%) with 54,438 (40%) of these finalised cases being substantiated. These 54,438 substantiations involved 40, 844 children. (Child Family Community Australia, 2015a) During the period 2013–2014, the total number of substantiations increased nationally by 1.4%, much less than in the previous year when there had been a 10% increase in substantiations.

The Australian data does not record "false allegations" (perhaps more accurately called "erroneous concerns" by Oates et al. 2000) in cases of sexual assault, although a review of over 500 notifications investigated in the USA showed that this is a relatively small number, comprising 2.5% of child sexual abuse reports with only 1% being false allegations made by the child (Oates et al. 2000).

Child abuse notifications that are thought to be of less risk and so not investigated are often referred to other helping agencies (including charitable organisations) where practical support or the provision of advice to the family can be given. However, this involves a quick assessment being made based on the initial notification, with the possibility that at times potentially serious cases go un-investigated.

The Australian Institute of Health and Welfare uses the following definitions:

Emotional abuse: as any act that results in a child suffering significant emotional deprivation or trauma. Children who witness domestic violence are now categorised as having experienced emotional abuse. This is probably one of the main reasons for the high proportion of substantiations of emotional abuse in the national figures.

Neglect: the failure to provide for a child's basic needs, including failure to provide adequate food, shelter, clothing, supervision hygiene and medical attention. Poverty is not a major problem in Australia, although it is a significant one, raising the importance of awareness that poverty and neglect is not the same thing.

Physical abuse: any non-accidental physical act inflicted upon a child by a person having the care of a child.

Sexual abuse: any act by a person having the care of a child that exposes the child to, or involves the child in, sexual processes beyond his or her understanding or contrary to accepted community standards.

2.3.3 The Most Common Types of Substantiated Reports

Of the types of maltreatment reported in 2013–2014, the largest category amongst the 54,438 children with substantiated reports was emotional abuse (40%), followed by neglect (27%), physical abuse (19%) and sexual abuse (14%). As in other countries around the world and confirmed by retrospective studies where adults have been asked about their childhood experiences, it is recognised that the majority of cases of child abuse, particularly sexual abuse are never reported.

Although reporting legislation varies across the States, in general, the terminology of notification, investigation and substantiation are defined as:

Notification: An allegation of child abuse, neglect, child maltreatment or harm to a child.
Investigation: Notifications are assessed to determine whether an investigation is required. If an investigation is not required, a notification may be referred to one of several support services.
Substantiation: A substantiation indicates that there was sufficient reason after an investigation to believe the child has been abused, neglected or is in danger of harm.

There is over-representation of indigenous children in substantiation rates. The rate for non-indigenous children is 5.7/1000 children compared with 45.3/1000 indigenous children. This is a major problem for Australia. The possible reasons and the complexity of this issue are discussed below.

2.3.4 *Characteristics of Children Who Are the Subject of Substantiated Reports*

Nationally, girls (18%) were almost twice as likely as boys (10%) to be the subject of a sexual abuse substantiation, although this varied considerably across the nation, being up to 28% for girls in Western Australia. Boys were more likely to be the subject of a substantiation for the other three reportable categories: physical abuse, emotional abuse and neglect.

The rate of substantiation decreases as the age of the child increases. Children under 1 year are more likely to be the subject of a substantiation at 14.7/1000 children, followed by children aged 1–4 years at 8.4 per 1000 children with children aged 15–17 years being the least likely (3.5 substantiations per 1000 children).

2.3.5 *Children in Out of Home-Care*

In some cases children who have been harmed or who are thought to be at serious risk of serious harm are removed from the care of their parents and placed in out of home care (OOHC). This type of care may be provided by government agencies, volunteer organisations, and foster parents or may be kinship care, something which is particularly important for indigenous families.

OOHC may be:

Residential care, where paid staff care for a number of children; in a family group home that has live-in, non-salaried carers who are reimbursed or subsidised for providing care;
Home based (foster) care, in the home of a carer who is reimbursed for expenses related to the care of the child. Sometimes this is kinship care, a factor of particular importance to indigenous families. Ninety three per cent of OOHC occurs in home based care;
Independent living, this may be appropriate for older children and may involve private board.
Depending on the circumstances and availability of resources other placements can involve boarding schools, hospital and hotels or motels.

The number of children living in OOHC has risen each year from 2010 to 2014 and is now 20% higher than in 2010. In 2014, 43,009 children were in OOHC, a rate of 8.1 per 1000 children. This figure is influenced by the fact that the rate of OOHC for Aboriginal and Torres Strait Islander children in 51/1000 children, ten times higher than the rate for other children.

Over time, the children admitted to OOHC are becoming increasingly younger and are remaining in care for longer. It is not surprising that the younger age group predominates in OOHC as this is the most vulnerable age group, particularly to the effects of physical abuse and neglect. In 2013–2014 the median age of admission was 6 years with 44% of children placed in OOHC being under 5 years of age.

2.4 Abuse Suffered by Aboriginal Children

Aboriginal and Torres Strait Islanders comprise 2.5% of the Australian population. The history of relations between white settlers and Australia's original inhabitants has been a troubled one, often leading to community breakdown, a paternalistic approach and loss of culture.

It was only in 1967 that legislation was passed to include all indigenous Australians in the official estimates of the Australian population and not until 1992 that Australian courts overturned the concept of Terra Nullius (that the aborigines were too primitive to actually be owners of the land), accepting that the land had been continuously owned and populated for over 50,000 years, the world's longest continuous living culture.

Aboriginal children are over-represented in substantiated reports of children at risk. For example, in NSW the rate of substantiated reports of aboriginal children in 2013–4 was 51 cases per 1000, compared with 6.5 cases per 1000 for non-indigenous children, a ratio of almost 8:1. More startling is Western Australia, where the ratio of indigenous substantiated reports (29/1000 children) is 13 times higher than for non-indigenous children (5.2/1000 children) (Child Family Community Australia 2015b).

At first glance, this would simply suggest that something is wrong with parenting in these communities. But such a simplistic view ignores the complex underlying reasons. Between 1910 and 1970, over 100,000 aboriginal children were forcibly taken from their parents or removed under duress (Wilson 1997). Whole communities lost their children, resulting in destruction and loss of culture for these communities and their children.

Removal was based on the erroneous idea that full blood aboriginals would simply die out and that any children of mixed blood should be removed and placed in institutions or with white families so that they could assimilate and be raised as whites. As a result, in addition to the mental health problems caused to the stolen generation and their parents, there developed a deep distrust, fear and loss of confidence in the police, the justice system and government agencies.

While the underlying causes for the over representation of Aboriginal and Torres Strait Islander children are complex, involving a range of historical, community, individual and family factors, the report of the Human Rights an Equal Opportunities Commission (Wilson 1997) suggests that they include:

Cultural differences in child rearing practices, not well understood by white welfare officers;
The legacy of past policies of forced removal and cultural assimilation;
A historical pattern of marginalisation and racism that have led to high levels of unresolved trauma and grief, leading to intergenerational cycles of adversity, violence, poverty, family dysfunction and community dysfunction. These include: overcrowding and poor housing; family violence; pornography; gambling; alcohol and drug abuse and a tendency to take a punitive rather than a therapeutic approach.

Several inquiries over the last 20 years have highlighted that in some Aboriginal and Torres Strait Islander communities, children are at higher risk of abuse and neglect (Anderson and Wild 2007; Scott and Higgins 2011). This is for complex reasons described above.

A major problem with most of these enquiries is that there has been little involvement of the Aboriginal community in implementing recommendations with, at times, attempts to impose recommendations upon them without involving Aboriginal communities in meaningful, effective implementation.

2.5 Court Systems That Deal with Child Abuse

Because child protection is regarded as a matter for states and territories, each of the six states and two territories has its own legislation.

2.5.1 Children's Court

The Children's court is used when the investigating agency determines that a child is at risk and needs intervention to ensure that child's safety. Depending on the circumstances, the agency may not use court but may refer the family to a voluntary agency that can provide support services for the family, such as childcare, parenting classes and access to social service benefits. Parents may do this voluntarily with the support of the social services agency or the agency may obtain an order from a Children's court to mandate this involvement.

If the agency determines that the child is in danger it can commence proceedings in the Children's court to remove the child from the parent(s) and place the child in out-of-home care on either a temporary, long term or permanent basis, depending on the circumstances.

Shorter-term removals are to allow sufficient time for interventions to be put in place to support parents in their role and to protect the child. Decisions in the Children's Courts are made by the court examining the evidence and weighing it up on the "balance of probabilities". This is in contrast to Criminal Court determinations, which are made on the basis of "beyond reasonable doubt". A key consideration in the Children's Courts is that decision making should be guided by what is in the child's best interests.

The generally held view of the Children's court is to try to balance three distinct but overlapping areas:

1. The state or territory Child Family Welfare Department (the name varies across states) is obliged to protect children from harm.
2. Parents have an interest in preserving the family unit and generally do not want their children to be harmed or to suffer.
3. Children have interests of their own (such as wanting to remain part of a family while at the same time not being harmed) which may not always be the same as those of their parents or of the state.

All relevant state, territory and commonwealth legislation notes the importance of involving children and young people in decision-making, to the extent that their age and maturity enables, and to seek the views of children on issues affecting their lives. As an example, The *Children, Young Persons and Their Families Act* in the state of Tasmania states "In any exercise of powers under this Act in relation to a child, if a child is able to form and express views as to his or her ongoing care and protection, those views must be sought and given serious consideration, taking into account the child's age and maturity." (Child Family Community Australia 2014).

2.5.2 Criminal Court

For serious injury to a child, murder and for cases of sexual abuse the police become involved and cases go before the criminal court so that the offender can be tried. The criminal court has a higher standard of proof, a fact that makes child sexual abuse cases harder to prove.

2.5.3 Family Court

The Family court is under commonwealth government jurisdiction and has a different focus. There is often a poor fit with the state-based interventions as these only intervene when a parent is unwilling or unable to a child from harm. In contrast, the Family court has a focus on resolving disputes between parents who are divorced or separated on which care arrangements are in the best interests of the child or children from that family (Higgins and Kaspiew 2008).

Family court cases can be extremely complex involving allegations about abuse particularly when it is also about parents separating or divorcing. In recognition of this complexity an interagency collaborative model, known as Magellan, has been introduced into all Australian Family courts.

An evaluation of Magellan found that, compared with normal Family court proceedings in these complex cases: cases were settled more quickly; fewer court appearances were required; there was more involvement and better cooperation with the statutory child protection bodies in the states; children were more likely to have independent legal representation and there was a focus on what was in the best interests of the child. It was found that Magellan could be a successful case-management process for responding to allegations of child abuse in matters involving the separation of parents (Higgins 2007).

2.6 Abuse of Children in Immigration Detention

Abuse of children in immigration detention is a particular problem. In 1992 Australia adopted a mandatory detention policy whereby all persons entering Australia by small boat without a valid visa are detained while their claim for refugee status, along with security and health checks are undertaken. The majority of these people are asylum seekers fleeing from persecution with over 90% eventually being determined to be genuine refugees. However, the policy is one of indefinite detention, processing is slow and some politicians have vilified these asylum seekers as "illegal immigrants". A system of off shore detention was introduced in the belief that processing within Australia's borders was encouraging refugees to choose Australia as their destination for seeking asylum. The policy is a controversial one that has divided the Australian community and has been the subject of adverse reports from human rights organisations.

From the point of view of child protection, it has been documented by the Australian Human Rights Commission that children living in off shore detention, in facilities originally built exclusively for adults, are particularly vulnerable to emotional trauma, to physical abuse and sexual abuse and that the conditions in these centres contravene the UN Convention on the Rights of the Child. Successive Australian governments have been unresponsive to these concerns, an anomalous reaction when they have initiated and embraced a National Framework for protecting children.

2.7 Abuse in Religious and Other Institutions

All countries recognise that while the majority of child abuse, particularly sexual abuse, occurs in the home or in the homes of trusted family members and friends, it also occurs in a variety of institutions. These are usually institutions trusted by the family and where the family believes that the child will benefit by being involved with the institution, be it a school, a secular youth group or a religious organisation.

Concern about reports of sexual abuse by church employees caused the Australian Anglican church, Australia's largest protestant denomination, to commission a report into the extent of the problem. A retrospective study of cases of child sexual abuse complaints made against clergy, other church employees and volunteers between 1990 and 2001 found 191 allegations against 135 individuals. Fifty-nine per cent of offenders were clergy; most of the non-clergy were youth workers, often leaders of church youth groups.

Unlike the Catholic Church, the Anglican Church does not have a requirement of celibacy. Because of this, it was it was hypothesised that the gender of victims would be similar to that for extra familial abuse in the community (more girl victims than boys). However, it was found that 67% of the victims were boys, a figure similar to that found in the Catholic Church (Terry 2008). One possible explanation was that parents supervised their daughters more carefully, taking them to and from functions whereas there were more opportunities for offenders to be alone with boys (Parkinson et al. 2012).

During the late 1990s and early 2000s, allegations of child sexual abuse within the Roman Catholic Church surfaced, similar to those made in the United States, Canada and Ireland. There was concern that many complaints were not adequately investigated, or ignored and that no efforts were made to prevent the perpetrators committing further acts of abuse.

Consequently, in 2013 the Australian government established a Royal Commission (a special enquiry with extensive powers to obtain documents and to require witnesses to appear before it) to enquire into how institutions, including a wide range of non-religious institutions, responded to allegations of child sexual abuse. In addition to obtaining evidence from organisations, members of the public were invited to make submissions in public or in private. Legal and support services were provided for victims who wished to make a submission. Regular interim reports were issued. There was considerable public interest. Many reforms have been proposed. The final report of the commission is expected to be released in 2018. There is no doubt that the Commission has been helpful in exposing past practices and putting safe protocols in place. It has been extremely stressful for survivors who gave evidence, even though giving evidence was voluntary for them.

One downside is that with the considerable publicity that has been generated there is the danger that the public may think that child sexual abuse is a problem that is "out there" in churches and institutions that work with children whereas the reality is that abuse in institutions represents only a small proportion of child sexual abuse. Most of it occurs within the context of relationships within family and extended family.

2.8 Economic Costs of Abuse in Australia

The most recent figures are for 2013–2014, showing that approximately $3.3 billion was spent on child protection and out-of–home care services, the latter consuming 65% of this expenditure. Expenditure has been increasing annually at a rate 2–4%, depending on the year. For every child in Australia aged up to 17 years, recurrent expenditure on intensive support services, out of home services and child protection is approximately $686 per child and young person, representing an average increase of 2.9% per year over 5 years (Child Family Community Australia 2015c). Intensive family support services are defined as "services designed to prevent the imminent separation of children from their primary care-givers as a result of child protection concerns and to reunify families where separation has already occurred".

The above figures are for government expenditure in response to an identified risk. There is much less information on the amount spent of prevention. Based on limited data, Taylor et al. (2008) estimated that the total Australian spending on child abuse prevention across all government departments was approximately $1.16 billion, with only 35% of that spent on services.

It seems likely that the amount currently spent on prevention would be greater if governments had a greater awareness of the long-term costs of child abuse: mental illness; poor health; juvenile offending; homelessness; drug and alcohol abuse; criminality and incarceration. Taylor et al. (2008) estimate long term costs to be $6 billion annually. Another study, using a broader definition estimated the annual cost to be $9 billion (Child Family Community Australia 2015c). Add to this the estimated $7.7 billion for lifetime costs of unemployment or under employment for some victims, as well as economic costs related to mental anguish, difficulty sustaining relationships and parenting difficulties, the total annual burden, using Taylor's more conservative estimate, is close to $14 billion.

To put this in perspective, in terms of annual health costs during the same period, total annual Australian health expenditure was $103 billion, demonstrating that the total cost of child abuse is a major economic burden.

While the direct economic costs of child abuse are substantial, the addition of the indirect costs should make prevention a priority. Quite apart from the economic aspects, the devastating effects of abuse on individual lives should alone be enough to make this a national priority. This has now happened with the introduction of a National Framework.

2.9 A National Framework for Protecting Australia's Children

In Australia, child protection is a state government responsibility, with laws and procedures varying across different states. A significant breakthrough occurred in 2009 when the Council of Australian Governments, the nation's peak intergovernmental forum, decided for the first time to work together to reduce child abuse and neglect in Australia (Protecting Children is Everyone's Business, 2009). It agreed to develop a National Framework with the key message that the protection of children is everyone's responsibility. It is an ambitious, long-term approach (2009–2020) with a process of regular, rolling 3 year Action Plans and annual reports to government. As well as government agencies, the Framework took an approach that communities, children and young people, non-government organisations, as well as business and the corporate sector all have a role to play.

The starting point for the Framework was that Australia needed to move from seeing "protecting children" merely as a response to abuse and neglect to one of promoting the safety and well-being of children. A public health model was adopted, where there was greater emphasis placed on assisting families early enough to prevent abuse and neglect. Priority was placed on having universal supports available for all families. More intensive secondary prevention interventions were provided to families needing additional assistance with a focus on early intervention. Tertiary services were to be seen as a last resort, being the least desirable option for families as well as for governments. The ultimate aim of the National Framework is to reduce the occurrence of child abuse and neglect by providing the most appropriate responses to vulnerable families and those in which abuse or neglect had already occurred.

While these concepts were not new, the national approach was in contrast to the situation in the states where, as the demand for child protection services grew, the size of those services also grew, leaving no resources or ability to have a wider focus on all vulnerable children. Also new was that for the first time Australia had a national, coordinated commitment.

As in many countries, states are reluctant to give up their responsibilities to national governments. However, under the National Framework there is a commitment by all parties to work together in areas of shared responsibility, to deliver more integrated services and to avoid duplication.

The Framework listed six ambitious supporting outcomes to measure its effectiveness:

1. Children will live in safe and supportive families and communities
2. Children and families will be able to access adequate support to promote safety and intervene early
3. Risk factors for abuse and neglect will be addressed.
4. Children who have been abused or neglected will receive the support and care they need for their safety and wellbeing.
5. Indigenous children will be supported and safe in their families and communities
6. Child sexual abuse and exploitation will be prevented and survivors will receive adequate support.

While the Framework acknowledged that it aimed for a substantial and sustained reduction in child abuse and neglect over time, it did acknowledge that measuring reduction would be difficult as there are currently no robust data on incidence and prevalence. Although each state and territory has mandatory reporting, there is wide variation in figures, definitions and interpretation across states, making comparisons and overall measurement difficult.

2.9.1 Is the National Framework Effective?

The Framework is a 12-year strategy for reform, supported by rolling 3-year action plans to evaluate progress towards the six supporting outcomes listed above. It aims to identify specific actions to achieve these outcomes and the responsibilities and timeframes for their implementation.

In 2013 the First Action Plan running from 2009 to 2012, had been completed. The Second Action Plan (Protecting Children is Everyone's Business 2012). recognises some of the achievements, some of the ongoing challenges and incorporates some of the lessons learned in the previous 3 years.

Some achievements:

1. A national Children's Commissioner was appointed
2. National standards for out of–home care were implemented.
3. A national consistent approach to Working with Children Checks
4. A program to help transition young people from out-of-home care to independence
5. A national agreement to share information between child support and social service agencies
6. A priority to ensure that indigenous children would be at the forefront of future service planning
7. The development of a common assessment tool
8. A national research agenda with agreed research priorities: effectiveness of preventive strategies; effectiveness of therapeutic responses; how different types of maltreatment interact and how to improve delivery of services across agencies. However, despite these ambitious research aims, only $600,000 [$US 450,000] was allocated to be spread over 3 years. In the author's view, this disappointing amount and unlikely to achieve meaningful results
9. A national study on responding to sexualised or sexually abusive behaviours in children and young people
10. A network of 98 parenting support services for indigenous families
11. A network of 38 Child and Family Centres

Some ongoing challenges:

1. Substantiation rates have not fallen; instead there has been a rise.
2. The rate of children in out-of-home care has risen
3. There is still a need for uniform reporting data

4. It remains to be seen whether any of the achievements listed above have an impact on reducing abuse and neglect and improving the welfare of all Australian children.

The Framework's most recent annual report was released in 2016, reviewing the progress made in the Second Three-year Action Plan (Protecting Children is Everyone's Business 2016).

Of concern is that the reports show an observed increase in the rate of children 0–17 years who were the subject of a child protection substantiation, rising from 6.2/1000 children in 2010–2011, to 7.4/1000 in 2011–2012, to 7.8/1000 children in 2012–2013 and again in 2013–2014. The rate of substantiation for indigenous children has not fallen and has remained seven times higher than for non-indigenous children since 2010. The report speculates that enhanced public awareness and changes to policy, practice and legislation since the start of the National Framework may be contributing factors.

The rate of children residing in out of–home care has also increased from 7.1/1000 children in 2010 to 8.1/1000 in 2014. In addition, the numbers of children recorded as victims of sexual assault have not fallen either.

Since the first action plan, a range of initiatives to support families continues to be initiated. These are long term projects where it may take more time to see major improvement. While family support, community awareness and inter-agency cooperation have improved following introduction of the National Framework, it is of concern that to date no improvement is showing in the national figures.

2.9.2 The Response of Pediatricians to the National Framework

In Australia, pediatricians are consultants. The majority of primary paediatric care is provided by family doctors (general practitioners). When a paediatric problem seems complex or outside the expertise of the general practitioner, the child is referred to a paediatrician. This is quite different to the USA model and more akin to the model in the UK. Family doctors may initially see child abuse, with paediatricians seeing cases referred on to them by family doctors or by child welfare agencies.

In 2015 the Paediatricians belonging to the Royal Australasian College of Physicians endorsed the common approach to assessment and support outlined in the National Framework, emphasising that inter-professional and interagency partnership is crucial at all levels if children are to be protected (Royal Australasian College of Physicians 2015). It recognised the value of the public health model in primary and secondary child protection in addition to tertiary level services. It encouraged paediatricians to take on stronger primary and secondary roles than previously, where most of the child protection work of paediatricians had been at the tertiary level. They recommended to their members that central to the primary and secondary roles is the conduct of a comprehensive psychosocial assessment and the subsequent provision of appropriate services or referral to such services. This is somewhat at odds with traditional paediatrics training in Australia where there has been emphasis on acute hospital paediatrics, although in the mid 1970s training started to be provided in community paediatrics and child protection. Experience in child protection has now become a mandatory component of training to become a consultant paediatrician.

The College reminded paediatricians that there are some particular population groups that are more vulnerable. These include:

Refugee groups, where children have often already experienced a variety of trauma, where families may be fragmented, where there may be over-crowding in refugee hostels and where schooling may have been disrupted.

And

Children living in situations where there is intimate-partner (domestic) violence. Children are known to be present in 65–85% of homes where there is domestic violence, with the majority of these children being under five years of age. Australian figures show that in 55% of physical assaults on children and 40% of sexual abuse, domestic violence co-exists.

2.10 Conclusion

We have learned a great deal about child protection in the relatively short period since the First Fleet arrived in Australia. From a time of seeing neglected children as a threat to society, through to denial of abuse, there has gradually been increased recognition of the extent and serious impact of the problem, the mobilisation of the medical, social work and justice professions, amongst others, the introduction of legislative changes and a national government commitment to provide safety for all children.

But there is still a long way to go.

References

Anderson, P., & Wild, R. (2007). Little children are sacred. In *Report of the Northern Territory Board of Inquiry into the protection of aboriginal children from sexual abuse*. Darwin: Northern Territory Government.

Australian Bureau of Statistics. (2006). *Personal safety survey* (ABS Cat. No 4906.0). Canberra: Australian Government Printer.

Bialestock, D. (1966). Neglected babies: A study of 289 babies admitted consecutively to a reception centre. *Medical Journal of Australia, 2*, 1129–1133.

Birrell, R., & Birrell, J. (1966). The maltreatment syndrome in children. *Medical Journal of Australia, 2*, 1134–1113.

Birrell, R., & Birrell, J. (1968). The maltreatment syndrome in children: A hospital survey. *Medical Journal of Australia, 2*, 1023–1029.

Child Family Community Australia. (2013). *The prevalence of child abuse and neglect* (Australian Institute of Family Studies). Canberra: Australian Government printer.
Child Family Community Australia. (2014). *Australian child protection legislation* (Australian Institute of Family studies). Canberra: Australian Government printer.
Child Family Community Australia. (2015a). *Child abuse and neglect statistics* (Institute of Family Studies). Canberra: Australian Government printer.
Child Family Community Australia. (2015b). *Child protection and Aboriginal and Torres Strait islander children* (Australian Institute of Family Studies). Canberra: Australian Government printer.
Child Family Community Australia. (2015c). *The economic cost of child abuse and neglect* (Australian Institute of Family Studies). Canberra: Australian Government printer.
Child Family Community Australia. (2016). *Mandatory reporting of child abuse and neglect* (Australian Institute of Family Studies). Canberra: Australian Government printer.
Higgins, D. (2007). *An evaluation of the family court of Australia's Magellan case-management model* (Australian Institute for Family Studies). Canberra: Australian Government printer.
Higgins, D. J., & Kaspiew, R. (2008). 'Mind the gap': Protecting children in family law cases. *Australian Journal of Family Law, 22*, 235–258.
Kempe, C. H., et al. (1962). The battered-child syndrome. *Journal of the American Medical Association, 181*, 17–24.
Mathews, B. (2014). *Mandatory reporting laws for child sexual abuse in Australia: A legislative history* (Royal Commission into Institutional Responses to Child Sexual Abuse). Sydney.
Mathews, B., Lee, X. J., & Norman, R. E. (2016). Impact of a new mandatory reporting law on reporting and identification of child sexual abuse: A seven year time trend analysis. *Child Abuse and Neglect, 56*, 62–79.
Najman, J., et al. (2005). Sexual abuse in childhood and sexual dysfunction in adulthood: An Australian population-based study. *Archives of Sexual Behavior, 34*, 517–526.
Oates, K. (2014). Role of the medical community in detecting and managing child abuse. *Medical Journal of Australia, 1*, 7–8.
Oates, K., & Yu, J. (1971). Children with non-organic failure to thrive: A community problem. *Medical Journal of Australia, 2*, 199–203.
Oates, K., et al. (2000). Erroneous concerns about child sexual abuse. *Child Abuse and Neglect, 24*, 149–157.
Parkinson, P., Oates, K., & Jayakody, A. (2012). Child sexual abuse in the Anglican church of Australia. *Journal of Child Sexual Abuse, 21*, 553–557.
Protecting Children is Everyone's Business. (2009). *National framework for protecting Australia's children, 2009–2020*. Canberra: Australian Government printer.
Protecting Children is Everyone's Business. (2012). *National framework for protecting Australia's children, 2009–2020* (Second Action Plan). Canberra: Australian Government printer.
Protecting Children is Everyone's Business. (2016). *National framework for protecting Australia's children, 2009–2020* (Third Action Plan). Canberra: Australian Government printer.
Royal Australasian College of Physicians. (2015). *Protecting children is everyone's business: Paediatricians responding to the challenge of child protection*. Sydney: Royal Australasian College of Physicians.
Scott, D. A., & Higgins, D. J. (2011). *Supporting families in northern territory emergency response: Evaluation report* (Department of Families Housing, Community Services and Indigenous Affairs). Canberra: Australian Government printer.
Segal, L. (2015). Economic issues in the community response to child maltreatment. In B. Mathews & D. Bross (Eds.), *Mandatory reporting laws and the identification of severe child abuse and neglect* (pp. 193–218). Dordrecht: Springer.
Taylor, P., et al. (2008). *The cost of child abuse in Australia*. Melbourne: Australian Childhood Foundation and Research Centre.
Terry, K. (2008). Stained glass: Child sexual abuse in the Catholic Church. *Criminal Justice and Behavior, 35*, 549–569.

Wilson, R. D., & Australia Human Rights and Equal Opportunity Commission. (1997). *Bringing them home: Report of the National Inquiry into the Separation of Aboriginal and Torres Strait Islander Children from their Families*. Sydney: Human Rights and Equal Opportunity Commission.

Wurfel, L., & Maxwell, G. (1965). The battered child syndrome in South Australia. *Australian Paediatric Journal, 1*, 127–130.

Kim Oates is a pediatrician who trained in the Sydney, London and Boston. Most of his professional work has been associated with The Children's Hospital at Westmead and the University of Sydney. He was the Sydney University foundation Burrows Professor of Pediatrics and Child Health (1985–1997) and was simultaneously Chairman of the Hospital's Division of Medicine. He was the Hospital's Chief Executive from 1997–2006. He was the inaugural chair of the New South Wales Child Death Review Team and founding Chair of the Federal Government's National Council on the Prevention of Child Abuse. He has received a range of national and international awards for his services to and advocacy for children. He served on the Council of the International Society for the Prevention of Child Abuse and for 24 years, including terms as President and Treasurer. He has published widely on child abuse, particularly its longer-term effects, in general pediatrics and in patient safety.

He is currently Emeritus Professor of Pediatrics at the University of Sydney, Director of Undergraduate Quality and Safety Education at the New South Wales Clinical Excellence Commission and co-leader of a course in medical education and research for emerging health leaders in Vietnam.

Chapter 3
Child Welfare Services in Canada

Nico Trocmé, Tonino Esposito, Jennifer Nutton, Valerie Rosser, and Barbara Fallon

3.1 Introduction

In Canada, the responsibility for protecting and supporting children at risk of abuse and neglect falls under the jurisdiction of the 13 provinces and territories and a system of Indigenous child welfare organizations, which have increasing responsibility for protecting and supporting Indigenous children. Across Canada, over 230,000 child maltreatment investigations are conducted every year, and on any one day, over 62,000 children are in out-of-home care; these figures correspond to rates of 39.16 child maltreatment investigations and 8.5 children in out-of-home care per every 1000 children (Jones et al. 2015, Table 1, p. 2 and Fig. 1, p. 3; Trocmé et al. 2010, Table 3-1, p. 23). While there is significant variation in the structure and organization of services and in the statutes defining investigation procedures and intervention mandates, these systems nevertheless share many common characteristics, including mandatory reporting of suspected child abuse and neglect; child maltreatment investigations and risk and safety assessments as a primary framework for determining service eligibility; the option to use court orders to enforce services; and the placement of children and youth in a range of out-of-home care settings, from kinship care to foster homes to group homes to residential treatment facilities. In comparison to several other jurisdictions, the Canadian child welfare system is usually described as having a safety orientation as opposed to a child and family

N. Trocmé (✉) · J. Nutton · V. Rosser
School of Social Work, McGill University, Montreal, QC, Canada
e-mail: nico.trocme@mcgill.ca; jennifer.nutton@mail.mcgill.ca; valerie.rosser@mail.mcgill.ca

T. Esposito
School of Social Work, University of Montreal, Montreal, QC, Canada
e-mail: tonino.esposito@umontreal.ca

B. Fallon
Factor-Inwentash Faculty of Social Work, University of Toronto, Toronto, ON, Canada
e-mail: barbara.fallon@utoronto.ca

L. Merkel-Holguin et al. (eds.), *National Systems of Child Protection*, Child Maltreatment 8, https://doi.org/10.1007/978-3-319-93348-1_3

welfare orientation (Fallon et al. 2012; Gilbert et al. 2009). Several provinces and territories are attempting to broaden to a child and family welfare approach with the introduction of differential or alternate response models (Mansell 2006; Merkel-Holguin et al. 2014; Waldfogel 2009), a shift that is also stressed in emerging Indigenous service delivery models.

3.2 Key Characteristics and Trends in Investigated Maltreatment

The Canadian Incidence Study of Reported Child Abuse and Neglect (CIS), a periodic survey of child welfare investigations conducted across Canada, is the only Canada-wide source of data on child maltreatment investigations. The most recent full national survey was conducted in 2008 and found that, of an estimated 235,842 child-maltreatment-related investigations conducted that same year, 74% focused on possible incidents of abuse or neglect that may have already occurred (174,411 child maltreatment investigations or 28.97 investigations per 1000 children) and 26% were concerns about risk of future maltreatment (61,431 investigations or 10.19 investigations per 1000 children) (see Table 3.1). Thirty-six percent of the investigations were substantiated. In a further 8% of investigations, there was insufficient evidence to substantiate maltreatment, but maltreatment remained suspected by the worker at the completion of the intake investigation. Thirty percent of investigations were unfounded.

The inclusion of investigations for risk of future maltreatment in the CIS 2008 reflects a general expansion, across Canada, in the scope of child protection mandates (Fallon et al. 2011a, b). Amongst the risk only investigations, 19% were judged to involve significant risk of future maltreatment, while two-thirds were judged to not involve significant risk. In another 16%, the level of future risk was not determined (see Table 3.1).

The relatively broad scope of protection mandates across Canada is also apparent if one examines rates of documented injuries in cases of substantiated maltreatment. Only 8% of substantiated investigations, involving an estimated 7069 child investigations at a rate of 1.17 per 1000 children, involved situations where some type of physical harm had been noted, two-thirds of these injuries being minor bruises, cuts or scrapes that did not warrant medical intervention (Trocmé et al. 2010, Table 4-3, p. 33). Head trauma was documented in an estimated 325 substantiated maltreatment incidents, broken bones in an estimated 175 incidents, and burns or scalds in an estimated 172 incidents (Trocmé et al. 2010, Table 4-3, p. 33).

The three national cycles of the CIS conducted in 1998, 2003 and 2008, document the expansion in the scope of child protection mandates across Canada, more specifically an expansion that occurred in the early 2000s, with the total number of child investigations increasing from an estimated 135,261 in 1998, a rate of 21.47 investigations per 1000 children, to 235,315 in 2003, a rate of 38.33 investigations

Table 3.1 Estimated Number of Maltreatment-Related Investigations in Canada in 2008 by Investigation Outcome and Primary Form of Substantiated Maltreatment

	# of Investigations		Incidence per 1000 children		% of all investigations	
Risk of maltreatment investigations	61,431		10.19		26%	% of Risk investi-gations
Risk of future maltreatment		12,018		2.00		19%
Unknown risk of future maltreatment		10,1224		1.68		16%
No risk of future maltreatment		39,289		6.52		64%
Maltreatment investigations	174,411		28.97			
Unfounded maltreatment	71,053		11.80		30%	% of Substan-tiated Investi-gations
Suspected maltreatment	17,918		2.91		8%	
Substantiated maltreatment	85,440		14.19		36%	
Physical abuse		17,212		2.86		20%
Sexual abuse		2607		0.43		3%
Neglect		28,939		4.81		34%
Emotional maltreatment		7423		1.23		9%
Exposure to intimate partner violence		29,259		4.86		34%
Maltreatment and risk of maltreatment investigations	235.842		39.16		100%	

Note: Based on a sample of 15,980. Adapted from Trocmé et al. (2010), Fig. 3-1, p. 24 and Table 4-1, p. 31

per 1000 children (see Fig. 3.1). In Ontario, Canada's largest province, where Ontario Incidence Studies (OIS) have been conducted since 1993 on a 5-year cycle through to 2013, this increase is even more dramatic: rates of investigation increased from an estimated 21.32 investigations per 1000 children in 1993 to 53.32 in 2013, with the sharpest increase occurring between 1998 and 2003 (see Fig. 3.1).

These increases have been primarily driven by investigations involving concerns about exposure to intimate partner violence, emotional maltreatment and investigations of risk of maltreatment, while there has been little change over time in the number of investigations involving serious injuries or child sexual abuse (Fallon et al. 2011a; Trocmé et al. 2011, 2013). Analysis of investigations re-classified as urgent or chronic on the basis of injury, child age and severity of maltreatment from the 1998, 2003 and 2008 Canadian Incidence Studies shows urgent protection cases have dropped from 28% of all investigations in 1998, to 19% in 2003, to 15% in 2008. In 2008, 7% of cases involved neglect of a child under four, 4% of cases

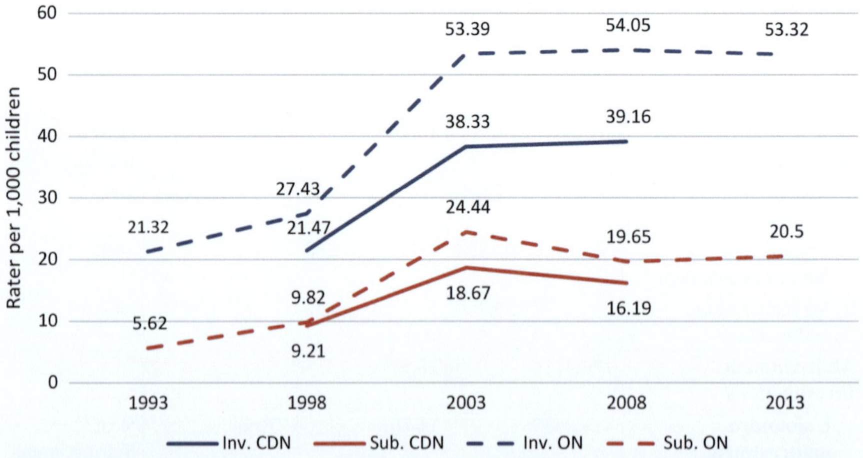

Fig. 3.1 Child Maltreatment-Related Investigations and Substantiations in Canada and Ontario, 1993–2013. (Data for investigation rate in Canada adapted from Trocmé et al. (2010), Table 3-1, p. 23, and for substantiation rate in Canada from Table 3-3, p. 25. Data for investigation rate in Ontario adapted from Fallon et al. (2015), Fig. 3-1, p. 41, and for substantiation rate in Ontario from Table 3-3, p. 46)

involved sexual abuse, 2% of cases involved physical abuse of a child under four and 1% of cases involved children who had sustained severe enough physical harm that medical treatment was required. The other 85% of maltreatment investigations involved situations where concerns appear to focus less on immediate safety and more on the long-term effects of a range of family related problems. These findings underscore the importance of considering the dual mandate of Canadian child welfare authorities: protecting children from imminent harm and supporting the development and well-being of children living in difficult circumstances (Fallon et al. in press; Trocmé et al. 2014).

3.2.1 Children in Out-of-Home Care

There are limited Canada-wide data on the number and characteristics of children in out-of-home care. The CIS tracks placement of children in out-of-home care during the investigation period, typically the first 30–60 days of a child and family's involvement with child welfare services. At that initial point of contact, 4% of children investigated by child welfare services are formally placed in out-of-home care. Of these placements, over 85% are in relative or non-relative foster care, and less than 15% involve group homes or residential treatment facilities (Trocmé et al. 2010). Across Canada in 2008, this translated into close to 11,000 children, or 1.8 child investigations per 1000 children, a rate that has not changed over the three cycles of the CIS (1998, 2003 and 2008) (Trocmé et al. 2001, 2005, 2010). These

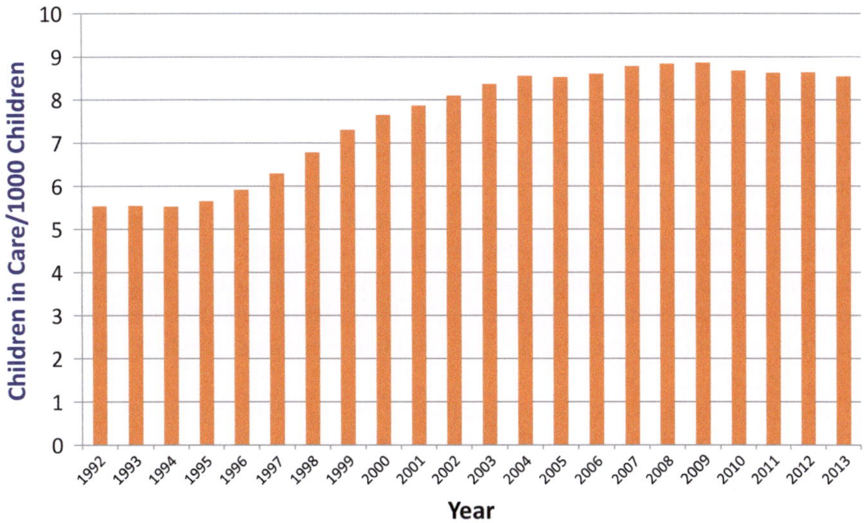

Fig. 3.2 Children in care (1992–2013). (Adapted from Jones et al. (2015), p. 3)

numbers, however, significantly underestimate the placement rate, since many of the children in care are placed after the initial investigation.

A second source of estimation is a compilation of the number of children in care reported by each provincial and territorial jurisdiction. Compiling these figures, Jones et al. (2015) report that there were an estimated 62,428 children in out-of-home care in 2013, a rate of 8.5 children in care per every 1000 children (pp. 2–3); since each jurisdiction defines placement in different ways, these figures must be treated as estimates. Consistent with the increase documented by the CIS and the OIS, placement rates increased from the mid-1990s to the mid-2000s (see Fig. 3.2).

One of the challenges with using cross-sectional counts is that they confound two very different populations: children placed in short-term care because of a short-term family crisis, and children who end up in long-term care. While there are no national longitudinal data tracking different types of placement trajectories, analysis of administrative placement data from Quebec describes the range of these different trajectories in Canada's second largest province. Following a cohort of 127,181 children investigated for maltreatment-related concerns between 2002 and 2010, Esposito et al. (2013) found that 22.8% of investigated children experience at least one out-of-home placement lasting more than 72 h. Further analysis of the children who experienced at least one placement shows that over 80% were reunified with their family, half of these within 175 days of their initial placement (Esposito et al. 2014). At the population level, a study from Manitoba, the province with one of the highest rates of out-of-home placement, found that by age 12, 9.4% of all children born between 1998 and 2001 had been placed in out-of-home care at least once (O'Donnell et al. 2016, p. 81).

3.2.2 Overrepresentation of FN Children

First Nations children are significantly overrepresented in the Canadian child welfare system. Using data from the 2008 CIS, Sinha et al. (2011) show that, in the population served by sampled agencies, the rate of investigations for First Nations children was 4.2 times that of non-Aboriginal children, with First-Nations children being investigated at a rate of 140.6/1000 versus 33.5/1000 for non-Aboriginal Children (p. 48). Overrepresentation increases even further when comparing children who are placed in out-of-home care following the investigation, with rates being over 12 times higher: 13.6 per 1000 First Nations children were placed in out-of-home care, compared to 1.1 per 1000 non-Aboriginal children (Sinha et al. 2011, Table 6.7, p. 81).

In a recent analysis of children identified as foster children by respondents of the 2011 Census and the National Household Survey (NHS), Sinha and Wray (2015) examined disparities between the rates of Aboriginal and Non-Aboriginal foster children and found that, despite the fact that Aboriginal children (ages 0–15) make up only 7% of the child population in Canada, they represent 49.1% of the children in foster care. By Aboriginal identity group, the NHS data indicate that the rate of children in foster care was 45.2 per 1000 First Nations children, 28.3 per 1000 Inuit children, and 17.2 per 1000 Metis children, while only 2.9 of every 1000 non-Aboriginal children were identified as foster children. The NHS data also show that over-representation was particularly marked for First Nations children in Western Canada, where the rate of First Nations foster children was between 16.6 and 33.9 times the rate of non-Aboriginal foster children.

3.2.3 Childhood Prevalence of Physical and Sexual Abuse

Child victimization identified through the child welfare system represents only a small portion of the rate of victimization in the general population. Several community surveys document rates of childhood physical and sexual abuse victimization as reported by adults recalling such incidents from their childhood. However, direct comparisons between the number of incidents investigated by the child welfare system and these childhood prevalence figures cannot be made, since the former count reported incidents during a year and the latter document prevalence over a whole childhood. Using data from the 2012 Canadian Community Health Survey, Afifi et al. (2014) report that 10.1% of respondents reported at least one incident of sexual victimization before the age of 16, with prevalence rates being 5.8% for males and 14.4% for females (p. 2). Rates of childhood physical abuse victimization were reported to be 26.1% overall—31.0% for males and 21.3% for females. These rates of victimization remain similar across a range of different surveys (Burczycka and Conroy 2017, p. 6; Shields et al. 2016).

3.2.4 *Child Homicides*

A total of 319 children and youth (0–17) were victims of familial homicide between 2003 and 2013, according to data collected through the Statistics Canada Homicide Survey (Canadian Centre for Justice Statistics 2015). Over 60% of the deaths resulted from beating, shaking, suffocating or strangulating. Over that 10 year period, infants were at greatest risk of death at the hands of family members (20 per million), followed by children under five (6 per million); children over five were even less likely to be killed by a family member. The rate of familial homicide against children and youth has fluctuated since 1974 without a discernable pattern through to the early 2000s; since then, there has been a slight decline (Canadian Centre for Justice Statistics 2007, p. 25; Wegner-Lohin and Trocmé 2016).

3.3 Historical Context: The Moral and Colonial Roots of Canada's Child Welfare Systems

To understand the structure of Canada's current child welfare systems, it is important to consider how the moral "child saving" movement of the late 19th and early twentieth century and the colonization of Indigenous peoples have shaped these systems.

3.3.1 *The Development of Mainstream Child Welfare Services in Canada*

Canada's child welfare system emerged at the end of the nineteenth century through the reorganization of church-run orphanages and the growing movement of "child saving" societies for the prevention of cruelty to children. The Toronto Humane Society, founded in 1887 for the protection of women, children and animals, renamed the Children's Aid Society in 1891, was modeled on the New York Society for the Prevention of Cruelty to Children (1875) and the American Humane Association (1877), and was the first such child protection organization in Canada. Similar societies developed in a number of municipalities across Canada, eventually seeking provincial legal mandates that gave them the power to remove children who were victims of abuse or neglect (Bala et al. 2004). In the 1950s and 1960s, jurisdictions across Canada started developing a comprehensive network of provincially regulated or provincially run child welfare agencies, by establishing the legislative, regulatory and financial frameworks required to transform these organizations from voluntary societies to professionally organized bureaucracies. The various child protection statutes that shaped these frameworks maintained much of the late nineteenth century child-saving language. For instance, the purpose of Quebec's *Youth Protection Schools Act* of 1951 was to protect children "exposed to moral or physical dangers" (a. 15). Similarly, Ontario's Child Welfare Act (1970) included, in its definition of a child in need of protection, situations where: "a child [was] found associating with an unfit or improper person" (s. 20 [1] [b] [v]) or "a child [was] found begging or receiving alms in a public place" (s. 20 [1] [b] [vi]).

Jurisdictions across Canada sought to modernize their child welfare statutes in the 1970s and 1980s by replacing explicit reference to morality with terminology reflecting the emerging focus on research and practice in child maltreatment, including physical and sexual abuse and child neglect (Bala et al. 2004; Trocmé 1991). The new provincial child welfare statutes also included more specific procedures to protect parent and child rights and shifted the onus onto child welfare authorities to ensure that in-home family support services were provided as an alternative to placement whenever possible. Ontario's 1984 *Child and Family Services Act*, which served as a model for other provinces, required that agencies demonstrate that they were employing the "least disruptive course of action that is available and is appropriate" (*Child and Family Services Act* 1990, s. 1 [2]). This period also marked a dramatic shift in practice in child welfare organizations. In Ontario, for example, the number of children placed in out of home care on December 31st dropped from 17,807 in 1977 to 9712 in 1988, while the number of families receiving services increased from 28,323 to 74,116 during the same timeframe (Trocmé 1991, Table 4.1).

The shift to a less intrusive approach came under fire following a series of inquests and inquiries in British Columbia, Manitoba, Ontario, Quebec and New Brunswick. The Gove Inquiry into the death of five-year-old Matthew Vaudreuil at the hands of his mother provided detailed documentation of a disorganized health and social service system in which dozens of professionals failed to share their concerns and appeared more concerned about minimizing intrusion than responding to alarming signs of serious neglect and abuse (Gove 1995). The Gove Inquiry led to a complete restructuring of British Columbia's Ministry-run child welfare system. Similar concerns about the balance between child protection and parental rights were raised in Ontario, leading to a "re-balancing" of the legislation to ensure that child protection and well-being were clearly identified as the primary consideration (Bala 1999). To underscore the primary importance of child safety, several jurisdictions also adopted risk assessment tools, service eligibility, and triage guidelines. This shift towards a lower threshold for intervention was compounded by a significant expansion in child welfare mandates in response to the growing body of research on the effects of child neglect and emotional maltreatment—especially in the context of children's exposure to intimate partner violence. (Brassard et al. 1987; Erickson and Egeland (2002); Wolfe et al. 2003). The increase in child abuse and neglect investigations, and in the number of children placed in out-of-home care between 1998 and 2003, can be largely attributed to shifts in intervention thresholds and expanding mandates (Fallon et al. 2011a; Trocmé et al. 2011; see Figs. 3.1 and 3.2).

The sharp increase in investigations and out-of-home placements that occurred in the late 90s and early 2000s led to calls across Canada for once again finding the right balance between protection and over-intervention (Dumbrill 2006; Freymond and Cameron 2006; Trocmé et al. 2014). Reviews and inquests focusing on the conditions for children and youth placed in out-of-home care have led to calls for developing family support services that can provide less-intrusive alternatives to removal (British Columbia Ministry of Family Development 2011; Contenta n.d.; Gharabaghi et al. 2016; Government of New Brunswick 2015; Graff 2017; Milward 2016). As will be discussed in the following section of this chapter, the call for more family and community-based alternatives has gained even more momentum in the face of growing evidence that Indigenous children are dramatically over-represented across Canada, to the extent that in some provinces they represent over 75% of all children in out-of-home care.

3.3.2 The History of Child Welfare Services for First Nation, Metis and Inuit Communities

The development of child welfare services for Indigenous communities, which in Canada includes First Nations, Inuit and Metis communities,[1] has followed a very different trajectory, shaped by the history of colonizing the peoples who first lived in North America. The history of colonialist child welfare for Indigenous peoples in Canada began in the nineteenth century with the introduction of the residential school system, one of many colonial policies meant to eradicate Indigenous culture (language, traditions and beliefs) by assimilating Indigenous peoples into Canadian culture (Indigenous and Northern Affairs Canada 1996; Miller 1996). Beginning in 1879, the Canadian government (in partnership with Christian churches) began to systematically remove Indigenous children from their families and communities and place them into residential schools (Indigenous and Northern Affairs Canada 1996; Sinha and Kozlowski 2013). Residential schools did not only serve assimilative and educational functions but also served as state care for Indigenous children living on reserve who were suspected of being abused and/or neglected (Milloy 2017).

Residential schools were chronically underfunded, which often led to failure to provide students with basic necessities, such as medical care, clothing, and food

[1] In reference to the Aboriginal groups who historically lived in North America, the three broad categories of Indigenous groups that are referred to are the Inuit, First Nations and Métis. A plain language definition used by the Government of Canada is that "First Nations are those peoples who historically lived in North America, from the Atlantic to the Pacific, below the Arctic. Inuit historically lived along the coastal edge and on the islands of Canada's far north. The Métis descend from the historical joining of First Nations members and Europeans." https://www.aadnc-aandc.gc.ca/eng/1303147522487/1303147669999. These three broad categories of Indigenous peoples have different histories with respect to negotiation and recognition of their rights, and each includes many very different communities. There are, for instance, over 600 First Nations across Canada speaking more than 50 distinct languages.

(Hamilton and Sinclair 1991; Sinha et al. 2011), and demands by parents to return their children home to live in better conditions went unanswered. Many children died of disease and neglect (Hamilton and Sinclair 1991; Milloy and McCallum 2017; Sinha et al. 2011) or were physically, emotionally and sexually abused (Hamilton and Sinclair 1991; Milloy and McCallum 2017), and were disciplined harshly for using their language (Johnston 1983). In some schools, children tried to escape and many died from drowning or freezing in remote or water-locked areas (Indigenous and Northern Affairs Canada 1996; Milloy and McCallum 2017).

By the time the last residential school closed in 1986 (Indigenous and Northern Affairs Canada 1996; Milloy and McCallum 2017), over 150,000 Indigenous children in Canada had attended (Truth and Reconciliation Commission of Canada [TRC], n.d.). The mass removal of Indigenous children who were sent to residential schools over several generations meant that, when Indigenous children returned to their communities as young adults, many were confused about their identities—belonging neither to their community nor white society (Kirmayer et al. (2003).

In 1951, the Indian Act was amended to include language under Section 88, which stated that "all laws of general application from time to time in force in any province are applicable to and in respect of Indians in the province" (*Indian Act* 1985, s. 88). This section has been interpreted to mean, in the absence of any explicit mention of child protection, that provincial child welfare laws and services would be extended to Indigenous children on reserve (Auditor General of Canada 2008; Hamilton and Sinclair 1991). With the 1951 amendment to the Indian Act and with federal and provincial governments coming to agreement over time on funding issues, provincial child welfare services expanded onto reserves (Bennett et al. 2005). This led to the next period of mass removal of Indigenous children from the 1960s to 1980s, commonly referred to as the 'Sixties Scoop' (Sinclair 2007). This term originated from an interview Patrick Johnston (1983) had with an employee from the Ministry of Human Resources in British Columbia, who commented that "provincial social workers would, quite literally, scoop children from reserves on the slightest pretext" (p. 23).

For many Indigenous children, being removed from their families and communities was made permanent—with over 11,000 Indigenous children put up for adoption between 1960 and 1990 (Ontario Ministry of Children and Youth Services 2016). Once placed in foster care or adopted out, few would ever return home, and most were sent to live with non-Indigenous families, often in other provinces and (less frequently) in the United States (Bennett et al. 2005; Fournier and Crey 1997; Johnston 1983). By the 1970s, foster care placement and adoption had replaced residential schools as the primary child protection and out-of-home care system for Indigenous children (Libesman 2014).

The history of child welfare services for Indigenous peoples in Canada is complex (Johnston 1983). The beginning of (colonial) Indigenous child welfare policy was influenced by countless treaties and agreements between hundreds of Indigenous communities and successive Canadian governments across 13 provinces and territories over several hundred years. Many political, economic, social and cultural factors impacted the ways in which Indigenous child welfare has been shaped over time. Although the Canadian government may no longer explicitly engage in deliberate acts of assimilation that would be considered cultural genocide, this history of explicitly racist colonial policies continues to have an impact on child welfare systems across Canada. The mass removal of Indigenous children from their families and communities is not only a tragic period of history but persists with the overrepresentation of Indigenous children in the child welfare system. Conceding that it is likely that some of these placements are appropriate to keep children safe from harm, there are certainly structural problems, such as poverty, and likely cultural conflicts that play a part in the significant numbers of Indigenous children placed in out-of-home care.

3.4 Legislative and Administrative Structure of Child Welfare Services Across Canada

In Canada, the responsibility to protect children is delegated to the country's ten provinces and three territories. With the exception of funding services to First Nations children and families living on reserves, the Canadian federal government has no direct funding nor policy-making jurisdiction in child welfare.

3.4.1 Structure of Child Welfare Service Delivery Systems

Canada's decentralized child welfare system has led to a range of child welfare service delivery models. In some provinces, most notably Ontario, where child welfare services are provided by 48 delegated community-run child welfare agencies (Ontario Association of Children's Aid Societies n.d.; Wegner-Lohin et al. 2014), agencies provide a broad spectrum of services, ranging from the core investigative function to providing on-going supervision, counselling and some out-of-home care services. Many of these agencies were initially founded over a century ago as Children's Aid Societies (CAS) (Jones and Rutman 1981). In some communities, these were faith-based organizations that continue to maintain service on a religious basis, notably agencies serving the Catholic and Jewish communities. Children's Aid Societies manage all child welfare services including investigations, family support services, case-management and many foster homes. Group and residential care services are, however, mostly provided by a range of private for-profit and not-for-profit organizations (Gharabaghi et al. 2016).

In most other provinces and territories, services are provided through government offices with varying levels of local independence and of service contracted with non-government organizations. In Quebec, for example, child welfare services are provided through 16 regional Integrated Health and Social Services Centres (IHSSC), with child protection, investigation, and service oversight functions delegated to a local Director of Youth Protection, while all on-going case-management, family support, out-of-home care and other specialized services are provided by a range of youth service departments subsumed under the IHSSCs (Lajoie 2006). Most out-of-home care services are also run through the IHSSCs, including group homes and treatment homes. Quebec is also the first province in Canada to have a union representing all foster parents. Unlike most other jurisdictions, Quebec's IHSSCs also run services for youth involved with criminal justice. In Alberta, the investigation and case-management functions are also provided through regional government-run offices; however, many ongoing treatment, family support and out-of-home placement services are contracted out to a mix of private for-profit and not-for profit organizations (Kyte and Wegner-Lohin 2014).

A number of jurisdictions are moving towards differential response models emphasizing more collaborative and community-based approaches in situations where forensically focused maltreatment investigations are not required (Kyte et al. 2013). In jurisdictions like Quebec and Ontario, the shift away from an investigation-driven approach has been primarily developed in the form of a statement of principles about the importance of collaboration and flexibility (Wegner-Lohin et al. 2014). Other jurisdictions have developed more formal separations between child protection and family support streams. The Alberta Response Model (ARM) has two legislated streams of activity: family enhancement services and protection services (Kyte and Wegner-Lohin 2014) with three quarters of investigations being streamed to child protection (Alberta Human Services n.d.). In British Columbia, low-risk cases are diverted to a Family Development Response (FDR) that provides community-based resources (Kozlowski et al. 2014). The proportion of reports streamed to the FDR track has steadily increased, with over 75% of reports being referred to FDR in 2015 (British Columbia 2016).

3.4.2 Legislation

Child welfare intervention mandates and services are governed through provincial and territorial legislative frameworks. However, as noted earlier in this chapter, these child welfare statutes share a common legislative history and, as a result, share many features. All statutes, for instance, identify both child safety and child well-being as the paramount principles of their legislation (Trocmé et al. 2014, Table 1). All include some type of mandatory reporting requirement which, at a minimum, apply to professionals working with children—and often extend to all members of the public (Gough et al. 2009). All statutes define child maltreatment in relatively broad terms, including physical abuse, sexual abuse, neglect and emotional maltreatment. Many also include exposure to intimate partner violence, and Quebec includes situations where a child has serious behavior problems (Hélie et al. 2017). These definitions apply to situations where children have been harmed or are at risk of harm. As described above, the vast majority of investigations involve situations in which demonstrable harm has not yet occurred. These broad intervention mandates are usually balanced by reference to the principle of providing the least intrusive or least disruptive services.

The age range for investigating maltreatment covered by each jurisdiction varies, with some jurisdictions limiting child protection mandates to children and youth under 16 (for example, Saskatchewan and Newfoundland), others under 18 (for example, Quebec and Alberta), while British Columbia extends its legislation to youth under 19 (Gough et al. 2009). Ontario's coverage was limited to children and youth under the age of 16, but will be revised to 18 in 2018. Similarly, in terms of service provided to youth in long-term care, age and conditions for provision of ongoing services varies considerably, with extended care and maintenance being conditionally up to the ages of 18–21 depending on the province (Reid and Dudding 2006).

In addition to provincial and territorial child welfare statutes, the Federal Criminal Code covers a range of criminal activities, such as physical assault, sexual assault, abduction, exploitation and trafficking (*Criminal Code* 1985). Unlike child welfare statutes that follow the balance of probability family court evidentiary rules, the Criminal Code requires a much higher level of evidence beyond a reasonable doubt, and does not cover services to children (Bala et al. 2004). In cases of physical abuse involving an injury, sexual abuse and some cases of serious neglect, as well as situations involving domestic violence, child welfare and criminal proceedings may proceed concurrently, usually through joint protocols between child welfare and the police. In 2008, 22% of child maltreatment-related investigations were referred by the police, the majority of these situations involving intimate partner violence; 14% of maltreatment investigations involved some type of joint police investigation (Fallon et al. 2013).

Section 43 of Canada's Criminal Code provides explicit permission to school-teachers, parents or persons standing in the place of the parent to use "force by way of correction (…) if the force does not exceed what is reasonable under the circumstances." Section 43 has come under criticism because it is inconsistent with provincial child welfare statutes and violates children's rights under the Canadian Charter of Rights and Freedoms and the United Nations Convention on the Rights of the Child (Durrant et al. 2009). The confusion created by the Federal legislation is reflected by the finding that 74% of cases of physical abuse investigated and substantiated by child welfare authorities in Canada in 2008 were considered by the investigating worker to have occurred in a context of punishment, an estimated rate of 2.3 cases of substantiated punitive physical abuse per 1000 children in Canada (Jud and Trocmé 2012).

3.4.3 First Nations Federally Funded Services

Unlike services to non-Indigenous Canadians, the Federal government is responsible for funding services for many Indigenous children and families. The structure of that funding arrangement varies on the basis of a range of historical, treaty and regional factors. As of 2011, there were 121 Indigenous child and family services agencies (First Nations, Metis and urban Aboriginal agencies) in Canada (Sinha and Kozlowski 2013). As of 2008, these agencies have provided at least partial services to approximately 442 of the 606 nations covered by the First Nations Child and Family Services Program (Auditor General of Canada 2008). Indigenous communities have negotiated for varying levels of jurisdiction over the provision of child welfare services that have led to signed agreements. There are five types of agreements that govern the provision of child welfare services to Indigenous communities.

Provincial and Territorial Authority This model does not involve the transfer of jurisdiction over child welfare services to Indigenous communities. Similar to child welfare services for non-Indigenous children and families, the majority of Indigenous children living off reserve receive services under provincial or territorial authority and legislation (Sinha and Kozlowski 2013). The majority of provincial and territorial legislation, however, now include specific language that specifies that Indigenous children and families should receive culturally appropriate services and programs (Bennett et al. 2005; Libesman 2014; Sinha and Kozlowski 2013). For example, most provincial or territorial legislation requires Indigenous bands be notified of any court hearings involving Indigenous children and if an Indigenous child is placed in out-of-home care (Sinha and Kozlowski 2013).

Delegation Under delegated authority, Indigenous communities negotiate agreements with provincial or territorial governments to take responsibility for a range of specified child welfare services in accordance with provincial or territorial legislation (Sinha and Kozlowski 2013). Funding for Indigenous child welfare agencies will come from the province or territory if off reserve and from the federal government on reserve. The delegation model for structuring Indigenous child welfare agencies is common. For example, in 2011, there were 17 First Nations child welfare agencies operating under delegated authority agreements in Saskatchewan (Kozlowski et al. 2011a). Other provinces also have high numbers of First Nations child welfare agencies operating under delegated authority (see Sinha and Kozlowski 2013).

Integrated Governance In this model, governance over child welfare is not delegated to but formally shared between Indigenous communities and the provincial or territorial government (Sinha and Kozlowski 2013). Manitoba is an example where Indigenous communities moved beyond delegated authority to a model for Indigenous communities to take greater authority over the care and wellbeing of children (Libesman 2014). In Manitoba, child welfare agencies are overseen by four regional authorities, two of which are First Nations, one Metis, and one non-Indigenous (Kozlowski et al. 2011b). The integrated model of Indigenous child welfare in Manitoba has been lauded for the level of Indigenous control over child welfare and the willingness of the Manitoba provincial government to share jurisdiction (Libesman 2014).

Band-by-Law In 1980, the Spallumcheen Indian Band in British Columbia took complete control and responsibility for providing child welfare services for all Spallumcheen Band members (Bennett et al. 2005; Johnston 1983; Libesman 2014). The by-law, which is legally recognized by the British Columbia and federal government, gave the Band exclusive authority over the care of all Spallumcheen First Nations children, whether living on or off reserve (Bennett et al. 2005). The Spallumcheen Indian Band is the only Indigenous community in Canada to have full jurisdiction over child welfare services and not bound by provincial legislation (Bennett et al. 2005; Sinha and Kozlowski 2013).

Despite a long history of Indigenous communities actively seeking full jurisdiction, most authority continues to be delegated, which means that most Indigenous child welfare agencies operate under provincial or territorial legislation (Blackstock and Trocmé 2005; Libesman 2014). Indigenous child welfare professionals who have worked under delegated models report concerns of perpetuating colonialism upon their own people (Strega and Esquao 2009). While provincial and territorial legislation have become more culturally sensitive and contain specific provisions for Indigenous children, families and communities, they cannot represent fully the needs of Indigenous communities, by virtue of the fact that they are not laws derived by Indigenous peoples.

Child and family services within First Nations communities are funded by the Canadian federal government through Indigenous and Northern Affairs Canada (INAC) under the First Nations Child and Family Services (FNCFS) Program. The stated goal of the FNCFS Program was to promote the development of culturally appropriate child welfare services controlled by First Nations communities for the benefit of children and their families living on reserve (Auditor General of Canada 2008). However, INAC's funding mechanisms have been criticized in many reports over the past two decades (Indigenous and Northern Affairs Canada n.d.). For example, the funding models developed through Directive 20-1 have been found, in several independent reviews, to be seriously flawed because: (1) they are based on child population not actual costs; (2) in-home prevention services that are not adequately covered, leaving out-of-home placement as the only option for intervention; and (3) FNCFS agencies are required to comply with provincial or territorial legislation to be eligible for funding, making it impossible for First Nations' to develop service delivery models that are tailored to their communities traditions, needs and assets (Bennett et al. 2005). Directive 20-1 is being replaced with a new funding policy, the Enhanced Prevention Focused Approach (EPFA) designed to allow service providers to use funds for prevention and early intervention services, as well as alternatives to traditional institutional care or foster care. However, the amount of funding available for these enhanced services has not kept pace with the needs of communities. In 2007, First Nations organizations brought forth a case against the Government of Canada to the Canadian Human Rights Tribunal (CHRT) on the grounds that child welfare services provided to Indigenous children and families on reserve are under-funded (Blackstock 2011; Sinha and Kozlowski 2013). On January 26, 2016, the CHRT found that the Government of Canada was racially discriminating against

163,000 First Nations children and their families and ordered the Government to significantly increase funding and develop more equitable funding models. Unfortunately, the situation remains unresolved and the CHRT has subsequently issued several non-compliance orders.

3.5 Child Welfare Service Outcomes

With over 230,000 children investigated by child welfare authorities every year in Canada, approximately 65,000 children in out-of-home care, and over $5 billion spent on child welfare services, surprisingly little is known about the outcomes of these services. A 2005 review of Canadian experimental and quasi-experimental evaluations of program impact in child welfare found only 10 published evaluations using comparison groups, four of which used a randomized design (Flynn and Bouchard 2005). More recently, a Royal Society of Canada panel concluded that "despite consistent evidence of the severe and long-lasting effects of child maltreatment, research on how best to intervene to prevent maltreatment and its recurrence is surprisingly limited" (Boivin and Hertzman 2012, pp. 102–103). When rigorous evaluation designs have been implemented, the results have been disappointing. A randomized controlled trial of an intensive home visitation program for children receiving child welfare services as a result of abuse or neglect found no statistically significant differences in maltreatment recurrence rates (MacMillan et al. 2005).

Beyond outcome studies specifically designed to evaluate intervention efficacy, a growing number of jurisdictions are reporting on outcomes of child welfare services. Using the National Outcomes Matrix (NOM) framework, several jurisdictions are reporting on the recurrence of maltreatment, which is measured as the proportion of child protection cases that are reopened as a result of a substantiated incident of maltreatment with 12 months of case closure (Trocmé et al. 2009). The reported rate of recurrence for Quebec was 9.3% for cases closed during the fiscal year 2012–2013, 11.2% in BC, for protection investigations and 3.6% of FDR cases in 2014–2015, and 19% in Ontario for protection cases closed in 2014–2015 (British Columbia 2016; Esposito et al. 2017; Ontario Ministry of Children and Youth Services 2017).

Two key outcome indicators reported for children and youth in out-of-home care are placement stability and permanency. Unfortunately, because of differences in definitions of placement, permanence, and follow-up timeframes comparisons between jurisdictions are difficult to make. However, placement stability can be measured by the number of significant placement changes. For example, using data from Quebec, Esposito et al. (2017) report that, tracked over a period of up to 36 months, children who came into care in 2010 and 2011 moved an average of 1.87 times, with 31% of children experiencing no changes within 36 months, 25% having one change in placement, 27% having two-three changes, and 18% with four or more changes. Tracking placement changes during a 12-month period, British Columbia (2016) reports that 68.7% of children did not move, 22.7% moved once, and 8.6% moved two or more times. Permanency is measured by tracking the proportion of children who end up returning home, are adopted, or are in a placement considered to be permanent. Reported rates of permanency range from a low of 21.8% in BC (British Columbia 2016, p. 55), measured as the proportion of all children in care who exit care to a permanent arrangement, to between 60% and 70% in Quebec measured by tracking the placement status of children 36 months after they enter care (Esposito et al. 2017).

Educational outcomes, which provide a more direct measure if success, are starting to be tracked in jurisdictions that link child welfare service and educational data. British Columbia provides the most extensive set of annually reported indicators, showing that 86% of children and youth in out-of-home care who are at school are in an age-appropriate grade, but that only 52.7% of youth in care who turned 19 had high school credentials (British Columbia 2016, p. 79). Analysis of school and placement trajectories of children and youth in Manitoba provide the most comprehensive portrait of the educational challenges faced by children and youth in child welfare: while 85% of youth in the general population tested in Grade 8 were competent in reading and writing, only 66% of youth who had received family support services through child welfare tested as competent, while only 49% of youth who had been in out-of-home care met the Grade 8 reading and writing level of competency (Houden 2015).

The extent of the overrepresentation of Indigenous children and youth in out-of-home care discussed earlier in this chapter, is a key indicator being tracked by a growing number of jurisdictions. Alberta and British Columbia, the two provinces with the most comprehensive reports tracking child welfare outcomes, breakdown most of their statistics by comparing outcomes for Indigenous and non-Indigenous children and youth. 69% of children in care in Alberta were Indigenous in 2016; over time the rate of overrepresentation has been increasing (Alberta Human Services n.d). In BC, 61% of children in out of home care are aboriginal, a proportion that has also been increasing (British Columbia 2016). Additional analysis of trends in BC show that the number of Aboriginal children in care has remained the same or increased, while the number of non-Aboriginal children has declined; however, the rate of Aboriginal children in care per 1000 Aboriginal children in the population has been declining. Consistent nation-wide monitoring of the placement of First Nations children in out-of-home care is one of the key recommendations from the TRC (2015).

3.6 Conclusions

Canada's provincially organized child welfare system has been profoundly shaped by its roots in late nineteenth century morally driven child saving movements and colonial assimilationism of indigenous communities. Modernization of child welfare statutes and programs have shifted the language to concepts of child maltreatment and an emphasis on less intrusive family and community centered approaches.

Despite these changes child welfare mandates have been expanding across Canada; rates of investigation nearly doubled from 2003 to 2008, the number of children in out of home care has increased continuously, as have rates of overrepresentation for Indigenous children. Closer examination of these increases show that they do not appear to be driven by situations where there is immediate concern for child safety, but rather the concerns relate to the well-being of children living in difficult conditions. While the number of investigations involving serious abuse has not changed, the number of children referred for risk of abuse and neglect, emotional maltreatment, or exposure to violence has increased dramatically.

In contrast to many European jurisdictions that emphasize family support services over child maltreatment investigations, child welfare systems across Canada continue to function primarily through a child protection framework characterized by mandatory reporting, centralized responses by mandated agencies, and investigations focused on substantiation and risk assessment (Gilbert et al. 2009). Efforts are being initiated across Canada to develop a broader array of options to meet the diverse needs of child welfare engaged families, a shift that is most notably needed for children and families from Indigenous communities. Continued monitoring of investigation and placement trends, in particular with respect to Indigenous children, are key indicators of the extent to which Canadian child welfare systems are able to shift from a safety orientation to a broader child and family support orientation.

References

Afifi, T. O., MacMillan, H. L., Boyle, M., Taillieu, T., Cheung, K., & Sareen, J. (2014). Child abuse and mental disorders in Canada. *CMAJ: Canadian Medical Association Journal, 186*(9), E324–E332. https://doi.org/10.1503/cmaj.131792.

Alberta Human Services. (n.d.) *Child intervention information and statistics summary 2017/18, First Quarter (June) Update*. Retrieved from http://www.humanservices.alberta.ca/documents/child-intervention-info-stats-summary-2017-18-q1.pdf

Auditor General of Canada. (2008). First nations child and family services program—Indian and northern affairs Canada (Chapter 4). In *Report of the auditor general of Canada to the house of commons*. Retrieved from http://www.oagbvg.gc.ca/internet/English/parl_oag_200805_04_e_30700.html

Bala, N. (1999). Reforming Ontario's child and family services act: Is the pendulum swinging back too far? *Canadian Family Law Quarterly, 17*, 121–172.

Bala, N., Zapf, M. K., Williams, R. J., Vogl, R., & Hornick, J. P. (Eds.). (2004). *Canadian child welfare law: Children, families and the state* (2nd ed.). Toronto: Thompson Educational Publishing.

Bennett, M., Blackstock, C., & De La Ronde, R. (2005). *A literature review and annotated bibliography on aspects of Aboriginal child welfare in Canada*. Ottawa: First Nations Child and Family Caring Society of Canada.

Blackstock, C. (2011). The Canadian human rights tribunal on first nations child welfare: Why if Canada wins, equality and justice lose. *Children and Youth Services Review, 33*(1), 187–194. https://doi.org/10.1016/j.childyouth.2010.09.002.

Blackstock, C., & Trocmé, N. (2005). Community-based child welfare for aboriginal children: Supporting resilience through structural change. *Social Policy Journal of New Zealand, 24*, 12–33.

Boivin, M., & Hertzman, C. (Eds.). (2012). *Early childhood development: Adverse experiences and developmental health* (Royal Society of Canada—Canadian academy of health sciences expert panel [with Ronald Barr, Thomas Boyce, Alison Fleming, Harriet MacMillan, Candice Odgers, Marla Sokolowski, & Nico Trocmé]). Ottawa: Royal Society of Canada. Retrieved from https://rsc-src.ca/sites/default/files/pdf/ECD%20Report_0.pdf

Brassard, M. R., Germain, R., & Hart, S. N. (1987). *Psychological maltreatment of children and youth*. New York: Pergamon Press.

British Columbia. (2016). *Performance management report* (Volume 8, March 2016, Reporting October 2015 – March 2016). Ministry of Children and Family Development. Retrieved from https://www2.gov.bc.ca/assets/gov/family-and-social-supports/services-supports-for-parents-with-young-children/reporting-monitoring/00-public-ministry-reports/volume_8_draftv7.pdf

British Columbia Ministry of Family Development. (2011). *Residential review project: Phase one—Findings report*. Retrieved from https://www2.gov.bc.ca/assets/gov/family-and-social-supports/services-supports-for-parents-with-young-children/reporting-monitoring/02-residential-review-project/residential_review_phase_1_findings.pdf

Burczycka, M., & Conroy, S. (2017). *Family violence in Canada: A statistical profile, 2015* (Statistics Canada, Canadian Centre for Justice Statistics, *Juristat* article, Catalogue no. 85-002-X). Ottawa: Minister of Industry. Retrieved from http://www.statcan.gc.ca/pub/85-002-x/2017001/article/14698-eng.pdf

Canadian Centre for Justice Statistics. (2007). *Family violence in Canada: A statistical profile, 2007* (Statistics Canada, Catalogue no. 85-224-XIE). Ottawa: Minister of Industry. Available from http://publications.gc.ca/Collection/Statcan/85-224-X/85-224-XIE.html

Canadian Centre for Justice Statistics. (2015). *Family violence in Canada: A statistical profile, 2013* (Statistics Canada, *Juristat* article, Catalogue no. 85-002-X). Ottawa: Minister of Industry. Retrieved from http://www.statcan.gc.ca/pub/85-002-x/2014001/article/14114-eng.pdf

Child and Family Services Act, R.S.O. (1990) c. 11 (CanLII). Retrieved from http://canlii.ca/t/4m7#sec1subsec2

Child Welfare Act, R.S.O. (1970) c. 64.

Contenta, S. (n.d.). Children's aid society (Investigative series). *The Toronto star*. Retrieved from https://www.thestar.com/news/cas.html

Criminal Code, R.S.C. (1985) c. 46, s. 231(6).

Dumbrill, G. C. (2006). Ontario's child welfare transformation: Another swing of the pendulum? *Canadian Social Work Review, 23*(1–2), 5–19.

Durrant, J. E., Trocmé, N., Fallon, B., Milne, C., & Black, T. (2009). Protection of children from physical maltreatment in Canada: An evaluation of the supreme court's definition of reasonable force. *Journal of Aggression, Maltreatment & Trauma, 18*(1), 64–87. https://doi.org/10.1080/10926770802610640.

Erickson, M. F., & Egeland, B. (2002). Child neglect. In J. Myers, L. Berliner, J. Briere, C. Hendrix, C. Jenny, & T. Reid (Eds.), *The APSAC handbook on child maltreatment* (2nd ed.). Thousand Oaks: Sage.

Esposito, T., Trocmé, N., Chabot, M., Shlonsky, A., Collin-Vézina, D., & Sinha, V. (2013). Placement of children in out-of-home care in Québec, Canada: When and for whom initial out-of-home placement is most likely to occur. *Children and Youth Services Review, 35*(12), 2031–2039. https://doi.org/10.1016/j.childyouth.2013.10.010.

Esposito, T., Trocmé, N., Chabot, M., Collin-Vézina, D., Shlonsky, A., & Sinha, V. (2014). Family reunification for placed children in Québec, Canada: A longitudinal study. *Children and Youth Services Review, 44*, 278–287. https://doi.org/10.1016/j.childyouth.2014.06.024.

Esposito, T., Trocmé, N., Chabot, M., Robichaud, M.-J., Léveillé, S., Desmarais, S., … Sirois, M.-C. (2017). *Gestion fondée sur les indicateurs de suivi clinique (GFISC) en protection de la jeunesse: Rapport synthèse*. Available from https://mcgill.ca/crcf/channels/news/recently-released-gestion-fondee-sur-les-indicateurs-de-suivi-clinique-gfisc-synthesis-report-269155

Fallon, B., Trocmé, N., & MacLaurin, B. (2011a). Should child protection services respond differently to maltreatment, risk of maltreatment, and risk of harm? *Child Abuse & Neglect, 35*(4), 236–239. https://doi.org/10.1016/j.chiabu.2011.03.001.

Fallon, B., Trocmé, N., MacLaurin, B., Sinha, V., & Black, T. (2011b). Untangling risk of maltreatment from events of maltreatment: An analysis of the 2008 Canadian incidence study of reported child abuse and neglect (CIS-2008). *International Journal of Mental Health and Addiction, 9*(5), 460–479. https://doi.org/10.1007/s11469-011-9351-4.

Fallon, B., Trocmé, N., Fluke, J., Van Wert, M., MacLaurin, B., Sinha, V., et al. (2012). Responding to child maltreatment in Canada: Context for international comparisons. *Advances in Mental Health, 11*(1), 76–86. https://doi.org/10.5172/jamh.2012.11.1.76.

Fallon, B., Lefebvre, R., Seto, M., & Van Wert, M. (2013). *Cases involving multiple sectors of the justice system: Information from the 2008 Canadian Incidence Study of Reported Child Abuse and Neglect* (Internal report for the Department of Justice Canada).

Fallon, B., Van Wert, M., Trocmé, N., MacLaurin, B., Sinha, V., Lefebvre, R., … Goel, S. (2015). *Ontario incidence study of reported child abuse and neglect-2013 (OIS-2013)*. Toronto: Child Welfare Research Portal. Retrieved from http://cwrp.ca/sites/default/files/publications/en/ois-2013_final.pdf

Fallon, B., Trocmé, N., Filipelli, J., Black, T., & Joh-Carnella, N. (in press). Responding to safety concerns and chronic needs: Trends over time. *Child and Adolescent Psychiatry and Mental Health.*

Flynn, R., & Bouchard, D. (2005). Randomized and quasi-experimental evaluations of program impact in child welfare in Canada: A review. *Canadian Journal of Program Evaluation, 20*, 65–100.

Fournier, S., & Crey, E. (1997). *Stolen from our embrace*. Vancouver: Douglas & McIntrye.

Freymond, N., & Cameron, G. (Eds.). (2006). *Towards positive systems of child and family welfare: International comparisons of child protection, family service, and community caring systems*. Toronto: University of Toronto Press.

Gharabaghi, K., Trocmé, N., & Newman, D. (2016). *Because young people matter: Report of the residential services review panel*. Toronto: Ontario Ministry of Children and Youth Services.

Gilbert, R., Kemp, A., Thoburn, J., Sidebotham, P., Radford, L., Glaser, D., & MacMillan, H. L. (2009). Recognising and responding to child maltreatment. *The Lancet, 373*(9658), 167–180. https://doi.org/10.1016/S0140-6736(08)61707-9.

Gough, P., Shlonsky, A., & Dudding, P. (2009). An overview of the child welfare systems in Canada. *International Journal of Child Health & Human Development, 2*(3), 357–371.

Gove, T. J. (1995). *Executive summary: Report of the Gove inquiry into child protection in British Columbia*. Victoria: BC Government.

Government of New Brunswick. (2015). *Keeping children and youth safe from harm in New Brunswick: A five year strategy by New Brunswickers*. Fredericton: Province of New Brunswick. Retrieved from http://www2.gnb.ca/content/dam/gnb/Departments/cya-dej/pdf/ChildrenYouthSafeFromHarm.pdf

Graff, D. (2017). *Three young children: An investigative review* (Report prepared by the Office of the Child and Youth Advocate, Alberta). Retrieved from http://www.ocya.alberta.ca/wp-content/uploads/2014/08/InvRev_Three-Young-Children_2017July.pdf

Hamilton, A. C., & Sinclair, C. M. (1991). The justice system and aboriginal people: Report of the aboriginal justice inquiry of Manitoba. In *The Queen's Printer* (Vol. 1). Winnipeg.

Hélie, S., Collin-Vézina, D., Turcotte, D., Trocmé, N., & Girouard, N. (2017). *Étude d'incidence québécoise sur les situations évaluées en protection de la jeunesse en 2014 (ÉIQ-2014): Rapport final.* Retrieved from http://cwrp.ca/sites/default/files/publications/en/eiq-2014_rapport_final.pdf

Houden, M. (2015). *Manitoba can do better for kids in care* (Summary of Manitoba Centre for Health Policy report, *The Educational Outcomes of Children in Care in Manitoba*, by Marni Brownell, Mariette Chartier, Wendy Au, Leonard MacWilliam, Jennifer Schultz, Wendy Guenette, and Jeff Valdivia). University of Manitoba, Faculty of Health Sciences. Retrieved from http://mchp-appserv.cpe.umanitoba.ca/reference/CIC_summary.pdf

Indian Act, R.S.C. (1985). c. I-5 (CanLII). Retrieved from http://canlii.ca/t/52fln
Indigenous and Northern Affairs Canada (1996). *Highlights from the report of the Royal Commission on aboriginal peoples: People to people, nation to nation.* (Catalogue no. Z1-1991/1-6E). Ottawa: Minister of Supply and Services Canada. Retrieved from http://www.aadnc-aandc.gc.ca/eng/1100100014597/1100100014637
Indigenous and Northern Affairs Canada. (n.d.). *First nations child and family services.* Retrieved from https://www.aadnc-aandc.gc.ca/eng/1100100035204/1100100035205
Johnston, P. (1983). *Native children and the child welfare system.* Toronto: Canadian Council on Social Development in association with James Lorimer &.
Jones, A., & Rutman, L. (1981). *In the children's aid: J.J. Kelso and child welfare in Ontario.* Toronto: University of Toronto Press.
Jones, A., Sinha, V., & Trocmé, N. (2015). *Children and youth in out-of-home care in the Canadian provinces* (CWRP Information Sheet #167E). Montréal: Centre for Research on Children and Families. Retrieved from http://cwrp.ca/sites/default/files/publications/en/167e.pdf
Jud, A., & Trocmé, N. (2012). *Physical abuse and physical punishment in Canada* (CWRP Information Sheet #122E). Montréal: Centre for Research on Children and Families. Retrieved from http://cwrp.ca/infosheets/physical-abuse-and-physical-punishment-canada
Kirmayer, L., Simpson, C., & Cargo, M. (2003). Healing traditions: Culture, community and mental health promotion with Canadian aboriginal peoples. *Australasian Psychiatry, 11*, 2–9. https://doi.org/10.1046/j.1038-5282.2003.02010.x.
Kozlowski, A., Sinha, V., Hartsook, G., Thomas Prokop, S., & Montgomery, H. M. (2011a). *First Nations child welfare in Saskatchewan* (CWRP Information Sheet #99E). Montreal: Centre for Research on Children and Families. Retrieved from http://cwrp.ca/infosheets/first-nations-child-welfare-saskatchewan
Kozlowski, A., Sinha, V., Petti, T., & Flette, E. (2011b). *First Nations child welfare in Manitoba* (CWRP Information Sheet #97E). Montreal: McGill University, Centre for Research on Children and Families. Retrieved from http://cwrp.ca/infosheets/first-nations-child-welfare-manitoba
Kozlowski, A., Milne, L., & Sinha, V. (2014). *British Columbia's child welfare system* (CWRP Information Sheet #139E). Montreal: Centre for Research on Children and Families. Retrieved from http://cwrp.ca/sites/default/files/publications/en/BC_final_infosheet.pdf
Kyte, A., & Wegner-Lohin, J. (2014). *Alberta's child welfare system* (CWRP Information Sheet #137E). Montreal: Centre for Research on Children and Families. Retrieved from http://cwrp.ca/sites/default/files/publications/en/AB_infosheet_final.pdf
Kyte, A., Trocmé, N., & Chamberland, C. (2013). Evaluating where we're at with differential response. *Child Abuse & Neglect, 37*(2), 125–132. https://doi.org/10.1016/j.chiabu.2012.10.003.
Lajoie, J. (2006). *Quebec's child welfare system* (CECW Information Sheet #35E). Montreal: McGill University, School of Social Work. Retrieved from http://cwrp.ca/sites/default/files/publications/en/QueChildWelfareSystem35E.pdf
Libesman, T. (2014). *Decolonising indigenous child welfare.* Oxon: Routledge.
MacMillan, H. L., Thomas, B. H., Jamieson, E., Walsh, C. A., Boyle, M. H., Shannon, H. S., & Gafni, A. (2005). Effectiveness of home visitation by public-health nurses in prevention of the recurrence of child physical abuse and neglect: A randomised controlled trial. *The Lancet, 365*(9473), 1786–1793. https://doi.org/10.1016/S0140-6736(05)66388-X.
Mansell, J. (2006). The underlying instability in statutory child protection: Understanding the system dynamics driving risk assurance levels. *Social Policy Journal of New Zealand, 28*, 97–132.
Merkel-Holguin, L., Yuan, Y. T., Jowers, K., Hollinshead, D., Fluke, J., & Hahn, A. (2014). *Final report: QIC-DR cross-site evaluation.* Available from Quality Improvement Center on Differential Response website: www.differentialresponseqic.org
Miller, J. R. (1996). *Shingwauk's vision: A history of native residential schools.* Toronto: University of Toronto Press.
Milloy, J. S. (2017). *A national crime: The Canadian government and the residential school system* (p. 464). Winnipeg: University of Manitoba Press.
Milloy, J. S., & McCallum, M. J. (2017). *A national crime: The Canadian government and the residential school system, 1879 to 1986.* Winnipeg: University of Manitoba Press.

Milward, D. (2016). *Children need families, not courtrooms: Alternatives to adversarial litigation in child welfare* (A special report by the Office of the Children's Advocate, Manitoba). Retrieved from http://www.childrensadvocate.mb.ca/wp-content/uploads/MILWARD-FULL-web.pdf

O'Donnell, M., Maclean, M., Sims, S., Brownell, M., Ekuma, O., & Gilbert, R. (2016). Entering out-of-home care during childhood: Cumulative incidence study in Canada and Australia. *Child Abuse & Neglect, 59*, 78–87. https://doi.org/10.1016/j.chiabu.2016.07.011.

Ontario Association of Children's Aid Societies. (n.d.) *OACAS operational plan 2016–2017: Message from Chief Executive Officer*. Retrieved from http://www.oacas.org/oacas-operational-plan-201617/

Ontario Ministry of Children and Youth Services. (2016). *The aboriginal advisor's report on the status of aboriginal child welfare in Ontario*. Queen's Printer for Ontario. Retrieved from http://www.children.gov.on.ca/htdocs/English/professionals/indigenous/child_welfare-2011.aspx

Ontario Ministry of Children and Youth Services. (2017). *Safety*. Queen's Printer for Ontario. Retrieved from http://www.children.gov.on.ca/htdocs/English/professionals/childwelfare/societies/publicreporting/safety.aspx

Reid, C., & Dudding, P. (2006). *Building a future together: Issues and outcomes for transition-aged youth*. Ottawa: Centre of Excellence for Child Welfare.

Shields, M., Tonmyr, L., & Hovdestad, W. (2016). Is child sexual abuse declining in Canada? Results from nationally representative retrospective surveys. *Health Promotion and Chronic Disease Prevention in Canada: Research, Policy and Practice, 36*(11), 252–260. https://doi.org/10.24095/hpcdp.36.11.03.

Sinclair, R. (2007). Identity lost and found: Lessons from the sixties scoop. *The First Peoples Child & Family Review, 3*(1). Retrieved from http://journals.sfu.ca/fpcfr/index.php/FPCFR/article/view/25

Sinha, V., & Kozlowski, A. (2013). The structure of aboriginal child welfare in Canada. *The International Indigenous Policy Journal, 4*(2), 1–21. https://doi.org/10.18584/iipj.2013.4.2.2.

Sinha, V., & Wray, M. (2015). *Foster care disparity for Aboriginal children in 2011* (CWRP Information Sheet #165E). Montréal: Centre for Research on Children and Families. Retrieved from http://cwrp.ca/sites/default/files/publications/en/165e.pdf

Sinha, V., Trocmé, N., Fallon, B., MacLaurin, B., Fast, E., Thomas Prokop, S., … Richard, K. (2011). *Kiskisik Awasisak: Remember the children. Understanding the overrepresentation of first nations children in the child welfare system*. Ontario: Assembly of First Nations. Retrieved from http://cwrp.ca/sites/default/files/publications/en/FNCIS-2008_March2012_RevisedFinal.pdf

Strega, S., & Esquao, S. A. (Carrière, J.). (Eds.). (2009). *Walking this path together: Antiracist and anti-oppressive child welfare practice*. Halifax: Fernwood.

Trocmé, N. (1991). Child welfare services. In D. Barnhorst & L. Johnson (Eds.), *State of the child in Ontario* (pp. 63–91). Toronto: Oxford University Press.

Trocmé, N., MacLaurin, B., Fallon, B., Daciuk, J., Billingsley, D., Tourigny, M., … McKenzie, B. (2001). *Canadian incidence study of reported child abuse and neglect: Final report*. Ottawa: Minister of Public Works and Government Services Canada. Retrieved from http://cwrp.ca/sites/default/files/publications/en/cis1998.pdf

Trocmé, N., Fallon, B., MacLaurin, B., Daciuk, J., Felstiner, C., Black, T., … Cloutier, R. (2005). *Canadian incidence study of reported child abuse and neglect – 2003: Major findings*. Ottawa: Minister of Public Works and Government Services Canada. Retrieved from http://cwrp.ca/sites/default/files/publications/en/cis2003.pdf

Trocmé, N., MacLaurin, B., Fallon, B., Shlonsky, A., Mulcahy, M., & Esposito, T. (2009). *National child welfare outcomes indicator matrix (NOM)*. Montreal: McGill University Centre for research on children and families. Retrieved from https://www.mcgill.ca/crcf/files/crcf/NOM_09Final.pdf

Trocmé, N., Fallon, B., MacLaurin, B., Sinha, V., Black, T., Fast, E., … Holroyd, J. (2010). *Canadian incidence study of reported child abuse and neglect – 2008: Major findings*. Ottawa:

Public Health Agency of Canada. Retrieved from http://cwrp.ca/sites/default/files/publications/en/CIS-2008-rprt-eng.pdf
Trocmé, N., Fallon, B., Maclaurin, B., Chamberland, C., Chabot, M., & Esposito, T. (2011). Shifting definitions of emotional maltreatment: An analysis child welfare investigation laws and practices in Canada. *Child Abuse & Neglect, 35*(10), 831–840. https://doi.org/10.1016/j.chiabu.2011.05.015.
Trocmé, N., Fallon, B., Sinha, V., Van Wert, M., Kozlowski, A., & MacLaurin, B. (2013). Differentiating between child protection and family support in the Canadian child welfare system's response to intimate partner violence, corporal punishment, and child neglect. *International Journal of Psychology, 48*(2), 128–140. https://doi.org/10.1080/00207594.2013.765571.
Trocmé, N., Kyte, A., Sinha, V., & Fallon, B. (2014). Urgent protection versus chronic need: Clarifying the dual mandate of child welfare services across Canada. *Social Sciences, 3*(3), 483–498. https://doi.org/10.3390/socsci3030483.
Truth and Reconciliation Commission of Canada. (2015). *Truth and Reconciliation Commission of Canada: Calls to action.* Retrieved from http://www.trc.ca/websites/trcinstitution/File/2015/Findings/Calls_to_Action_English2.pdf
Truth and Reconciliation Commission of Canada. (n.d.). *Reconciliation…Towards a new relationship*. Retrieved from http://www.trc.ca/websites/reconciliation/index.php?p=312
Waldfogel, J. (2009). Differential response. In K. A. Dodge & D. L. Coleman (Eds.), *Preventing child maltreatment: Community approaches* (pp. 139–155). New York: Guilford Press.
Wegner-Lohin, J., & Trocmé, N. (2016). *Injuries and death of children at the hands of their parents* (CWRP Information Sheet #174E). Montreal: Canadian Child Welfare Research Portal. Retrieved from http://cwrp.ca/sites/default/files/publications/en/174e_0.pdf
Wegner-Lohin, J., Kyte, A., & Trocmé, N. (2014). *Ontario's child welfare system* (CWRP Information Sheet #138E). Montreal: Centre for Research on Children and Families. Retrieved from http://cwrp.ca/sites/default/files/publications/en/ON_infosheet_final_0.pdf
Wolfe, D. A., Crooks, C. V., Lee, V., McIntyre-Smith, A., & Jaffe, P. G. (2003). The effects of children's exposure to domestic violence: A meta-analysis and critique. *Clinical Child and Family Psychology Review, 6*(3), 171–187. https://doi.org/10.1023/a:1024910416164.

Nico Trocmé, MSW, PhD, TS, FRSC, is the Director of the School of Social Work and the Philip Fisher Chair in Social Work at McGill University. Dr. Trocmé is the principal investigator for the Canadian Incidence Study (CIS) of Reported Child Abuse and Neglect (1993, 1998, 2003 & 2008), was the lead researcher for a Federal-Provincial-Territorial initiative to develop a common set of National Outcomes Measures in child welfare, directs the Canadian Child Welfare Research Portal (cwrp.ca), and is conducting a research capacity development and knowledge mobilization initiative involving child welfare and Aboriginal service provider agencies in Quebec.

Tonino Esposito, MSW, PhD, is an Assistant Professor at University of Montreal and Adjunct Professor at McGill University and, recipient of a Tier II Canada Research Chair in Social Services for Vulnerable Children. Dr. Esposito is the lead researcher for province-wide longitudinal studies on children's service trajectories in the Quebec child welfare system and principal investigator a Canadian Social Sciences and Humanities Research Council Grant on neighborhood socioeconomic disadvantages and child protection service outcomes. The work for this chapter was also supported by Dr. Esposito's Canada Research Chair (SSHRC # 950-230680).

Jennifer Nutton is currently a PhD Candidate in the School of Social Work at McGill University, and works out of the McGill Centre for Research on Children and Families. Jennifer conducts community-based partnership research with Indigenous communities as well as non-Indigenous community and public service agencies serving Indigenous children and families. Jennifer has worked with child welfare systems since 2005 including as a training coordinator under a United

States federally funded grant to develop and deliver child welfare training in Nevada. Her research interests include Indigenous research methodologies, decolonization and Indigenization, child welfare and social policy, participatory action research, social justice and qualitative inquiry.

Valerie Rosser is currently a Masters of Social Work student and research assistant in the School of Social Work at McGill University. With a professional background in Nutrition and Dietetics and a history of anti-poverty volunteerism, Valerie's research interests include accessibility of mental health services, systems of marginalization and oppression, decolonization and Indigenization, participatory action research, social justice, food security, and child welfare.

Dr. Barbara Fallon, for the past 20 years, has worked to bridge that knowledge gap by collecting reliable national and provincial child welfare data across Canada and mining it with innovative statistical techniques to help policymakers determine what works and is needed to best help children based on evidence, not perceptions. Dr. Fallon has received over 11 million dollars in research grants and contracts as a Principal Investigator or Co-Investigator. These research grants include provincial-wide studies such as the Ontario Incidence Study of Reported Child Abuse & Neglect (2008 & 2013) as well as several knowledge mobilization grants have allowed her to capitalize on the analytic potential of child welfare's administrative data. She is a Canada Research Chair in Child Welfare and the Factor-Inwentash Chair in Child Welfare.

Chapter 4
Balancing Prevention and Protection: Child Protection in England

Nina Biehal

4.1 Introduction

According to a recent prevalence study, one-quarter of children in the UK experience physical, sexual or emotional abuse or neglect by a parent or caregiver at least once before they reach the age of 18. Furthermore, interviews with 2,275 children and young people (or their parents or caregivers) revealed that 2.5% of under 11 year-olds and 6% of 11–17 year olds in the sample had experienced at least one type of maltreatment in the previous year alone (Radford et al. 2013). Unsurprisingly these self-reported rates are much higher than those that come to the attention of services, as child maltreatment often goes unreported and may be undetected for many years, if at all. The incidence of *recorded* maltreatment is therefore much lower. Official statistics indicate that in 2015–2016, 1.7% of all under-18 year olds in the general population were assessed as needing support due to concerns about abuse or neglect (Department for Education 2016a). However, these figures are not strictly comparable, as the prevalence study reported the incidence of maltreatment over the course of a year whereas official statistics record the number of children involved in the child welfare system due to abuse or neglect on an annual census date. Furthermore, official statistics record only abuse and neglect assessed as sufficiently severe to make children eligible for services whereas not all self-reported maltreatment will reach that service threshold.

The scope of child protection activity has expanded over time. Although the principal focus has been on four broad categories of intra-familial maltreatment, namely physical, sexual and emotional abuse and neglect, over the last 30 years or so a number of other problems have also come to be conceptualised as forms of abuse. These include institutional abuse in residential institutions such as children's homes and boarding schools, where physical, sexual and emotional abuse remained hidden,

N. Biehal (✉)
University of York, York, UK
e-mail: nina.biehal@york.ac.uk

L. Merkel-Holguin et al. (eds.), *National Systems of Child Protection*, Child Maltreatment 8, https://doi.org/10.1007/978-3-319-93348-1_4

or unchallenged, for many years, and the less widespread problem of abuse in foster care (Biehal 2014; Sen et al. 2008). Female genital mutilation (FGM) has been prohibited in the UK since 1985 but penalties were increased in 2003 and since 2015 it has been mandatory for health and social care professionals, teachers and the police to report any cases of FGM they identify in the course of their work. Witnessing domestic violence was for the first time legally defined as a form of child maltreatment by the *Adoption and Children Act 2002* and child trafficking for the purposes of sexual and non-sexual exploitation was defined as abusive and prohibited by law in 2003 and 2004. More recently, child sexual exploitation (CSE) has received growing attention. Until relatively recently this was viewed as prostitution or as a lifestyle choice by young people but it has since been redefined as a form of sexual abuse. Today many local authorities have specialist child protection teams with a specific remit to deal with CSE. Most recently of all, the scope of child protection activity has been widened to include anti-radicalisation to safeguard children and young people from being drawn into Islamic terrorism or far-Right groups through online grooming or by other means. Constructions of abuse have therefore broadened over time, with a wider range of issues now defined as abusive.

This chapter draws on work undertaken for the *Hestia* study which compared child protection systems and practice in England, Germany and the Netherlands, funded by Norface, a European funding body. Both the *Hestia* study and this chapter focus on England rather than the UK as a whole because, while there are many similarities, there are also a number of important differences in legal and institutional frameworks for child protection between England, Scotland, Northern Ireland and Wales as the latter three countries have devolved parliaments responsible for some aspects of policy.

The chapter is principally concerned with the contemporary child protection system in England but begins with a brief account of its development, as the operation of child protection systems is often influenced by the legacy of earlier arrangements. The chapter therefore discusses how the policies and priorities which have shaped the English child protection system have developed over time before examining the key policy principles that underpin child protection activity today. It also discusses the institutional characteristics of the system and the responsibilities of social workers and other professionals. Finally, it explores the current operation of the system through an analysis of patterns of intervention and discusses the challenges it currently faces.

4.2 Development of the Policy Framework

The origins of the English child protection system lie in the work of charitable and religious organisations in the mid- to late- nineteenth century, which drew attention to the neglect and ill-treatment of children. Their work contributed to the development of the first legislation to protect children from abuse and neglect in 1889 (amended in 1894), which for the first time allowed state intervention in family life and also gave recognition to mental cruelty. This was followed by further legislation over the next few years including the *Children Act 1908* and the *Punishment of Incest Act 1908*. All existing legislation on children was subsequently consolidated in the *Children and Young Persons Act 1933*. However, although physical, sexual and emotional abuse had been given legal recognition by the early twentieth century, the main form of maltreatment recorded from the late nineteenth century onwards was neglect, and neglect still accounted for around 90% of cases of child maltreatment dealt with by state and voluntary agencies until the early 1970s (Ferguson 2011).

The modern child welfare system has its origins not only in these earlier developments but also in the post-war legislative programme which set up the British welfare state. This included the passing of the *Children Act 1948,* which gave local authorities new responsibilities for children who were neglected or otherwise vulnerable and whose parents were unable to care for them adequately. The 1948 Act set up a new child care service, that was to be provided by the Children's Departments to be established in every local authority, and gave local authorities a new duty to 'receive children into care' on a voluntary basis and to assume parental rights if children had been lost or abandoned or if their parents were 'unfit or unable' to care for them (Ball 1998; Hughes 1998). Much of the emphasis in the 1948 Act was on removing neglected children from families unable to provide adequate care but, by the early 1950s, there was growing recognition of the link between neglect and material deprivation, leading to calls for professionals to be given statutory powers to undertake preventive work (Biehal 2005; Heywood 1978). The *Children and Young Persons Act 1963* was the first legislation in England to set out a duty to provide support to families to prevent admission to out of home care and also delinquency, marking a shift to a greater emphasis on supporting families in order to prevent abuse, neglect and youth offending. This approach was also strongly in evidence in the *Children and Young Persons Act 1969*, which set out a broad commitment to preventing deprivation and delinquency through working with the whole family.

However, parallel developments during the 1960s and in the decade that followed led to heightened concern about physical abuse and paved the way for a shift to a more interventionist approach to protecting children. This was prompted initially by the publication of Kempe's research on the 'battered baby syndrome' and, from the early 1970s, by a number of widely-reported inquiries into child deaths from abuse (Kempe et al. 1962). The public inquiry into the death of Maria Colwell at the hands of her stepfather in 1973 was followed by 29 other inquiries into cases of child deaths due to abuse by 1985 (Secretary of State for Social Services 1974). Since that time there have been recurrent policy tensions between the 'defenders of the birth family', who emphasise the importance of family support to prevent child maltreatment and the placement of children in out of home care, and those proposing a more interventionist approach to child protection with 'the state as parent' (Fox-Harding 1991).

From the late 1970s there was also a growing recognition (or rather, a rediscovery) of sexual abuse within the family. By the 1990s there was increasing attention to emotional abuse and, since the mid-2000s, there has been renewed attention to neglect. The growing acknowledgement of the needs and rights of children to protection was also the product of wider social developments in the mid-twentieth century, including the highlighting of family violence by the women's movement in the 1970s and increasing attention of children's rights during the development of the United Nations Convention on the Rights of the Child (UNCRC) in the 1980s (Frost and Parton 2009).

These developments contributed to a shift towards a stronger child orientation and more legalistic, interventionist approaches to child protection during the 1970s, but there was nevertheless continuing attention to prevention. By the 1980s, concern about the rise in the number of children in care and evidence of poor outcomes for children who had been in care contributed to calls for more attention to work with families to prevent the need to remove children from their parents (Parker 1980; Fisher et al. 1986; Holman 1988). These debates about the need for more, or alternatively less, state intervention in family life, an accompanying desire to achieve a balance between protecting children and preserving family autonomy, along with a perceived need to consolidate existing legislation, led to the *Review of Child Care Law* in 1985. This considered what the role of the state should be in relation to vulnerable children and, significantly, questioned the value of the distinction between the needs of the child and the needs of the family.

4.3 The *Children Act 1989*

These developments shaped the *Children Act 1989*, which still provides the core legal framework for the English child welfare system, which includes preventive services, child protection services, out of home care and services for disabled children. 'Children' are defined as all those under 18 years old. The 1989 Act tried to achieve a new balance between supporting families and protecting children. Safeguarding the welfare of children is therefore defined very broadly, with the protection of children from maltreatment located within a wider framework of services to support children and families.

The *Children Act 1989* represented an attempt to reconcile the two main value positions regarding state intervention in family life that had underpinned the development of policy in the post-war years: a more legalistic, protectionist approach to children at risk of maltreatment and a less interventionist, preventive approach. It therefore sought to integrate a new duty to protect children from significant harm with a wider duty to support families in order to safeguard and promote the welfare of children. The Act states that children are best looked after by their families and makes it clear that legal proceedings to protect them should be taken only as a last resort.

The role of local authorities was no longer simply to prevent children coming into out of home care but instead to actively promote their upbringing by their families, insofar as this was consistent with their parallel duty to promote the welfare of children in their area. This approach was reflected in the new concept of **parental**

responsibility, which included the collection of duties, rights and authority held by a parent and which parents continue to hold even if a child is placed in out of home care on a court order. Consistent with this approach, official guidance to the 1989 Act emphasised the value of negotiation with families, recommending that local authorities should work in **partnership with parents** in order to promote both the welfare of children and their upbringing by their families. These provisions were underpinned by the view that most parents will want what is best for their children. The 1989 Act also required professionals to ascertain **children's wishes and feelings** if they are in care and to take these into account. In 2004 this requirement was extended to all children in contact with social work services, including those who are the subject of child protection investigations.

The *Children Act 1989* tried to achieve a new balance between supporting families and protecting children. It introduced the concept of **family support**, a positive term which represented a shift away from the narrower, more negative concept of prevention. Providing family support services was entirely consistent with the anti-collectivist policies of the Conservative government of the time, with their emphasis on family responsibility and on the need to reduce the role of the state. At the same time it satisfied many of those with more liberal views, who were calling for more support to disadvantaged families to enable them to care safely for their children (Jack and Stepney 1995). However,1989 Act's key underlying principle was that the child's best interests and welfare must be the first and paramount consideration when decisions are taken (the '**paramountcy principle'**) and there may, at times, be a tension between its twin concerns with supporting children in their families and protecting them from harm.

The 1989 Act placed a general duty on local authorities to 'safeguard and promote the welfare of children' within their area who are 'in need,' a duty that was underpinned by the Act's focus on child development. It stated that a child should be considered a **child in need** if:

- He or she is unlikely to achieve or maintain, or to have the opportunity of achieving or maintaining, a reasonable standard of health or development without the provision of services by the local authority;
- The child's health or development is likely to be significantly impaired, or further impaired, without the provision of such services;
- The child is disabled (Section 17 (1), *Children Act 1989*.

S.17 of the 1989 Act therefore allows for the provision of non-stigmatising, voluntary family support services not only in response to concerns about abuse and neglect but also in the context of a wider range of circumstances which may undermine child health or development. It was envisaged at the time that compulsory intervention would occur only as a last resort and that, in most cases, professionals would use S.17 of the Act to work in partnership with parents on a voluntary basis to safeguard and promote children's welfare.

The *Children Act 1989* also introduced the new concept of **significant harm** to set a clear threshold for compulsory intervention in family life where there is evidence of abuse or neglect. The criteria for significant harm were deliberately broad: ill treatment, the impairment of physical or mental health and the impairment of the child's physical, intellectual, emotional or behavioural development. The Act required local authorities to make enquiries if a child was thought to be suffering, or likely to suffer, significant harm and tightened the grounds for the compulsory removal of children. The aim was to provide a consistent definition of the circumstances in which compulsory intervention to protect children is allowed. The *Children Act 1989* therefore aimed to promote the welfare of a wide group of children who were defined as being in need of services, with specific legal provisions for children at risk of abuse or neglect nested within this wider framework. It encouraged parents of children in need to look to local authorities for non-stigmatising support services without fear of losing their parental responsibility, which they retain even if the child is taken into care on a court order (Harwin and Madge 2010).

4.4 Policy Development Since the Children Act 1989

Although other important legislation on child welfare has followed (the *Children (Leaving Care) Act 2000*, *Adoption and Children Act 2002* and further Acts in 2004, 2008, 2014 and 2017), the *Children Act 1989* (as amended by subsequent Acts) remains the core legal framework for child protection in England. However, despite its emphasis on supporting children and families on a voluntary basis, within a few years of its passing concerns were being expressed about the continuing prioritisation of child protection work and the marginalisation of family support services (Audit Commission 1994; Aldgate and Tunstill 1995). In 1995, a report on a collection of government-funded studies of child protection argued that the research highlighted an over-emphasis on forensic investigation and too little attention to preventive work. Some studies had found that persistent physical or sexual abuse was evident in relatively few cases and that many more children were experiencing emotional neglect and were growing up in environments of 'low warmth and high criticism.' The report argued that forensic investigation to gather evidence was not always the best way to bring about change and that there should therefore be a re-focusing of child protection services, which should provide voluntary support to improve parenting in cases of this kind (Department of Health 1995).

This reinforcement of the 1989 Act's emphasis on supporting children in their families may have had some impact on practice, as a government report a few years later noted that the threshold for compulsory intervention in cases of abuse and neglect had risen. This was consistent with the intentions behind the legislation which had intended that this threshold should be more clearly defined, with family support provided to prevent unnecessary compulsory intervention wherever possible. This rise in the threshold for compulsory intervention meant that statutory intervention to remove children from their families was now focusing on a narrower group of children, who came from families with persistent and serious problems (Department for Education and Skills 2002). This shift to a greater emphasis on family support was reflected in a fall in the number of children entering care from the early 2000s (the 'flow' into the care system). However, between the mid-1990s and the early 2000s there was a rise in the total number in care at any time (the 'stock' of children), because those who entered care were being admitted for more serious reasons and were therefore staying longer. Children with less serious problems were receiving alternative forms of support in the community.

4.4.1 Prevention and Protection Under the Every Child Matters Programme

However, as the 2000s progressed, extensive media attention to further child deaths from abuse led to concern that children were not being sufficiently protected. An official inquiry into the killing of Victoria Climbié led to a major overhaul of child welfare policy, the *Every Child Matters* policy programme (Lord Laming 2003). *Every Child Matters* was a wide-ranging policy document which set out the Labour government's vision for services for all children. It was nested within the wider Labour policy of 'progressive universalism,' which aimed to prevent social exclusion by improving the wellbeing of *all* children in five outcome areas (being healthy, staying safe, enjoying and achieving, economic wellbeing and making a positive contribution). The idea was to promote the wellbeing of children with different levels of need through universal services (most commonly through health and education services), more targeted secondary preventive services if needed and through specialised services such as social work or mental health interventions for those with the highest level of need.

Every Child Matters aimed to achieve a better balance between prevention and protection through 'a shift to prevention while strengthening protection' (Department for Education and Skills 2004). The government viewed early intervention as the most effective way of tackling problems such as abuse, neglect, school failure and involvement in crime and therefore aimed to address risk factors in children's lives and enhance protective factors at an early stage, before problems became more serious. It emphasised the need both for early intervention, which has remained a continuing policy theme, and for effective protection. These were to be achieved through support to parents, integration of services and reform of the social work workforce. The legal framework for *Every Child Matters* was provided by the *Children Act 2004*, which mainly focused on organisational change. This Act also updated the legislation on physical punishment so that the defence of reasonable punishment could no longer be used when people are charged with child cruelty, wounding or causing actual or grievous bodily harm to a child.

4.4.2 The Shift to Protection

However, another high profile tragedy, the death of the baby Peter Connelly, followed in 2007, despite 78 contacts by a variety of professionals in his short life. The official inquiry into the 'Baby Peter' case which followed marked a return to the use of the term 'child protection' in policy discourse instead of the wider concept of safeguarding employed in the Children Act 1989 (Lord Laming 2009). A separate inquiry by a Select Committee of the UK parliament noted the lack of a decisive response to cases where there was a risk of significant harm and concluded that thresholds for admission to out of home care were too high. These inquiries marked a decisive shift back towards a greater emphasis on an interventionist approaches to protect children in cases of significant harm.

These concerns were reflected in practice, as the deaths of Victoria Climbié and Peter Connolly were followed by a steady rise in referrals to Children's Services departments and in the number of children entering care, suggesting that greater caution on the part of professionals and the courts was leading to a lowering of thresholds for compulsory intervention. However, despite the concerns about physical abuse raised by the Victoria Climbie and Baby Peter cases, the main change was that a higher number of applications for care were now being made in cases of long-standing neglect of children under 5 years old, a group that had for many years received relatively little attention (Hall and Guy 2009; Harwin and Madge 2010).

Child protection has remained high on the policy agenda since the election of the Conservative-led Coalition government in 2010 and subsequent Conservative governments in 2015 and 2017. Building on developments that had begun under the Labour government from 2008, the Coalition government brought a renewed focus on child protection work and on the value of skilled social work with families. There was also a continuing emphasis on the value of early intervention, previously highlighted by *Every Child Matters* in 2004, reinforced by two reports commissioned by the new government (Allen 2011a, b). However, some commentators were critical of these developments, conceptualising early intervention as a form of state surveillance that may divert services from providing direct work with children and families (Parton 2005). The new government also commissioned a review of child protection by Professor Eileen Munro, whose influential report, *A Child-Centred System*, was published in 2011 (Munro 2011). This argued that centralised systems, excessive bureaucracy and a target-driven culture were hampering the use of professional judgement and recommended a greater emphasis on professional judgement and the quality of frontline practice, with a focus on effectiveness and outcomes rather than on procedural or organisational issues.

Some of the recommendations of the Munro review echoed policies proposed in the Conservative pre-election manifesto on child protection, *Back to the Frontline*, but it was nevertheless welcomed across the political spectrum. Although not motivated by political Conservativism, aspects of the review fitted very well with the Conservative Party's political agenda, as its calls for less central prescription regarding service delivery, the local redesign of services and greater individual accountability for professionals were consistent with the Conservative Party's goal of moving to a 'small state', its localism agenda and the long-standing Conservative emphasis on individual, rather than state, responsibility.

4.4.3 Ensuring Permanence in the Child's Timeframe

The last 20 years or so have also seen a number of important policy developments regarding the placement of children in out of home care. Detailed discussion of these is beyond the scope of this chapter, but two key issues in relation to children entering out of home care are particularly relevant to policy on child protection: the principle of permanence and the (related) requirement that decision-making should be timely.

The principle of **permanence** for separated children has a long history in England. The permanency planning movement emerged in the USA and the UK in the early 1970s prompted by studies in both countries which revealed that children were drifting in care with no proper planning for their future and fuelled by concerns about the psycho-social development of children separated from their parents (Rowe and Lambert 1973; Fanshel and Shinn 1978; Goldstein et al. 1973; Maluccio and Fein 1983). Proponents of permanency planning argued for a focus on reunifying children with their families but, if this was not possible, suggested that the state should provide them with a permanent substitute family, either through adoption or, more commonly in England at the time, long-term foster care.

Government guidance to the *Children Act 1989* states that the concept of permanence provides an underpinning framework for all social work with children and families from family support through to adoption: 'Permanence is the framework of emotional permanence (attachment), physical permanence (stability) and legal permanence (the carer has parental responsibility for the child) which gives a child a sense of security, continuity, commitment and identity (Department for Education 2015). The goal of ensuring that children have a loving family to care for them in the long-term applies to all children, so the principle of permanence must underpin decisions about children who are supported at home, return home from care, remain in care or leave care through special guardianship (which allows relatives or former foster carers to become the child's legal guardian) or through adoption.

4.4.4 Reducing Delay

A second principle – the need for timely decision-making – is linked to the principle of permanence. It is informed by research in developmental psychology which has shown the long-term effects of lengthy exposure to abuse or neglect on children's emotional, behavioural, social and cognitive development. Many children brought up in abusive or neglectful environments develop insecure or disorganised attachment styles and these are strongly associated with later emotional and behavioural difficulties (Brown and Ward 2012). There is also evidence from neuroscience that relationships with primary caregivers, particularly in the first 3 years of life, may affect the physical development of the brain, although the impact of these physical changes on children's subsequent development is not yet fully understood (Woolgar 2013; Belsky and De Haan 2011). This research, plus evidence of lengthy delays in decision-making and the resulting delay in providing children with permanent placements, contributed to policy changes which aimed to align decision-making with the timeframe for the developing child.

These concerns, together with growing pressure on the court system, led to the publication of a new legal protocol, the *Public Law Outline* (PLO), which was piloted from 2008 and subsequently rolled out nationally. An amendment to the PLO in 2013 required courts to make their decisions within 26 weeks of the start of the application to the court, although in some circumstances this can be extended by 8 weeks (Masson et al. 2017). These changes reflected both older (though fluctuating) concerns about ensuring permanence for children and the more recent emphasis on the need for children to be placed in their permanent placement as early as possible. They were also prompted by concerns about resources. Rising numbers of applications for care during the early 2000s led to a sharp increase in the cost of the court process and a desire to ensure that all alternatives have been explored before local authorities seek court orders to remove children from their parents. Although the overriding concern, other than cost, is with protecting children and ensuring that their developmental needs are met, giving them every opportunity to remain within their family network if it is safe to do so, the PLO also represents a desire to treat parents in a just manner by systematically exploring alternatives to compulsory intervention prior to court proceedings. However, there is as yet no clear evidence as to whether parents are provided with sufficient support to make the changes needed to avoid compulsory intervention.

4.5 The Child Protection System: Context, Organisation and Scope

The English child protection system is nested within a wider child welfare system which provides services on voluntary basis to children who are assessed as 'children in need,' as defined by S.17 of the *Children Act 1989,* because their health or development is threatened or impaired (as noted above). This child welfare system is itself located within a welfare state which provides free universal services, the most relevant being schooling and health care. However, the provision of universal and secondary preventive services that might offer a public health approach, supporting children at risk of abuse while problems are at an early stage, has been much reduced since the election of the Conservative-led Coalition government in 2010 due to significant budget cuts imposed under the government's austerity programme. This policy programme has also resulted in a significant reduction in funding for voluntary agencies providing support to children and families.

The child welfare system is highly integrated, with the government Department for Education providing national policy and guidance and the 156 English local authorities holding lead responsibility for implementing these at local level. Local authorities are responsible for providing services for all 'children in need' of services from the ages 0–17 years (and up to the age of 25 for eligible young people who leave out of home care after the age of 16). Repeated calls for improved information sharing from official inquiries into child deaths from abuse have led to a strong focus on inter-agency information sharing and co-operation. This is now embodied in the multi-agency Local Safeguarding Children's Boards (LSCBs) set up in every local authority following the *Children Act 2004*, which hold overall responsibility for local safeguarding priorities and arrangements. As in other Anglophone countries, but unlike most other countries, children at continuing risk of serious maltreatment may, as a last resort, be adopted from care without parental consent.

Children's Services departments in each local authority are responsible for services for children in need. Within this broader duty, they have lead responsibility for investigating and responding to child maltreatment. Most local authorities provide at least some family support services and foster placements and some also provide their own residential care placements. These services may also be commissioned from charities (NGOs) or private providers but these agencies are not the main service providers as they are in European countries with traditions of subsidiarity in welfare provision, such as the Netherlands and Germany.

Decisions about compulsory intervention in family life may only be made by the family courts. The legislation on child welfare which underpins the operation of the family courts, including the *Children Act 1989*, falls within the framework of civil law. In addition, the criminal law allows police to prosecute anyone who has the care of a child or young person under 16 who 'wilfully assaults, ill-treats, neglects, abandons, or exposes him, or causes or procures him to be assaulted, ill-treated, neglected, abandoned, or exposed, in a manner likely to cause him unnecessary suffering or injury to health…' (*Children and Young Persons Act 1933*). The standard of proof in the criminal courts is 'beyond reasonable doubt,' a much higher evidential threshold than for civil law cases in the family courts, where the grounds for compulsory intervention are based 'on the balance of probabilities.'

There is no legal requirement for the mandatory reporting of suspected maltreatment in England, except in relation to female genital mutilation. However LSCBs and national professional bodies issue guidance emphasizing that professionals have a duty to make a referral if they hold a reasonable belief that a child is at risk of harm. All schools must have a designated teacher with responsibility for child protection and health services must have designated nurses and doctors responsible for dealing with child protection issues. Allegations of abuse by professionals who work with children (and adults) are referred for investigation to a Local Authority Designated Officer (LADO).

In many other European countries, the child welfare system is also responsible for young people involved in crime. This was also the case in England from the early 1960s to the late 1980s, before the *Children Act 1989* introduced changes which represented the first step in the separation of institutional responses to child welfare and youth offending. These changes were largely prompted by concerns that the 'welfare approach' to youth offending evident in the *Children and Young Persons Acts* of 1963 and 1969 had the unintended consequence of drawing more young people into the formal court system. The transfer of responsibility for young offenders from the child welfare system to the criminal justice system was completed by the *Crime and Disorder Act 1998,* which established both the Youth Justice Board (YJB), a new national body responsible for overseeing the youth justice system, and local Youth Offending Teams (YOTs). YOTs are multidisciplinary teams which include social workers and aim to take a child-centred approach. Young people found guilty of criminal behaviour may be sentenced to detention in one of a small number of a secure residential institutions for young offenders (separate from out of home care provision) or may alternatively receive a community-based sentence.

4.6 Operation of the Child Protection System

This section discusses the different elements of the child protection system, drawing on national administrative data published annually by government on children in the child protection system or in out of home care to describe the operation of the system (Department for Education 2016a, 2017a).

4.6.1 Referral and Assessment

Since children in England may be referred to local authorities not only for abuse or neglect but also because they may need support for a range of other reasons, the initial focus at referral is on assessment rather than investigation. Social workers in Children's Services departments must take the lead in carrying out assessments of children referred and consult with relevant local agencies, following any local procedures set by the LSCB and by national guidance, *Working Together to Safeguard Children* (HM Government 2015). This official guidance incorporates a framework for assessment, which is informed by ecological theory and stipulates that assessments must take account of children's needs, parenting capacity and family and environmental factors (the 'assessment triangle'). Assessments must be child-centred, rooted in an understanding of child development, informed by evidence, holistic in approach, consider parenting capacity, address the child's needs within the context of their families and local communities and be outcomes-oriented. The guidance places an emphasis on the timeliness of assessment, which may be critical if the child is at risk (HM Government 2015).

In 2015–2016, 401,600 children (3.4% of the population under 18 years old on the annual census date) were assessed as being children in need (CIN) and for half of these (1.7% of the child population), the primary need recorded at assessment was abuse or neglect. Other factors identified at assessment were domestic violence (in 50% of cases), mental health difficulties of the parent, child or other adult in the household (37%) and parental misuse of drugs (19%) or alcohol (18%).

4.6.2 Community-Based Support (Voluntary)

As already noted, voluntary support to children and families was a key element of the *Children Act 1989*. The *Munro Review of Child Protection* (Munro 2011) similarly emphasised the value of preventive approaches, calling for public agencies such as health or education services to provide **early help,** in the form of targeted services for children and families who have specific needs but who are not assessed as 'children in need' and are therefore ineligible for social work services. Children with needs that might be met by early help include those who are showing early signs of abuse or neglect or whose families have problems with mental health, domestic abuse or substance abuse, for example, as well as those with anti-social behaviour.

Children who are assessed as being 'in need' are eligible to receive **family support** services, which may include individual work to support parents and children in their homes and access to local children's centres, which provide support and may offer parenting programmes. However, national data do not indicate how many children in need actually receive family support services.

4.6.3 Investigation

In 2015–2016, 43% of children in need became the subject of a formal child protection investigation, known as a Section 47 enquiry (under S.47 of the *Children Act 1989*). During the investigation social workers must consult with other agencies and involve parents and keep them informed, unless this poses a risk to the child. Depending on the child's age and understanding, they must also ascertain children's wishes and feelings. The number of children becoming the subject of a S.47 enquiry has risen in recent years from 79.5 children per 10,000 during 2009–2010 to 147.5 per 10,000 during 2015–2016.

If a strategy group of relevant professionals considers that the child may be at continuing risk of harm, a multi-agency Initial Child Protection Conference (ICPC) must be convened within 15 working days. This must bring together family members and their advocates, relevant professionals from other agencies and children

Table 4.1 Children referred during year ending March 31st 2016

	Number March 31st 2016 (stock) *(Rate per 10,000 children under 18 years)*	Number starting 2015–16 (flow) *(Rate per 10,000 children under 18 years)*
All referrals (for any reason)	–	621,470 *(532)*
Children assessed as in need (CIN) for any reason	394,400 *(338)*	401,600 *(344)*
Children assessed as in need due to abuse or neglect	199,720 *(171)*	–
Investigations into abuse and neglect (s.47 enquiries)	–	172,290 *(148)*
Initial child protection conference (ICPC)	–	73,050 *(63)*
Child protection plans	50,310 *(43)*	63,310 *(54)*

Characteristics of children in need 2015–2016 (Department for Education 2016a). Rates are based on 2015 mid-year population estimate of 11,677,900 children in England age 0–17 years

(where appropriate). These case conferences may also take place before a child is born, for example if there are concerns about parental substance misuse *in utero*, domestic violence or the previous abuse of siblings.

4.6.4 *Formal Community-Based Supervision*

If an ICPC considers that a child is at continuing risk of significant harm, the child may be made the subject of a **Child Protection Plan (CPP)**. A CPP is a multi-agency plan to address problems leading to the maltreatment concerns and to support the child to remain at home. It is a quasi-compulsory measure rather than one imposed by the courts, although parents are undoubtedly aware that non-compliance might potentially result in an application to remove the child. Just over half of 1% of all children under 18 became the subject of a CPP during 2015–2016.

CPPs are typically a short- to medium-term measure. Over half last for 6 months or less and 84% last for less than a year (Department for Education 2016a). They set out a plan to ensure the safety and wellbeing of the child, including details of the changes needed to reduce the risk to the child (for example, that an abuser should leave the household, or that a parent should attend drug treatment) and the support that will be provided. The CPP's effectiveness in safeguarding the child is monitored by a core group of professionals within 3 months of the start of the CPP and then at intervals of no more than 6 months thereafter.

Children in need due to abuse or neglect accounted for half of all children in need in March 2016, represented 171 per 10,000 children in the general population (in other words 1.7% of all children under 18). However, less than a quarter of these children (0.43% of all under-18 year olds) were the subject of a CPP, as shown in Table 4.1.

Just over one quarter (172,290, 28%) of referrals in 2015–2016 resulted in a S.47 enquiry and just over one-third (63,310) of the children subsequently investigated became the subject of a CPP. Others investigated may have been placed in out of home care or received family support on a voluntary basis or possibly no intervention at all if they were not deemed to be at high risk of harm.

4.6.5 Care Proceedings and the Public Law Outline

If concerns about abuse or neglect cannot be resolved through voluntary intervention or within the framework of a CPP, the local authority may commence care proceedings, the legal process for obtaining a court order to remove the child (a Care Order). Parents involved in care proceedings have a right to legal representation funded by the state. Care proceedings are governed by procedures set out in the Public Law Outline (PLO), whose development is noted above. Local authorities must systematically explore options to avoid compulsory intervention with families and must make sure that all assessments and interventions to improve parenting have been completed before a decision is taken to apply for a Care Order. Family group conferences are often held to explore whether the wider family network can help to support the child and parents or provide an alternative carer if it is deemed necessary to remove the child.

During care proceedings the court appoints a **children's guardian** (an experienced social worker employed by Cafcass, an independent agency accountable to the Ministry of Justice) to consult all concerned, including the child if old enough, in order to represent the child's interests in court. Children's guardians provide independent advice to the courts regarding the best interests of children when local authorities seek a court order to allow the compulsory placement of a child in care, adoption or special guardianship.

4.6.6 Admission to out of Home Care

In some cases, parents may agree to their child being placed in care under a voluntary arrangement (**accommodated** under S.20, *Children Act 1989*). Both children who are accommodated and those on court-ordered Care Orders are defined as children **looked after** by local authorities. Parents of accommodated children retain full parental responsibility and may remove their child at any time, but for children on Care Orders parental responsibility is shared with the local authority and, in practice, the local authority has the power to determine how far parents can exercise this parental responsibility. If the child is at immediate risk the family court may grant an Emergency Protection Order, which allows the removal of the child for up to 8 days. Police also have powers to remove a child for up to 72 hours under a Police Protection Order.

Table 4.2 Children in out of home care ('looked after children') Year ending March 31st 2017

	Total on March 31st 2017 (stock) *(Per cent of all in out of home care)*	Number starting 2016–17 (flow) *(Per cent of all in out of home care)*
All children in out of home care	72,670	32,810
Children looked after due to abuse or neglect	44,600 *(61%)*	19,060 *(58%)*
In voluntary care (accommodated)	16,470 *(23%)*	17,540 *(53%)*
On a care order (or interim care order)	50,470 *(69%)*	10,130 *(31%)*
In foster placements	53,420 *(74%)*	–
In children's homes	6070 *(8%)*	–

Children looked after in England (including adoption), year ending 31 March 2017 (Department for Education 2017a). Rates are based on 2015 mid-year population estimate of 11,677,900 children in England age 0–17 years

Very few children referred become looked after. In 2015–2016, children who started to be looked after represented just 5% of all those referred during the course of the year (Department for Education 2016a, b). As noted earlier, the increase in the 'stock' of children in out of home care by 2001 was not due not to an increase in admissions but instead occurred because many of those admitted were staying longer due to the seriousness of their difficulties. Since that time the care system has largely remained a residual system which principally serves children at risk of serious abuse and neglect. In March 2017, 62 children per 10,000 were looked after in England, a lower rate than that found in several other European countries, including Germany, France, Denmark, Norway and Sweden, although higher than the rates for Italy and Spain. These variations reflect differences in the purposes for which out of home care is used in different countries (Thoburn 2010; Department for Education 2017a).

The majority (61%) of children looked after are placed due to abuse or neglect, as shown in Table 4.2. However the published data do not tell us whether these children were placed in out of home care on a voluntary basis (i.e. accommodated), removed following a S.47 investigation or removed at a later stage, after a voluntary intervention or a CPP has been tried. The other main reasons for admission recorded are family dysfunction (15%), acute family stress (8%) and absent parenting (7%). The vast majority of those looked after due to absent parenting are unaccompanied asylum-seeking children (UASC), whose number rose sharply from 2015 following a policy-driven decline during the previous few years.

As Table 4.2 shows, over half of children who start to be looked after are admitted on a voluntary basis. In contrast to this 'flow' of children into the care system, the 'stock' of children looked after on the annual census date (March 31st) includes those who stay longer due to the serious nature of their difficulties, so the proportion on a Care Order is higher.

Local authorities are accountable for the children they look after and have a statutory duty to behave as a parent acting in the children's best interests (the 'corporate parent.') There is a strong preference for foster placements and much less use of residential care than in many other European countries, with only 8% of looked after children placed in residential children's homes. These are mainly used for young people aged 12 years or over. Residents have an average age of 15 years and most stay a relatively short time, in most cases a matter of months rather than years (Berridge et al. 2012).

Only a small proportion (12%) of looked after children are placed in kinship foster care, but the number has been rising, partly due to recognition of the greater stability of kin placements. However, there has been a recent rise in the use of Special Guardianship Orders (SGOs) to arrange placements with relatives. These were introduced by the *Adoption and Children Act 2002* as a framework for long-term care by relatives or former foster carers outside the care system. However, concerns have been raised about the courts making SGOs to family members with no pre-existing social relationship with the children in question or who were not previously known to them (Masson et al. 2017).

The total time spent in out of home care may range from 24 hours to many years, although only 14% remain in out of home care for three or more years, with the majority (55%) remaining for 1–2 years. Around one third of those who ceased to be looked after in 2016–17 returned home, 15% aged out of care and moved to independent living, 16% left the care system on SGOs or similar orders granted to kin or other 'connected persons. Just under 6% of all children in out of home care 2016–2017 were adopted. These are typically very young children at high risk of continuing and serious abuse or neglect and for whom there is no realistic prospect of achieving a permanent home through reunification with parents or placement with relatives. There was a rising trend in the use of adoption from care from 1999–2015, which reflected successive governments' strong policy emphasis on the use of adoption since 1998. However the number adopted has been falling since 2015 largely as a result of two influential legal judgements by the national president of the family court.

4.7 Outcomes for Children in the Child Welfare System

Although the government collects extensive data on the flow of children through the children in need and out of home care systems, including data on child characteristics, reasons for referral, the volume of referrals and service use, it collects no data on the outcomes of services, except on patterns of educational attainment, absence from school and school exclusion for children in need and for looked after children. A number of research studies on outcomes for looked after children have been published since the mid-1980s, many of which were funded by government, but there has been barely any research on outcomes for children in need and those on CPPs.

4.8 Child Protection Today

4.8.1 Recent Trends

The population of children in need has been rising, increasing from 336 per 10,000 children in 2009–2010 to 344 per 10,000 in 2015–2016. The proportion with a CPP also rose during this period, from 39.4 to 54.2 per 10,000 (Department for Education 2016a). There has also been a sharp rise in the number of applications for Care Orders made to the courts. High profile inquiries into the deaths of babies and young children have almost certainly contributed to this rise, as the publicity surrounding the death of Baby Peter in 2007 fuelled an increase in referral and intervention (Jones 2014; Hall and Guy 2009). However research showed that these increases also reflected evidence of improvements in professional recognition of need, particularly in relation to the neglect of young children (Macleod et al. 2010). Growing recognition of new needs may also have increased the number of referrals as constructions of abuse have broadened over the last 30 years or so, as outlined above. Some local authorities have also reported that the increase in referrals in their areas was to some extent due to the arrival of families from Eastern Europe, some of whose parenting practices were at odds with child welfare legislation in England (Brookes et al. 2016; Brookes and Brocklehurst 2014).

The proportion of children in out of home care has also increased, rising from 54 per 10,000 in 2007–2008 to 62 per 10,000 in March 2017 (Department for Education 2010, 2017a). However, this rise has been part of a longer-term, albeit fluctuating, trend that began in 1994, a few years after the implementation of the *Children Act 1989* (Rowlands and Statham 2009). Although the initial rise from 2008 is likely to have been prompted by the death of Baby Peter, more recently this rise may to some extent reflect an increase in the number of adolescents in out of home care including unaccompanied asylum-seeking children (UASC), 90% of whom are 16–17 years old. Their number has risen in recent years and in 2015–2016 (though not in other years) the increase in the number of looked after children appeared to be largely due to a rise in the number of UASC placed during that year, (Department for Education 2016b, 2017a). Changes in the law to the effect that 12–17 year olds remanded to custodial institutions and homeless 16–17 year olds must be given the status of 'looked after children' may also have contributed to the rise in numbers [Southwark Judgement 2009 and the Legal Aid, Sentencing and Punishment of Offenders Act 2012]. In addition, there has been growing professional awareness of child sexual exploitation (CSE) following media attention to the trials of several groups of perpetrators and a widely-reported independent review of CSE (Jay 2014). However, an increase in adolescent placements cannot explain the rise in applications to the courts for care orders, as adolescents in out of home care for the above reasons are unlikely to be placed on a court order.

There is considerable local variation in rates of children in need, on CPPs and in out of home care. A national study in 2014 reported that nearly half of the local authorities surveyed had seen a decrease in the number of children in need in recent years while the others had seen an increase. Some professionals reported that early help services were identifying more children in need of support but others felt that these services were diverting children from the child protection system (Brookes et al. 2016; Godar 2017). To some extent this variation is likely to be due to local variation in patterns of deprivation (Bywaters et al. 2018). Variations in demand for services may also be shaped by patterns of migration, as most UASC are looked after by a small number of local authorities close to ports of entry and migrant families tend to cluster in certain local areas.

4.8.2 *The Impact of Wider Policy on Demand and Provision*

These increasing pressures on the child protection system have occurred in the context of the Conservative-led Coalition and subsequent Conservative governments' austerity programme from 2010, which has the expressed aim of reducing the budget deficit and the less explicit ideological goal of reducing the size of the state. Since then the safety net provided by universal health and education services, along with social work and other targeted services provided by local authorities and voluntary agencies, have been progressively undermined by substantial cuts to the budgets of all public services. Local authority budgets have been cut by up to 40% since 2010, with the result that spending on children's services fell by 18% between 2012 and 2015 (Puffett 2016). Many children's centres and other voluntary family support services have been cut, with local authority spending on early intervention services falling by 31% between 2010–2011 and 2015–2016, despite the fact that providing support at an early stage may potentially reduce referrals to child protection services (Action for Children et al. 2016).

Demand for child protection and other child welfare services has therefore increased at a time when local authorities' spending power has decreased (All Party Parliamentary Group for Children 2017). A recent national survey reported that four in ten local authorities were unable to meet at least one of their legal duties due to funding pressures and 30% said that they lacked the resources to support children on CPPs or in out of home care (Stevenson 2017). There is some evidence that, in the context of significant cuts to local authority budgets, interventions are increasingly being targeted on children at the greatest risk, although there is local variation in this respect. Consistent with this, planned local expenditure on children's centres and family support services has fallen and while that on child protection services and out of home care has risen slightly (Department for Education 2017b; All Party Parliamentary Group for Children 2017).

The rise in referrals may also reflect the impact of wider government reforms to a range of social security and housing benefits introduced under its austerity programme, which have increased families' levels of need. These reforms have led to a substantial rise in rates of child poverty from 2010, with the result that in 2014–2015, 29% of children in the UK (3.9 million) were living below the poverty line (Bradshaw et al. 2016). Unemployment and in-work benefits for the poorest families have been frozen and the level of housing benefits capped, irrespective of family size, with a resulting increase in the number of poor families struggling to pay their rent. These changes to social security and housing benefits have also led to the setting up of food banks providing free food parcels, which did not exist before 2010, with the number of emergency food supplies provided rising from just over 128,000 in 2011–2012 to over one million in 2016–2017 (Trussell Trust 2017).

These policy developments led to a sharp increase in local authority spending on essential items for children in need between 2010 and 2015, as Children's Services were increasingly obliged to exercise their statutory duty to prevent destitution. This rise was driven partly by the need to mitigate the impact of the government's social security and housing benefit reforms on children and partly as a result of immigration policy, which made 6000 children of refugee families destitute in 2015 by forbidding their parents to work or claim benefits while applying for British citizenship (Carter 2015; Price and Spencer 2015). Surveys of local authorities in 2014 and 2016 reported that rising family poverty, deprivation, homelessness, use of temporary accommodation and stress occasioned by the wider welfare reforms of Conservative governments since 2010 were having an impact on the number and nature of referrals. Respondents to the 2016 survey also ascribed the rise in referrals, investigations and CPPs to families' increasingly entrenched and complex problems, particularly domestic violence, parental mental health difficulties and substance misuse, which often occurred in combination (Brookes and Brocklehurst 2014; Brookes et al. 2016). These wider developments may therefore help to explain the increasing demands on the child protection system in recent years.

4.9 Conclusion

Like other child protection systems, the English system seeks to balance children's rights to protection with the rights of parents. However the system is, on balance, principally child-oriented, as the underpinning legal principle informing all decisions is that the child's welfare must be the paramount consideration. The key legislation underpinning the system, the *Children Act 1989*, was influenced by the development of the United Nations Convention on the Rights of the Child during the course of the 1980s, by research evidence on child development and by research on the importance of providing a permanent home for children who are separated from their parents. This is most commonly achieved by returning separated children to their parents or relatives, but this focus on permanence, alongside concern about poor outcomes for many children in care and pressures on the care system, has also been a key driver of adoption policy in England and of the rise in the use of Special Guardianship Orders. The focus on planning for permanence and the use of adoption without parental consent are both features of the English system which distinguish it from the child protection systems of its European neighbours and other non-Anglophone countries.

High profile child deaths from abuse and neglect, increasing professional recognition of child maltreatment and changing constructions of 'what counts' as child maltreatment are unlikely to fully explain the rise in the number of children involved in the child protection system in recent years, as wider austerity policies have almost certainly contributed to the increase in rates of referral and intervention since 2010. The economic and social impact of wider government reforms has significantly increased family poverty and the associated stresses on families, particularly those where children are already vulnerable due to other family difficulties, such as low income, parental health or mental health problems, disability, domestic violence, lone parenting and drug and alcohol misuse. Together, these developments have shaped the operation of the English child protection system today.

References

Action for Children, National Children's Bureau, & The Children's Society. (2016). *Losing in the long run. Trends in early intervention funding*. London: Action for Children, National Children's Bureau & The Children's Society.

Aldgate, J., & Tunstill, J. (1995). *Making sense of section 17. Implementing services for children in need within the Children Act 1989*. London: HMSO.

All Party Parliamentary Group For Children. (2017). *No good options. Report of the inquiry into children's social care in England*. London: National Children's Bureau.

Allen, G. (2011a). *Early intervention: Smart investment, massive savings*. London: HM Government.

Allen, G. (2011b). *Early intervention: The next steps*. London: HM Government.

Audit Commission. (1994). *Seen but not heard – Co-ordinating community child health and social services for children in need within the Children Act 1989*. London: The Audit Commission.

Ball, C. (1998). Regulating child care: From the Children Act 1948 to the present day. *Child & Family Social Work, 3*, 163–171.

Belsky, J., & De Haan, M. (2011). Parenting and children's brain development: The end of the beginning. *Journal of Child Psychology And Psychiatry, 52*, 409–428.

Berridge, D., Biehal, N., & Henry, L. (2012). *Living in children's residential homes*. London: Department for Education.

Biehal, N. (2005). Working with adolescents at risk of out of home care: The effectiveness of specialist teams. *Children and Youth Services Review, 27*, 1045–1059.

Biehal, N. (2014). Maltreatment in foster care: A review of the evidence. *Child Abuse Review, 23*, 48–60.

Bradshaw, J., Garnham, A., Lister, R., & Shaw, M. (2016). *Improving children's life chances*. London: Child Poverty Action Group.

Brookes, C., & Brocklehurst, P. (2014). *Safeguarding pressures Phase 4*. Manchester: Association of Directors of Children's Services.

Brookes, C., Brocklehurst, P., & Ellis, A. (2016). *Safeguarding pressures Phase 5*. Manchester: Association of Directors of Children's Services.

Brown, R., & Ward, H. (2012). *Decision-making within a child's timeframe. An overview of current research evidence for family justice professionals concerning child development and the impact of maltreatment*. London: Department for Education.

Bywaters, P., Brady, G., Bunting, L., Daniel, B., Featherstone, B., Jones, C., Morris, K., Scourfield, J., Sparks, T., & Webb, C. (2018). Inequalities in English child protection practice under austerity: A universal challenge? *Child & Family Social Work, 23*(1), 53–61.

Carter, R. J. (2015). Council spending on essential items for children in need rose 20% under coalition *Community Care* November 25th. http://www.communitycare.co.uk/2015/11/25/council-spending-essential-items-children-need-rose-20-coalition/
Department for Education. (2010). *Children looked after by local authorities including adoption: 2009–10*. London: Department for Education.
Department for Education. (2015). *Children Act 1989: Care planning, placement and case review*. London: Department for Education.
Department for Education. (2016a). *Characteristics of children in need: 2015 to 2016 Sfr 52/2016*. London: National Statistics.
Department for Education. (2016b). *Children looked after in England (including adoption) year ending 31 March 2016 Sfr 41/2016*. London: Department for Education.
Department for Education. (2017a). *Children looked after in England including adoption: 2016 to 2017*. London: Department for Education.
Department for Education. (2017b). *Planned expenditure on schools, education and children's services by local authorities in England, 2017–18. Sfr 48/2017, 21 September 2017*. London: Department for Education.
Department for Education and Skills. (2002). *The Children Act report 2002*. London: Department for Education and Skills.
Department for Education and Skills. (2004). *Every child matters: Change for children*. Norwich: The Stationery Office.
Department of Health. (1995). *Child protection. Messages from the research*. London: HMSO.
Fanshel, D., & Shinn, E. (1978). *Children in foster care: A longitudinal investigation*. New York: Columbia University Press.
Ferguson, H. (2011). *Child protection practice*. Basingstoke: Palgrave Macmillan.
Fisher, M. A., Marsh, P., & Phillips, D. (1986). *In and out of care*. London: Batsford.
Fox-Harding, L. (1991). *Perspectives in child care policy*. London: Longmans.
Frost, N., & Parton, N. (2009). *Understanding children's social care. Politics, policy and practice*. London: Sage.
Godar, R. (2017). *Child protection – A review of the literature on current systems and practice*. London: Research In Practice/Early Intervention Foundation/Local Government Foundation.
Goldstein, J., Freud, A., & Solnit, A. (1973). *Beyond the best interests of the child*. New York: Free Press.
Hall, E., & Guy, J. (2009). *The Baby Peter effect and the increase in section 31 Care Order applications*. London: CAFCASS.
Harwin, J., & Madge, N. (2010). The concept of significant harm in law and practice. *Journal of Children's Services, 5*(2), 73–83.
Heywood, J. (1978). *Children in care. The development of the service for the deprived child*. London: Routledge and Kegan Paul.
HM Government. (2015). *Working together to safeguard children. A guide to inter-agency working to safeguard and promote the welfare of children*. London: Department for Education.
Holman, B. (1988). *Putting families first. prevention and childcare*. Basingstoke: Macmillan.
Hughes, R. (1998). Children Act 1948 and 1989: Similarities, differences, continuities. *Child & Family Social Work, 3*, 149–151.
Jack, G., & Stepney, P. (1995). The Children Act 1989 – Protection or persecution? Family support and child protection in the 1990s. *Critical Social Policy, 43*, 26–39.
Jay, A. (2014). *Independent inquiry into child sexual exploitation in Rotherham (1997–2013)*. Rotherham: Rotherham Metropolitan Borough Council.
Jones, R. (2014). *The story of Baby P. setting the record straight*. Bristol: The Policy Press.
Kempe, C., Silverman, F., Steele, B., Droegemueller, W., & Silver, H. (1962). The battered child syndrome. *Journal of The American Medical Association, 81*, 17–24.
Lord Laming. (2003). *The Victoria Climbie inquiry: Report of an inquiry by Lord Laming (Cm 5730)*. London: Department for Education and Skills/The Stationery Office.

Lord Laming. (2009). *The protection of children in England: A progress report*. London: The Stationery Office.
Macleod, S., Hart, R., Jeffes, J., & Wilkin, A. (2010). *The impact of the Baby Peter case on applications for Care Orders*. Slough: NFER.
Maluccio, A., & Fein, E. (1983). Permanency planning: A redefinition. *Child Welfare, 62*, 195–201.
Masson, J., Dickens, J., Bader, K., Garside, L., & Young, J. (2017). How is the PLO working? What is its impact on court process and outcome? Family Law Week, 17th February.
Munro, E. (2011). *The Munro review of child protection: Final report. A child-centred system*. London: Department for Education.
Parker, R. (1980). *Caring for separated children*. London: Macmillan.
Parton, N. (2005). *Safeguarding childhood. Early intervention and surveillance in late modern society*. Basingstoke: Palgrave Macmillan.
Price, J., & Spencer, S. (2015). *Safeguarding children from destitution: Local authority responses to families with 'No recourse to public funds' COMPAS*. Oxford: University Of Oxford.
Puffett, N. (2016). DfE: 'No Link' between spending on children's social care and quality, Children and Young People Now, January 12th. https://www.cypnow.co.uk/cyp/news/1155494/dfe-no-link-between-spending-on-childrens-social-care-and-quality
Radford, L., Corral, S., Bradley, C., & Fisher, H. L. (2013). The prevalence and impact of child maltreatment and other types of victimization in the UK: Findings from a population survey of caregivers, children and young people and young adults. *Child Abuse & Neglect, 37*, 801–813.
Rowe, J., & Lambert, L. (1973). *Children who wait*. London: Association of British Adoption and Fostering Agencies.
Rowlands, J., & Statham, J. (2009). Numbers of children looked after in England: A historical analysis. *Child & Family Social Work, 14*, 79–89.
Secretary of State for Social Services. (1974). *Report of the inquiry into the care and supervision provided in relation to Maria Colwell*. London: HMSO.
Sen, R., Kendrick, A., Milligan, I., & Hawthorn, M. (2008). Lessons learnt? Abuse in residential child care in Scotland. *Child & Family Social Work, 13*, 411–422.
Stevenson, L. (2017). Four in ten children's services unable to meet legal duties due to funding pressures, finds survey. Community Care, October 31st. http://www.communitycare.co.uk/2017/10/31/four-ten-childrens-services-unable-meet-legal-duties-due-funding-pressures-finds-survey/
Thoburn, J. (2010). Achieving safety, stability and belonging for children in out-of-home care. The search for 'What Works' across national boundaries. *International Journal of Child and Family Welfare, 12*, 34–48.
Trussell Trust. (2017). UK foodbank use continues to rise as new report highlights growing impact of universal credit rollout on foodbanks, 25th April. https://www.trusselltrust.org/2017/04/25/uk-foodbank-use-continues-rise/
Woolgar, M. (2013). The practical implications of the emerging findings in the neurobiology of maltreatment for looked after and adopted children: Recognising the diversity of outcomes. *Adoption And Fostering, 37*, 237–252.

Nina Biehal is a Professor of Social Work at the Department of Social Policy and Social Work at the University of York. She has conducted many studies of children and young people involved with child protection services, in out of home care, at risk of entry to care or returning home from care. Her most recent study compared outcomes for children in out of home care to those for children supported at home due to abuse or neglect. She is currently completing the *Hestia* study of child protection policy, systems and practice in three European countries and the *Permanently Progressing* study of outcomes for children who are fostered or adopted.

Chapter 5
Child Protection in France

Flora Bolter and Gilles Séraphin

5.1 Child Protection in France

With the highest fertility rate of EU-28 countries in 2015 (Eurostat 2017a), France retains one of the highest natural population growth in the region (Eurostat 2015), despite its overall demographic ageing. At 16.4 million, under-20s represent nearly a quarter of the overall population (24.5%) on January 1, 2017 (Bellamy and Beaumel 2017). The social and demographic portrait of France, however, is a composite of widely diverging realities in the territories of France (Insee 2017a), and that is particularly true for children: 0-to-24 year-olds represent 23.0% of the population in rural Cantal but up to 60.6% in Mayotte and 49.5% in Guyane (Insee 2017b), overseas *départements* that also have the lowest *per capita* GDP (Insee 2017b) in the country.

Providing high-quality care and services for this demographic is therefore a crucial challenge, but also a particularly complex one in the context of France, one that needs to take into account very different local contexts. But France also has an intricate network of services and institutions that aim to help children and families, and an administrative organization that adapts national policies to the different territories. This is particularly true with child protection, around which very different services, each with its own organization and rules, collaborate – but over which the *département*[1] level has a preeminent role, not least because it has the charge of steering the partnership.

[1] *Départements* are a territorial unit created in 1789. They number 101 as of January 1, 2017. Since the first wave of the *décentralisation* (devolution) movement started in 1982, *départements* have

F. Bolter (✉)
Observatoire national de la protection de l'enfance (ONPE), Paris, France
e-mail: Flora.bolter@onpe.gouv.fr

G. Séraphin
University of Paris, Nanterre, France
e-mail: Gilles.seraphin@parisnanterre.fr

L. Merkel-Holguin et al. (eds.), *National Systems of Child Protection*, Child Maltreatment 8, https://doi.org/10.1007/978-3-319-93348-1_5

We will first present the intricate net of services and institutions for children and families that constitute a determining national context, before delving into the child protection system itself and finally illustrating the policy challenges that remain.

5.2 The Child Protection System in Context

5.2.1 A Strong Overall Public Investment in Families

National solidarity with families and vulnerable persons is strongly put forward as a principle within the French legislation, starting at constitutional level: Article 1 of the 1958 Constitution identifies France as an "indivisible, secular, democratic and social republic" (*"La France est une République indivisible, laïque, démocratique et sociale"*). The preamble to the 1946 French constitution (which, along with the 1958 Constitution and the 1789 Declaration of the rights of man and of the citizen, forms the current body of constitutional rules and principle in France) even states that

> The Nation shall provide the individual and the family with the conditions necessary to their development. It shall guarantee to all, notably to children, mothers and elderly workers, protection of their health, material security, rest and leisure. All people who, by virtue of their age, physical or mental condition, or economic situation, are incapable of working, shall have to the right to receive suitable means of existence from society. (para. 10–11)

This strong social focus is translated most clearly in overall social spending: France ranks highest among the Organization for Economic Co-operation and Development (OECD) countries for overall social spending with 31.5% of its GDP (the OECD average is 21%) – in-cash social benefits to households alone account for 19.84% of GDP, and family benefits for 2.914% (OECD 2017d). Child protective services proper, or *Aide sociale à l'enfance* (ASE), represent a sizeable expenditure with 7.725 billion EUR in 2015, all *départements* combined (Direction de la recherche, des études, de l'évaluation et des statistiques 2017).

France's prized healthcare system, famously ranked first in the world by the World Health organization in 2000, is based on compulsory social insurance and is funded by social contributions. It is co-administered by workers' and employers' organizations under State control, and relies on financial transfers[2]. It is a very complex system, which relies on a centralized public regulatory authority complemented by a mix of public, non-profit (*mutuelles*) and private health insurance providers and hospitals, with self-employed doctors being the main providers of primary care. Health coverage is universal since 1999, and a law promulgated on January 2016 has generalized a

---

become the main level in charge of organizing social services. This status has been explicitely confirmed for child protection by Law 2007–293 in which the president of the *département* council is described as having leadership over child protection policies at local level (*"chef de file de la protection de l'enfance"*).

[2]For an in-depth presentation of the French healthcare system and its limitations, please see Nay et al. (2016).

third-party payment management system that aims to reduce even more out-of-pocket spending for families (currently estimated at 6.8% of all health expenditures according to OECD 2017b). France has the lowest amenable mortality rate of the European Union in 2014 (77.7 per 100,000 inhabitants) and one of the lowest preventable mortality rates (181.0, well behind the EU-28 average of 213.9 – Eurostat, 2017c).

Children under the age of six and expectant women can also benefit from a specialized medico-social service, *Protection maternelle et infantile* (PMI, mother-and-child protection services). PMI is an important resource managed by medical doctors at *département*-level, heavily focused on prevention and early screening (with a number of mandatory visits organized at specific ages). With universal social services and ASE, PMI is the main relevant social service for children and families (all are directly managed by the *département*).

Outside of the social security network, national solidarity is also expressed through a variety of general interest services that are also mostly public in nature and universally accessible. For children and families, the emphasis on the school system is an important element, as most children are schooled early on (mandatory education only starts at 6, but schooling is a right for all children starting at age 3): 11.5% of all 2-year-olds in 2015 were already attending school in the public system, as well as virtually all 3-year-olds (Direction de l'évaluation, de la prospective et de la performance 2016). By and large, most children successfully finish secondary school (88.6% in 2014, higher than the EU average of 82.3 – Ministère de l'Éducation nationale, de l'enseignement supérieur et de la recherche 2015). Schools are an important part of the child welfare net, and doctors and social workers are based in the school premises to support children.

Overall, the institutional and administrative context that surrounds children and families is very diverse and comparatively strong. This accounts for a fairly effective system in terms of health and education, as well as for reducing monetary poverty (social transfers reduced child poverty by 48% in 2014 – UNICEF Office of research 2017, 14).

Despite these resources for children, there are two broad types of limitations that must be mentioned. The first is the prevalence and compounded effects of social inequalities. Although the education system is fairly successful, the number of young people not in employment, education or training (NEETs) remains high, in contrast with an EU-wide downward trend in recent years (16.6% in 2015 – OECD 2016). Moreover, France has the dubious distinction of having the most counterproductive school system in terms of reducing inequalities. In the OECD PISA study for 2015, a one-unit increase in the economic, social and cultural status (ESCS) index in France "is associated with an average improvement across the three subjects of 56 score points, the equivalent of almost two years' schooling" (UNICEF Office of research 2017, 41). In a system that is fairly complex, not knowing how institutions work or what one is entitled to increases inequalities, with many not knowing their social rights or how to access help. In terms of social protection, underutilized benefits is a significant problem, with for instance an estimated 23 to 26% of all persons entitled to free complementary health insurance not availing themselves of this possibility (Chauveaud and Warin 2016, 1). Inequality also affects territories. As we said previously, there is considerable variation between territories in terms of demographics and economy, but here again, inequality tends to get compounded: since those areas that need to give out more funding for social action are precisely the ones with least resources, they are also those where the fiscal burden concerns taxpayers (despite some corrective redistribution from the state). Overall, it should also be noted that the strong public service and benefits system in France has a cost: tax revenue represented 45.50% of France's GDP in 2015, second only to Denmark within OECD countries (OECD 2017c). In a context where public spending is mainly seen as a competitive disadvantage and where debt reduction is the foremost issue on the European political agenda, there are concerns over the long-term sustainability of this model (OECD 2017a): social investment may be one of the variables of this equation, in a positive or a negative way.

The second overall issue, which is related, is the complexity of the overall system, with different types of actors behaving in a way that is coordinated for each policy area at a different level and within a different administration (*départements* are the main operating level for social affairs, but health agencies are organized on a *région* basis, while schools have an entirely different administrative *échelon* called *académies*). The decentralization movement initiated in the 1980s has devolved many policies to the various administrative levels, but not necessarily in a coordinated way: institutions tend to follow a "silo" pattern (and therefore to focus mainly on their own hierarchy and procedures), creating an added layer of complexity when trying to set up partnerships. *Département*-levels information processing units (*cellules de recueil des informations préoccupantes*, CRIP), for instance, typically involve protocols defined and signed between child protection services, the judicial system, public schools (the most important provider of information giving rise to concern) and health institutions, all of which are organized according to a different administrative geography. These protocols ensure the smooth and homogenous transfer of information; setting them up is essential, but very complex.

5.2.2 Defining the Child Protection System in a Dense Network of Services

In this complex framework of services and realities, child protection in France has always been at the conjunction of different policies and services, as in many other countries. The rise of the modern child protection system[3] in France can be dated to the 1950s. ASE, the service that is specifically in charge of caring for children in

[3]The history of child protection in France is fairly ancient, and initiatives to protect orphans and abandoned children have been in existence since the middle ages. Legal texts organizing public interventions to help children in need had already been instituted, most notably in 1811. But we will focus here purely on the modern child protection system: ONPE's website has a chronology of the main historical texts that can be consulted – Observatoire national de l'enfance en danger/Observatoire national de la protection de l'enfance (ONPE), n.d.

danger, has its origin in the 1950s: the development of the medical and psychological consultations for families in Paris gradually led to the realization that a multi-dimensional type of intervention was needed.

Ordinance 58-1301, passed on December 23, 1958 has set the legal basis for an intervention by social services when there is a situation of "danger" as defined by article 375 of the Civil code; decree 58-101 (January 7, 1959) and completes the family and social action code to create a wider legal basis for preventive interventions that don't require judicial decisions.

From this period on, the child protection system was organized into two broad types of intervention,[4] a distinction that is still valid:

1. Judicial interventions: These are carried out by licensed private-sector agencies[5] under the authority of ASE. They require a decision by a juvenile justice judge (*juge des enfants*, who is in charge of both criminal justice for affairs involving minors and child protection cases). This decision means the judge acknowledges that a situation of danger as defined by article 375 of the Civil code is present. This articles states that in intervention should be initiated "if the health, security or morality of unemancipated minors are in danger, or if the conditions of his/her education or physical, affective, intellectual and social development are severely compromised". The intervention can take place even if the parents don't agree to it or are unreachable. Judicial interventions may include the placement of a child in a foster family or a residential home but are not limited to it: the judge can order an in-home intervention to take place (*action éducative en milieu ouvert*, AEMO). 69.8% of all in-home decisions are judicial orders as of December 31, 2013 (ONPE 2016d, p. 127)
2. "Administrative" interventions: These are carried out by social services (ASE) or by licensed private-sector agencies under the authority of ASE. They are not judicial in any way; a decision is taken by the president of the *département* council (following a request by the social workers and families or following an *information préoccupante* or IP). The decision to initiate an administrative intervention means that the social services think a situation of danger is possible considering the situation of the child in his or her family setting, in the framework of Article L221-1 of the Code for social action and families. This article indicates that administrative protection is warranted when "the health, security, morality of the minor" are at risk to be put in danger, as well as in situations that "may severely compromise his/her education or physical, emotional, intellectual and social development". This type of intervention requires the parents' agreement. Administrative interventions may include in-home interventions (*aide éducative à domicile*, AED) but are not limited to them: 11.7% of all placement decisions are administrative interventions as of December 31, 2013 (ONPE 2016d, p. 125).

[4] For clarity's sake, the acronyms used here are the current denominations of the services.

[5] Protection judiciaire de la jeunesse (PJJ), a specialized branch of the justice system, can also be tasked with carrying out a child protection intervention, but this is excessively rare. As of December 31st, 2013, PJJ interventions only represent 0.1% of all child protection interventions (see ONPE, 2016d, p. 121.)

The distinction between the two tracks of child protection is not mainly based on the immediacy or severity of the situation. The family's consent to work with the social workers is the central determining factor in identifying what type of intervention is appropriate (having no parents around is in itself considered a situation of danger).

Part I of Article L226-4 of the Code for social action and families clarifies in what circumstances the départements services must refer the situation to the judiciary:

> The president of the département council immediately notifies the public prosecutor for the purposes of initiating proceedings in a juvenile justice court when a minor is in danger according to Article 375 of the Civil code and:
>
> 1. The child has already undergone one or more interventions in the framework of Article L 222-3 and L 222-4-2 and Article L 222-5 (1) and these interventions have not remedied the situation;
> 2. Even if no previous intervention mentioned in section 1 has taken place, such interventions cannot take place because the family refuses to accept the help offered by ASE services or because there is no possibility to initiate a collaboration between the service and this family;
> 3. The danger in question is severe and immediate, particularly in situations of ill-treatment (*maltraitance*).
>
> The president of the département council also immediately notifies the public prosecutor when a child is reputed to be in a situation of danger according to Article 375 of the Civil code but it is impossible to assess the situation.
>
> The president of the *département* council informs the public prosecutor of actions that have already been taken with the minor and family in question. (Code de l'Action sociale et des familles, Art. L 226-4 I).

This means that all depends on an initial assessment of the situation and of the parents' intentions. This in turn requires some form of cooperation and clear communication between the branches of the system.

When child protection, along with social services, was devolved to the *départements* in 1983 (Laws No. 83-8 and 83-663), the cooperation and communication between administrative and judicial tracks progressively re-formed in each territory: the 1989 reform specified new procedures for the exchange of information, but the need progressively arose to streamline a more efficient system and to confirm the *département*'s preeminent role within the local child protection network.

Clarifying the information-sharing and assessment process was one of the main rationales behind the March 5, 2007 Law (No. 2007-293) reforming child protection. In order to do this, the law now confirms the status of the president of the *département* council as the local "leader" (*chef de file*) of child protection, who facilitates protocol-based partnerships through the creation of rules for "shared secrecy" (*secret partagé*) between professionals from various institutions, and mandates the creation of multi-disciplinary units inside each *département* to collect any and all information giving rise to concern (IP) at local level. Protocols have been very helpful in detecting situations, especially with the public school system, but there are still issues with the collaboration between child protection and heatlh-care services, particularly private practices.

Another aim of Law No. 2007-293 was to promote prevention measures and gradual intervention. PMI services were now fully placed under the purview of the département, and a number of mandatory health visits to pregnant women and young children were instituted, so as to give advice and detect as early as possible all sorts of medical or social problems the family may be experiencing. The creation of CRIP, the specialized units that collect and assess all "information giving rise to concern" (whose role and procedures are described below), was also seen as a way to help promote administrative interventions, with judicial intervention being now seen as the last resort.

Finally, the 2007 law mandated the creation of *département*-level observatories of child protection (*observatoires départementaux de la protection de l'enfance*, ODPE) and developed the missions of Oned (*observatoire national de l'enfance en danger*), which later became ONPE, the national observatory of child protection[6]. As of August 2017, there are (out of 101 *départements*) 68 functioning ODPE; and 22 are additionally being set up. Two of the 68 existing ODPEs are integrated inside broader social work observatories at territorial level.

A new reform, Law No. 2016-297 (March 14, 2016), has brought little change to the overall structure of the system. Its aim was to reframe the general principles of intervention by giving child protection a new definition centered on the child and his/her needs. Article L 112-3 of the Code for social action and families now states that child protection aims to "guarantee the fundamental needs of the child are met, to support his or her physical, emotional, intellectual and social development, and to preserve his or her health, security, morality and education, all the while respecting his or her rights". This law also promotes more overall coherence in the system by creating a national council of child protection (*Conseil national de la protection de l'enfance*, CNPE)[7], which brings together all actors involved at the national level.

5.3 The Child Protection System in Action

5.3.1 Functional Diagram (2017)

As a policy, child protection is constantly streamlining its processes to adapt to an evolving territorial context and a rich background of institutions and services that cater to children and families. Because this makes it a fairly complex system to

[6] For more information on the 2007 reform, please see ONPE, n.d.

[7] For more information on the 2016 reform, please see ONPE. P*rotection de l'enfant: les nouvelles dispositions issues de la loi n°2016-297 du 14 mars 2016 relative à la protection de l'enfant. Note d'actualité.* Retrieved from https://www.onpe.gouv.fr/system/files/publication/20160315_notedactu_loipe.pdf

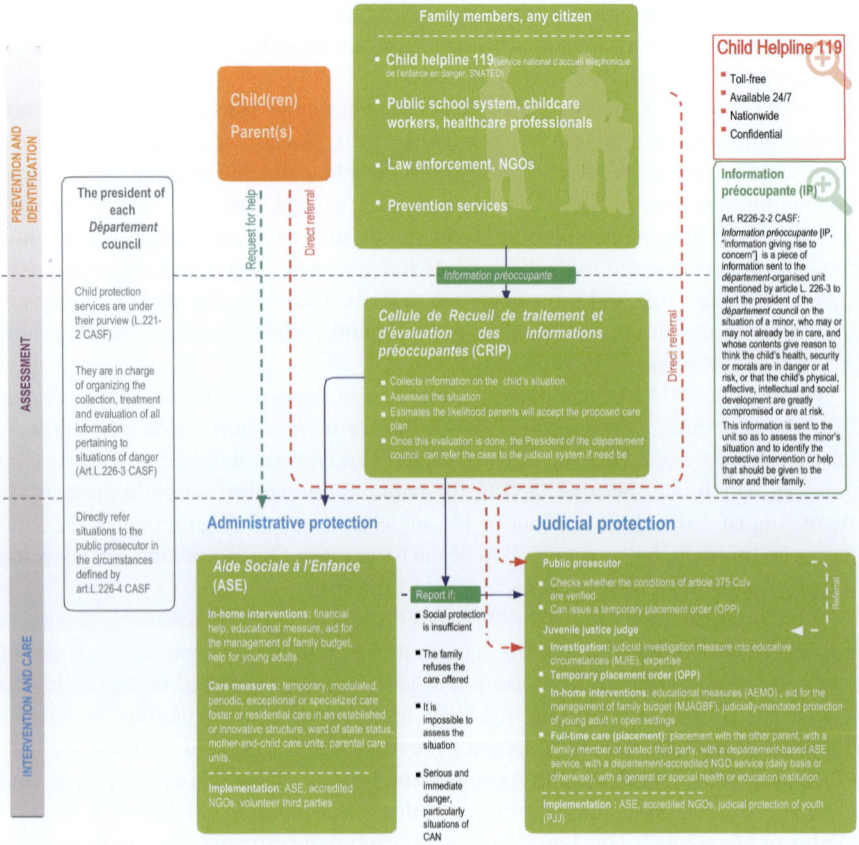

Illustration 5.1 The French child protection system (as of 2017)

understand at a glance, ONPE frequently uses the following diagram that we've translated into English for the purposes of this article (Illustration 5.1).

All persons who know of a child being in a situation of danger (as defined in the previous pages) have a duty to report their concerns to the local CRIP (Article 434-3 of the penal code institutes an obligation to report for "deprivations, maltreatment or sexual offenses inflicted on children under the age of 15 (…)". The penalty for failure to report can be up to 3 years in prison and a 45,000 EUR fine). Civil servants, teachers and professionals working with children have specific, more detailed obligations in their relevant professional codes that are similar. Even medical practitioners, despite some provisions for medical secrecy, are protected by article 226-14 of the Penal code if and when they decide to report situations of child abuse and neglect.

A variety of ways exist to report child maltreatment concerns. Professionals working with children usually have standardized procedures. Ordinary citizens who are worried can contact social workers, sometimes through a local helpline; and/or they can also call child helpline 119, which is an emergency number accessible for free 24/7 from any telephone in France (metropolitan and overseas)[8]. They also sometimes send the information to the judiciary, which they should only do in certain circumstances (CRIP were created in part because jurisdictions were overwhelmed).

In any event, the information[9] is collected by the CRIP and an initial assessment of the situation is conducted by using the information of the report that social services may have about the family, and ad hoc visits by social workers. Because there is the notion of "shared secrecy" (defined by article L 226-2-2 of the Code for social action and families), professionals from different services involved in child protection are allowed to share relevant information their services may have on this given situation.

The CRIP then assesses the pieces of information (reports by social services or by other institutions, claims made by the persons reporting the case…) it has on a given situation to determine what kind of intervention, if any, is warranted: general help from social services, or child protective (administrative) intervention. If the situation needs to be referred to the judiciary branch, then the *département* notifies the public prosecutor immediately.

When a judicial intervention is warranted, the judge decides what type of action should be taken (placement or in-home interventions), and for what duration (placement decisions need to be reviewed at least once every 2 years according to the law; in practical terms this review can also take place after 6 months or a year, depending on the situation's particulars). Licensed private-sector agencies under the authority of ASE carry out that decision in the conditions requested by the judge.

When an administrative intervention is initiated, ASE social workers (under the authority of the president of the *département* council) decides with the child(ren) and parents what needs to be done and for what duration. Some types of intervention, carried out by *technicien.ne.s de l'intervention sociale et familiale* (TISF), social workers whose intervention is mainly technical to help face a difficult situation, can last 3 months; most other types of administrative interventions, that involve educators and target more long-term problems, typically last 6 months or a year, and can be renewed..

Child protection interventions can be mandated for situations concerning children (under-18 s), but also, in a more limited way, for young adults (18-to-20-year-olds). When young adults are concerned, child protection interventions take place outside the framework of CRIP assessments (since there is no assessment to be made regarding parental capacities and/or willingness to work with social workers).

---

[8] This helpline is managed by SNATED, *service national d'assistance téléphonique à l'enfance en danger*, which like ONPE is a branch of GIPED, the public interest grouping for children in danger.

[9] Even when the judiciary initiates a procedure on the basis of information it has received directly, a copy of the information should be sent to the *département* services.

As of December 31, 2014, there were in all 290, 000 minors receiving help from the child protection system, which represents 19.8 per thousand (or 1.98%) of the total population of under-18 s in France. Young adults (from 18 to 20 included) were 21, 500, or 9.3 per thousand (0.93%) of the respective total population (ONPE 2016e).

More than half of the minors who receive some help from the child protection system reside with their parent(s): 10.7% of all children are involved in an in-home intervention by ASE as of December 31, 2014 (ONPE 2017b); slightly more than the proportion of children who are placed (9.8%); or to put it differently 52.3% of all child protection decisions concerning minors are in-home interventions (and the remaining 47.7% are placement decisions). This is an average: the proportion of placement at the level of the *départements*' ranges from 28.5 to 65.2% with a median of 47.1%(ONPE 2017b).

As of December 31, 2014, more than half (51.6%) of all minors and young adults who are placed outside of their parents' home by ASE are placed with a (mainly unrelated, professional) foster family (kinship care is very uncommon in France, except in some of the overseas *départements*); 37.5% live in a residential institution, 4% are living alone and 6.8% are in different living conditions. This is an average: the proportion of foster family placement decisions at the *département* level for minors and young adults ranges from 19.2 to 89.1% with a median of 56.3%. The proportion of residential placement similarly ranges from 10.9 to 65.7% with a median of 34.5% (ONPE 2017b). This is a rather high proportion of children in residential care. As the French committee of child protection institutions (Convention nationale des associations de protection de l'enfance, CNAPE) has pointed out in its 2012 Contribution to the European debate on de-institutionalization (CNAPE 2012), French law has instituted a number of participation mechanisms, both collective and individual, that allow children to have a fairly active role in residential institutions. In addition, the care that is provided there is tailored to each individual child in spite of the overall setting. For these reasons, residential care in child protection is not perceived in France in the same light as in Europe generally and remains comparatively common.

As of December 31, 2014, among minors, nearly 9 out of 10 placements have their origin in a judicial decision, as well as more than 7 out of 10 in-home interventions. Virtually all interventions concerning young adults stem from an administrative decision (ONPE 2016e). This is an average: the proportion of judicial interventions inside each *départements*' interventions with minors ranged on December 31, 2013 from 54.5 to 93.3% with a median of 77.1% (ONPE 2016d, and p. 123).

5.3.2 Practices in Child Protection

Statistical data shows the gulf that can exist between *départements*. The availability of institutions or foster families, the number of social workers, the different types of issues that can be found in different territories can explain these differences. It is also quite difficult to make broad generalizations on the decisions taken by judges and social workers for child protection in France. Local priorities and official partnerships are defined for each *département* in pluri-annual action plans called *schéma de protection de l'enfance*[10]. Decision makers at *département* level can use data from the ODPE to inform their choice.

A few general trends emerge nonetheless at national level: they correspond to broad directions taken over the years, directions which have helped motivate some of the more recent reforms.

The first trend is the desire to reduce the proportion of judicial measures. Until the early 2010s, many persons and professionals subscribed to the belief that it was best to send the information they had about possible child endangerment to the public prosecutor, the *procureur*. But this entailed three limitations:

- First and foremost, the information sent to the judiciary had all the weight of a judicial document (*signalement*), which could discourage persons to report when they weren't absolutely sure, or when the situation wasn't dire. Concern over the potential consequences led to the creation of "*information préoccupante*" (information giving rise to concern), a less intimidating expression, and to the idea that social services be sent this information as opposed to the judiciary branches. The idea was to take action as early as possible, before problems become entrenched.
- Second, the mass of information sent to the judicial branches needed to be dealt with by the judiciary before any other type of intervention could be considered, but the judiciary didn't necessarily have the personnel or expertise to assess all these situations in a timely fashion. There was concern that reports on non-immediately threatening situations would backlog the tribunals and wouldn't receive an adequate treatment. The 2007 law reform setting out that all information be sent to the CRIP (except for those that require immediate judiciary action) was enacted to make sure that a response would take place if necessary.
- Finally, since judiciary decisions don't require the parents' consent[11], social workers who implement them and work with the families could be seen as coercive, which could put a strain on the trust they needed to build with the families.

Administrative decisions, following the 2007 reform, were presented as the desirable option and judicial interventions as the last-resort fallback in most cases. This, however, is the theory; as data shows, judicial decisions remain the majority

[10] Mercifully, there is no acronym for these documents. Many *départements* make their *schémas* public on their website.

[11] Consent is the legal requirement for administrative intervention. In the framework of judicial interventions, social workers are required to obtain some form of "willingness" or "eagerness" (*adhésion*) of families toward the proposed intervention.

of all decisions in child protection, even when it comes to in-home interventions. In 2003, judicial decisions were the origin of 83% of all child protection interventions with children; in 2013, they are still 79% (ONPe 2016d, p. 122).

Another related trend of child protection services in France is the desire to protect family ties and therefore to avoid separating the child through placement. A joint report by the Inspectorate for social affairs (*Inspection générale des affaires sociales*, IGAS) and the Inspectorate for judicial services (*Inspection générale des services judiciaires*, IGSJ), penned by Naves and Cathala in 2000, concluded that placement, which had become the "center of gravity" of child protection, was seen as a form of violence and a threat to parents. This impacted the way parents interacted with services and led them to avoid help. To reclaim a positive relationship with families, the report and all subsequent policy announcements insisted on the central role of parents in preventing danger. In the framework of the subsidiarity principle put forward by French child protection, the protection that parents provide their children is paramount against danger; interventions by social services can only take place when this protection is defective or missing. Interventions should try to re-establish positive parenting roles, not do away with them altogether.

Finally, a tool has been set up that is promoted as a practical tool to make the intervention more child-centric, and that is the *Projet pour l'enfant* (PPE) or project for the child. Out of 96 *schémas* that were available in French *départements* in 2015 (i.e. in 96 of all 101 *départements*), 53 promoted PPE as a tool to be generalized all over the territory (ONPE 2016b). PPE was instituted by the 2007 reform, though its implementation has been very gradual. Further implementation of PPE also corresponds to one of the objectives of the 2016 Law. The idea is to ask practitioners to write down the specific aims of each intervention, following an assessment period that includes the points of view of parents and children. But the reality of what this tool represents varies considerably from one *département* to the other. As a study published by ONPE (2016b) has shown, PPE is the translation in terms of practices of the desire to tailor every single intervention around the needs and capacities of the child(ren) involved; although its principle is now accepted, its usage still has an important margin for progression, most notably because the overall legal and administrative framework remains hazy and because of emerging and competing tools and initiatives that divert attention from the structural nature of PPE.

5.4 Policy Challenges

5.4.1 An Emerging Concern: Unaccompanied Minors

Recent history has shown the French child protection system's capacity to adapt to shifting policy paradigms, albeit over a number of years. But it remains a system tailored to the needs of children experiencing hardship or educative difficulties within their family; it relies strongly whenever possible on the parent/child bond and when this bond cannot be maintained, it tries to substitute it. The focus on maintaining family ties, which is closely linked to the perception of child protection as a substitution or an alternative for parental care, goes very far in France: one form of intervention that can occur in some territories (11 *départements* as of 2015) is "placement without displacement" (*placement sans déplacement*), whereby a child is placed but inside his or her home, a foster carer being available to help the parents and house the child if need be. Another crucial element of child protection interventions in the French contact is that they rely on a local partnership that anchors it to the realities of relatively small territories.

But an emerging concern for this system is precisely a population that is not in a traditional family setting and that defies territorial boundaries: unaccompanied minors (UAMs). Europe has seen an expanding influx of migrants since 2013, and roughly a third of all asylum requests currently being treated in this framework are made by minors (Eurostat 2017b). Despite the insufficiencies of the European relocation programme, many minors arrive in France, with or without legal documents. The European Fundamental Rights Agency (2017) estimates that in 2017 "approximately 120 to 150 migrants entered France each week via the French–Italian border, according to organizations operating on the ground. This brings the total to between 480 and 600 arrivals for June." Although most are adults, many of them are children[12].

Even beyond intercultural issues and language problems, this is a very difficult population for child protection to work with: many children are trying to reach other countries and/or don't want to be cared for; many don't have reliable documents and can't prove they are minors; and they are frequently evasive about their journey and past experiences. Social workers of child protection services aren't typically trained on asylum legislation and aren't used to taking into account relocation projects the child may have[13].

An added problem lies in the territorial inequalities of France: while UAMs tend to be first identified and protected in *départements* with international borders, ports or airports, these are not necessarily the ones with the most resources to care for them. A tentative solution was proposed on May 31, 2013 with the creation of a national unit in charge of monitoring the number of UAMs in the different départements (*Cellule nationale MNA*) and deciding which *département* is responsible for the protection of any given UAM.

Until fairly recently, UAMs were cared for, but there was no systematic national framework detailing the process (despite the first elements given by EU directive 2011/95/UE). Law No 2016-297 explicitly confirms that UAMs fall under the scope of Article L 112-3 of the Code for social action and family and are therefore entitled

[12] According to Eurostat, under-18 s represent slightly under 20% of asylum requests in France in 2016, of which more than 90% are unaccompanied. But this is not a good indicator, as very few minors ask for asylum in France – in 2014, there were 4000 UAMs in care according to the ministry of justice, but OFPRA, the French asylum body, only received 273 requests from children – (ONPE 2017a, p. 63)

[13] A detailed description of the practical difficulties and promising practices for that public can be found in ONPE (2016b).

to protection by the *départements*. In July 2017, there were 6, 798 UAMs identified by the national unit in charge of redistributing UAMs in France (Ministère de la Justice 2017).

The legal limbo which used to surround the question of UAMs in France is now in many ways clarified thanks to the 2013 and 2016 reforms, but practices are still quickly evolving, and child protection is still struggling to reach and serve the many UAMs, as evidenced by the lack of proper care received by minors in the Calais camp, a situation that many human rights watchdogs including the French ombudsman have noted (Défenseur des droits 2017).

5.4.2 Quantifying Child Abuse and Neglect

Another challenge for policy in 2017 is remedying the lack of data concerning child abuse and neglect. The entry point into child protection isn't abuse and neglect as such, but "danger", a notion that deliberately includes a notion of parental protection that is not always operative in questions of child abuse or neglect (to be in danger, not only does there need to be child abuse or neglect, but also the lack of a proper parental response). As a result, the data that are available from child protection are not an overall indication of child abuse and neglect.

Very few quantified estimations of child and abuse exist in France, and there is therefore little information available on the victims, acts and perpetrators at national level. Clinical portraits, a wide range of tools and recommendations on identifying cases of CAN and providing adequate help, studies of the life trajectories of some children who have been abused or taken into care, and a number of completed studies on specific types of abuse and monographs detailing the life events and situations of young people in certain specific institutions and territories exist. ONPE (2016c) presents a detailed overview of the existing literature on child abuse and neglect, while ONPE (2016d) lists all existing data sources and surveys on child abuse and child endangerment in France today.

This lack of data is a difficult situation for all stakeholders of child protection (policymakers, government officials, professionals and advocates…). A very ambitious victimization survey has recently been launched by the *Institut national d'études démographiques,* VIRAGE (*Violences et rapports de genre: contextes et conséquences des violences subies par les femmes et par les hommes* – Violence and gender relations: context and consequences of the violence experienced by women and men). Although this survey focuses on gender-based violence, it does include elements connected to experiences of violence as a child and to children witnessing intimate partner violence. It was conducted from February to November 2015 on a representative sample of 27, 268 persons (15, 556 women and 11, 712 men) aged 20–69, living in metropolitan France (Hamel et al. 2016). The analysis is underway and the results should be available in November 2018.

The lack of data on child abuse and neglect is in itself a problem, but an exaggerated emphasis on the distinction between situations of danger and situations of abuse and/or neglect can also be a problem for social workers and their written reports, in which abuse tends to be absent. The ministry of social affairs has published a guide for practitioners regarding "information giving rise to concern", the new expression introduced in 2007 to clarify reporting procedures: this guide made no reference to abuse, but simply reminded practitioners to refer the situation to the justice system when a penal infraction is identified. This disconnect downplays the prevalence of abusive behavior and prevents ASE services from responding adequately (Corbet et al. 2015). Despite the fact that suspicions of abuse/neglect were noted in many assessment reports analyzed by Corbet, Séverac and Le Duff in their 2015 report on how child protection practitioners qualified abuse, it was rarely investigated or noted as an issue in the classification. This issue has been tentatively dealt with by Law No 2016-297 and its application decrees which require practitioners to explicitly name the types of abuse and neglect that they identify in the child's situation.

This is an increasingly emerging concern of professionals, researchers and decision-makers alike. To remedy this issue, ONPE is expected to promote and conduct research on these issues. Additionally, an inter-ministerial action plan against child abuse has thus been launched in March 2017 and some of its provisions could shed some light, mainly on suspicious deaths (Ministère des Familles, de l'enfance et des droits des femmes 2017).

Despite the policy challenges and gaps[14] that exist and need to be confronted, the French child protection system has shown a good capacity to adapt to its changing institutional and demographic context. New practices are being developed, such as the initiatives from the inter-ministerial action plan on child abuse and the consolidated framework for the protection of UAMs. However, the discrepancy between *départements* remains a concern that can have a real impact on situations that involve movement between territories and on the capacity to replicate promising practices.

References

Bellamy, V., & Beaumel, C. (2017, January 17). Bilan démographique 2016. *Insee Première,* 1630. Retrieved from https://www.insee.fr/fr/statistiques/2554860?sommaire=1912926

Chauveaud, C., & Warin, P. (2016, November). *Le non-recours à la Couverture maladie universelle complémentaire. Enquête auprès des populations précaires. Rapport d'étude.* Retrieved from https://www.cmu.fr/fichier-utilisateur/fichiers/ODENORE_Non-recours_CMUC_2016.pdf

Convention nationale des associations de protection de l'enfance. (2012, October). *Contribution de la CNAPE aux travaux européens relatifs à la dés institutionnalisation de la protection de l'enfance*. Retrieved from http://www.cnape.fr/files/news/1139.pdf

[14]The lack of data on children victims of trafficking, for instance, makes it difficult to raise awareness on this issue and to articulate informed policies.

Corbet, E., Séverac, N., & Le Duff, R. (2015, December). *Appréciation des situations de maltraitance(s) intrafamiliale(s).* Retrieved from https://www.onpe.gouv.fr/system/files/ao/creai_ra_rapport_etude_onpe_decembre.pdf

Défenseur des droits. (2017). *Décision du Défenseur des droits n° 2017-206*, 21 juin 2017. Retrieved from https://www.defenseurdesdroits.fr/sites/default/files/atoms/files/decision.pdf

Direction de l'évaluation, de la prospective et de la performance. (2016, June). La scolarisation à deux ans: en éducation prioritaire, un enfant sur cinq va à l'école dès deux ans. *Note d'information*, 19. Retrieved from http://cache.media.education.gouv.fr/file/2016/67/8/depp-ni-2016-19-scolarisation-a-deux-ans-en-education-prioritaire-un-enfant-sur-cinq-va-a-ecole-des-deux-ans_597678.pdf

Direction de la recherche, des études, de l'évaluation et des statistiques (Drees). (2017). *Études et résultats,* 991. Retrieved from http://drees.solidarites-sante.gouv.fr/IMG/pdf/er991.pdf

European Union agency for fundamental rights (FRA). (2017, July). *Monthly data collection on the migration situation in the EU. July 2017 monthly report.* Retrieved from http://fra.europa.eu/sites/default/files/fra_uploads/fra-2017-july-monthly-migration-report_en.pdf

Eurostat. (2015). *People in the EU – Statistics on demographic change.* [Data sets]. Retrieved from http:/ec.europa.eu/eurostat/statistics-explained/index.php/People_in_the_EU_%E2%80%93_statistics_on_demographic_changes

Eurostat. (2017a). *Fertility statistics.* [Data sets, March 2017]. Retrieved from http:/ec.europa.eu/eurostat/statistics-explained/index.php/Fertility_statistics.

Eurostat. (2017b). *Asylum statistics.* [Data sets, 13 March 2017]. Retrieved from http:/ec.europa.eu/eurostat/statistics-explained/index.php/Asylum_statistics.

Eurostat. (2017c). *Amenable and preventable deaths statistics.* [Data sets, June 2017]. Retrieved from http:/ec.europa.eu/eurostat/statistics-explained/index.php/Amenable_and_preventable_deaths_statistics

Hamel, C., Debauche, A., Brown, E., Lebugle, A., Lejbowicz, T., Mazuy, M., Charruault, A., Cromer, S., & Dupuis, J. (2016). Viols et agressions sexuelles en France: Premiers résultats de l'enquête Virage. *Population et Sociétés, 538.*

Insee. (2017a, February 6). *Population par sexe et par âge au 1er janvier 2016.* Comparaisons régionales et départementales. [Indicators]. Retrieved from https://www.insee.fr/fr/statistiques/2012692

Insee. (2017b, February 06). *Produit intérieur brut en 2014. Comparaisons régionales.* [Indicators]. Retrieved from https://www.insee.fr/fr/statistiques/2012723

Ministère de l'Éducation nationale, de l'enseignement supérieur et de la recherche. (2015). *L'éducation nationale en chiffres, 2015.* Retrieved from http://cache.media.education.gouv.fr/file/2015/58/6/DEPP_grands_chiffres_2015_482586.pdf

Ministère de la Justice. (2017). La mission "Mineurs non accompagnés". Tableau de suivi. Effectif MNA au 21 juillet 2017 – Exercice 2017. Retrieved from http://www.justice.gouv.fr/art_pix/tableau_mna.pdf

Ministère des Familles, de l'enfance et des droits des femmes. (2017). *Plan interministériel de mobilisation et de lutte contre les violences faites aux enfants. 2017–2019.* Retrieved from http://www.egalite-femmes-hommes.gouv.fr/wp-content/uploads/2017/02/PlanVIOLENCES_-ENFANTS_2017-2019.pdf

Naves, P., & Cathala, B. (2000). *Accueils provisoires et placements d'enfants et d'adolescents : des décisions qui mettent à l'épreuve le système français de protection de l'enfance et de la famille.* Paris: La Documentation française. Retrieved from http://www.ladocumentationfrancaise.fr/var/storage/rapports-publics/004001642.pdf

Nay, O., Béjean, S., Benamouzig, D., Bergeron, H., Castel, P., & Ventelou, B. (2016). Achieving universal health coverage in France: Policy reforms and the challenge of inequalities. *The Lancet, 387*(10034), 2236–2249.

Observatoire national de l'enfance en danger/Observatoire national de la protection de l'enfance. (n.d.). *La loi de réforme de la protection de l'enfance* [Presentation and selection of legal texts and analyses]. https://www.onpe.gouv.fr/loi-reforme-protection-lenfance

Observatoire national de la protection de l'enfance. (2016a, March). *Protection de l'enfant: les nouvelles dispositions issues de la loi n°2016-297 du 14 mars 2016 relative à la protection de l'enfant. Note d'actualité.* Retrieved from https://www.onpe.gouv.fr/system/files/publication/20160315_notedactu_loipe.pdf

Observatoire national de la protection de l'enfance. (2016b, July). *Le PPE: état des lieux, enjeux organisationnels et pratiques*. Paris. La Documentation française. Retrieved from https://www.onpe.gouv.fr/system/files/publication/rapport_ppe_2016.pdf

Observatoire national de la protection de l'enfance. (2016c, August). *Revue de littérature "La maltraitance intrafamiliale envers les enfants"*. Retrieved from https://www.onpe.gouv.fr/system/files/publication/revue_web_liens_actifs.pdf

Observatoire national de la protection de l'enfance. (2016d, October). *Enfants (en risque de) danger, enfants protégés: quelles données chiffrées ? Onzième rapport au Parlement et au gouvernement* (p. 121). Paris: La Documentation française.

Observatoire national de la protection de l'enfance. (2016e, November). *Estimation de la population des enfants et des jeunes pris en charge en protection de l'enfance au 31/12/2014. Note d'actualité.* Retrieved from https://www.onpe.gouv.fr/system/files/publication/20160927_note_estimation2014_ok.pdf

Observatoire national de la protection de l'enfance. (2017a, February). *Mineurs non accompagnés Quels besoins et quelles réponses ?* Paris: La Documentation française.

Observatoire national de la protection de l'enfance. (2017b, June). *La population des enfants pris en charge en protection de l'enfance au 31/12/2014: les disparités départementales Note d'actualité.* Retrieved from https://www.onpe.gouv.fr/system/files/publication/20170615_note_estimation2014_v2_revafletgs_1.pdf

Organization for Economic Co-operation and Development. (2016, October). *Society at a Glance 2016: OECD Social Indicators*. Paris: OECD Publishing. https://doi.org/10.1787/9789264261488-en.

Organization for Economic Co-operation and Development. (2017a). *France – Economic forecast summary.* Retrieved from http://www.oecd.org/economy/france-economic-forecast-summary.htm

Organization for Economic Co-operation and Development. (2017b). *Health spending* (indicator). https://doi.org/10.1787/8643de7e-en. Accessed on 03 Aug 2017.

Organization for Economic Co-operation and Development. (2017c). *Tax revenue* (indicator). https://doi.org/10.1787/d98b8cf5-en. Accessed on 03 Aug 2017.

Organization for Economic Co-operation and Development. (2017d). *Social spending* (indicator). https://doi.org/10.1787/7497563b-en. Accessed on 03 Aug 2017.

Preamble to the constitution of 27 October 1946. Retrieved from http://www.conseil-constitutionnel.fr/conseil-constitutionnel/root/bank_mm/anglais/cst3.pdf

UNICEF Office of Research. (2017). *Building the future: Children and the sustainable development goals in rich countries* (Innocenti Report Card 14). Florence: UNICEF Office of Research – Innocenti.

World Health organization (WHO). The world health report 2000: Health systems: Improving performance. Retrieved from: http://apps.who.int/iris/bitstream/10665/42281/1/WHR_2000.pdf

Flora Bolter is a political scientist currently working as a research officer for Observatoire national de la protection de l'enfance (ONPE, formerly Observatoire national de l'enfance en danger, ONED), the French observatory for child protection. As such, she most recently coordinated the publication of a thematic dossier for ONPE concerning gender in child protection, published in October 2017(*La prise en compte du genre en protection de l'enfance*, ONPE/La Documentation française - https://is.gd/V046SI). She specialises in comparative and European frameworks of child protection.

Gilles Séraphin, a sociologist, is a professor of Education sciences at Paris Nanterre- UPL University, with the Education and training research center (Centre de recherche Education et Formation – CREF-EA1589) where he oversees the Master's programme on family education and socio-educative interventions in Europe (Éducation familiale et interventions socio-éducatives en Europe – Efise). He is also the managing editor of *Recherches familiales*, as well as an expert member of the Conseil national de la protection de l'enfance (CNPE), and he coordinates the "From pregnancy to adulthood" committee of the French Council for mental health (Conseil national de la santé mentale, CNSM). Between 2012 and 2017, he was director of the French observatory of child protection (Observatoire national de la protection de l'enfance, ONPE – formerly ONED). His research mainly focuses on public policies targeting or involving families, as well as protection policies (for children and for adults). The last books he published or coordinated are *Comprendre la politique familiale*, Paris Dunod, 2013; *Articuler recherche et pratique en protection de l'enfance*, Oned/ONPE, La Documentation française, 2015; and *Religion, guérison et forces occultes en Afrique. Le regard du jésuite Éric de Rosny,* Karthala/Pucac, 2016. For a complete list of articles and chapters published, please see: http://www.gilles.seraphin.sitew.com/#Dernieres_publications.G

Chapter 6
Preventing Child Endangerment: Child Protection in Germany

Susanne Witte, Laura Sophia Miehlbradt, Eric van Santen, and Heinz Kindler

6.1 Introduction

Germany, first founded in 1871, has been a latecomer among European nation states and has been slow to adopt democratic values (Winkler and Sager 2006, 2007). With ties back to Bismarck's social legislation in the years after its founding, Germany has one of the oldest welfare systems in the world with a universal health care system, social security, as well as public schools and tuition-free university education (Stolleis 2013). Nowadays, Germany is a high-income country with a high standard of living (Baines et al. 2010). Life expectancy in Germany is higher than in most other European states and in the United States of America and neonatal and under-five mortality rate are well below comparable figures for other countries (WHO 2017). As in other high-income countries, child protection is considered a policy priority (Jud et al. 2013). This book chapter provides an overview of essential components of the child protection system in Germany. After a short introduction into different meanings of two key terms in the public discourse on child protection, an overview of developments and key concepts of child protection during the German history is provided.

S. Witte (✉) · L. S. Miehlbradt · E. van Santen · H. Kindler
German Youth Institute, Munich, Germany
e-mail: witte@dji.de; miehlbradt@dji.de; santen@dji.de; kindler@dji.de

L. Merkel-Holguin et al. (eds.), *National Systems of Child Protection*, Child Maltreatment 8, https://doi.org/10.1007/978-3-319-93348-1_6

6.2 Two Central Terms: Child Protection and Child Endangerment

The term 'child protection' is used in different ways in public discourse. Based on an analysis of policy documents and justifications of child protection laws, Kindler (2012) proposed a model of three different perceptions of the term: narrow, wide, and extensive.

In a *narrow sense,* child protection is defined as encompassing all organized activities aiming to detect and react to child maltreatment. Support measures and interventions are directed specifically at families in which a child has suffered or is very likely to endure maltreatment. In a *wider sense,* the term child protection incorporates all types of psychosocial support measures for families that may be able to prevent child maltreatment. The target groups for those support measures are more comprehensive and include parents with parenting problems, psychological problems, or other risk factors for child maltreatment. Support measures based on this definition have a lower threshold than those based on a narrow definition and aim to enhance child and family well-being and not only to avoid child maltreatment. Within the political discourse and in the mass media, the term child protection is sometimes used following a definition with a more *extensive sense*. This definition includes activities to protect children from violence in the media, peer violence, and sexual abuse by strangers. The activities and support measures on this level target all children. The narrow, broad and extensive definitions of child protection are not mutually exclusive, and approaches based on these different concepts are intertwining. In the following, the focus will be on child protection in the sense of a narrow definition. Links to wider concepts of child protection will be highlighted.

Within a narrow sense of child protection *child endangerment* (Kindeswohlgefährdung) is the key term focusing on the situation of children in their families and determining the threshold at which the state is allowed to use involuntary measures to protect children if parents are unwilling or unfit to improve their situation (§ 1666 I German Civil Code, BGB). The law itself does not provide further guidance on how to interpret the term child endangerment. Thus, the Federal Courts have defined child endangerment as an actual threat considered sufficiently severe to cause substantial harm to the child or that substantial harm can be foreseen with a high degree of certainty (BGH 1956; Schmid and Meysen 2006). The expression 'substantial harm' is used for imminent physical injury, serious avoidable pain, and serious impairment of mental health or mental capacity. It is also used for developmental trajectories that prevent children from becoming socially competent and self-reliant adults. To intervene in parental rights, three criteria have to be met: It has to be shown (1) that child endangerment is present, (2) that parents are unable or unwilling to avert actual danger although they have been offered support, and (3) that involuntary state intervention is adequate and proportionate (Schmid and Meysen 2006). The law itself does not differentiate between types of child maltreatment. Because the concept of child endangerment is holistic and does include substantial harm done to the physical, psychological, emotional, cognitive, and social well-being of children physical and psychological child abuse, child neglect, and child sexual abuse are all acknowledged as forms of child endangerment.

6.3 Historical Development of Concepts

The key concepts of child protection have changed considerably over the last centuries leading to the current child protection system. The overview of the history starts with the founding of the German Empire in 1871 although some child protection activities in the independent German states have existed before (Jacobi 2014).

6.3.1 *Rising Concern About the Moral Development of Children (1871–1914)*

In the second half of the nineteenth century, there was an increasing concern about the *Verwahrlosung* (moral and physical neglect) of children (Kindler and Borrmann 2012). This concern was based on the fear that rising juvenile delinquency would get out of control and could threaten social order (Elder 2014). Especially, children from lower social classes were considered at risk of neglect as well as severe physical abuse (Elder 2014). Causes for moral and physical neglect of children were attributed to lesser resources (Kindler and Borrmann 2012) and transmission of immoral behavior by criminal or indecent parents (Uhlendorff 2003), but also congenital factors (Kindler and Borrmann 2012).

The best interest of the child principle was emerging at that time together with the idea that under some circumstances the state has to act on behalf of those interests (Wapler 2015). The best interests of a child though were not thought of as being dependent on individual wishes but were derived from culturally formed ideals of morality, thus increasing the likelihood of children to become valuable members of society. Overall, child protection was part of a much broader movement of introducing regulations regarding child labor, schooling, and measures to improve child health. Two different concepts of child protection emerged: One was based on the idea of rescuing or saving innocent children from their immoral parents (Richter 2011), the other was conceptualized as disciplining children seen as antisocial in correctional institutions to prevent criminal behavior (Uhlendorff 2003).

With the introduction of the Civil Code Book (BGB) in 1900, a first legal definition of child endangerment was developed.§ 1666 BGB regulated that courts could intervene in families if fathers (as custody holders) neglected the child, misused custody, or behaved in an immoral way. The second possibility for state intervention was regulated in criminal law as well as in the introductory act to the Civil Code Book (§ 135) and allowed for the placement of children independent from parental behavior if this was seen as necessary to prevent children's moral ruin. In order to handle the rising number of cases, *Jugendämter* (local child and youth welfare authorities) were founded in some cities between 1900 and 1910. Still, services were mostly provided by non-governmental institutions, and service provision varied widely relying on staff and volunteers without professional training (Uhlendorff 2003).

6.3.2 *Increasing Responsibility of the State (1914–1933)*

During and immediately after World War I, large parts of the population suffered from hunger and poverty (e.g. Cox 2013). Child mortality rates and rates of nutritional deficiency diseases were rising (Demm 2001). As a reaction to this crisis, the state had to expand and reorganize child health care as well as child and youth welfare services. This included professionalization of staff and structured organization, e.g. more local child and youth welfare authorities (Jugendämter) were founded, which were assigned the task to coordinate, supervise, and organize services (Uhlendorff 2003).

In the constitution of the Weimar Republic, the right of parents to receive education for their children was granted, but this was formulated as parental duty and the state had the obligation to protect children from exploitation and "Verwahrlosung". Moreover, with the child and youth welfare law, a legal framework for child and youth welfare services was established in 1922 for the first time. For example, now all municipalities and counties had to establish a Jugendamt. The child and youth welfare law reflects intense political tensions of that time. Mainly, all political parties and the Christian Churches feared for their influence within the state (Dickinson 1996). This struggle led to subsidiarity as an organizing principle by law, which guaranteed partial independence to non-governmental organizations. Due to the economic crisis, the provision of many planed services was not made mandatory by law (Uhlendorff 2003). What had an impact, however, was a lowering of the threshold for placements in reformatories (Wapler 2015). Instead of averting "moral ruin" of children placement became already possible if there was some neglect due to inadequate parental behavior (sec. 63 RJWG). Thus, the number of children and adolescents placed in reformatories increased (Schmidt 2002b). Although some facilities developed more humanistic concepts (e.g. Lhotsky 1992), most children in reformatories were treated quite harshly or were even abused (Peukert 1986; Dickinson 2002). As expenditure rose, ideas about identifying "uneducatable" children were flourishing (e.g. Kölch 2002).

6.3.3 *"Child Protection" Based on National Socialist Ideology (1933–1945)*

After 1933, the National Socialist Party transformed the state into an instrument of totalitarian rule (Bracher et al. 1960). All governmental structures, including child protection law, were subordinated to ideological objectives, in particular the aim of strengthening the "Volksgemeinschaft" (Wapler 2015). Parents had to ensure that they educated their children in accordance with the National Socialist Ideology. Educational principles were guided by the idea to raise strong and fearless children, who would constitute the "Aryan master race" (Chamberlain 1998). There was a heavy emphasis on discipline, physical strengthening, and reinforcement of gender role conformity. In contrast, loving tenderness from parents was considered poor parenting weakening the child (Chamberlain 1998). Child protection law sometimes was used for sanctioning parents who did not adhere to these guidelines, e.g. children could be ruled as endangered if their parents did not let them participate in the Hitler Youth (Kindler and Borrmann 2012). Based on ideas of heredity, racial inequality, and racial purity exclusion and discrimination of children classified as inferior (e.g. Jewish or gypsy children, children with disabilities) were seen as necessary and justified (Benz 2009). Within a few years, strategies for exclusion grew more and more radical. They included forced sterilizations, starving or poisoning children with certain disabilities (Dahl 2001), as well as deportation and systematic murder of Jewish and gypsy children (Lewy 2000; Heberer 2011). The National Socialist party claimed to control all youth welfare services (Sachße and Tennstedt 1992). Nevertheless, most Christian charities stayed formally independent and some tried to distance themselves from certain elements of the National Socialist Ideology (van Vliet 2013).

6.3.4 Restrictive Approaches Aiming to Prevent Immoral Behavior (1945–1970)

After World War II, the economy of Germany prospered and the political system gained stability. A denial about the German National Socialist past during that time was often stated by historians and sociologists (Mitscherlich and Mitscherlich 1998). The Allies re-established the former Jugendämter and in 1953 the child and youth welfare law of the Weimar Republic – slightly changed – came into effect again. A majority of child and youth welfare services relied again on the services of non-governmental organizations. Concepts established earlier in this century continued to influence the practice of child protection (Kindler and Borrmann 2012). Therefore, decisions about child protection measures (e.g. out-of-home placement of children) again were based on a moral judgment of the behavior of children, adolescents, or parents (Runder Tisch Heimerziehung 2010). Many children's homes used extreme corporal punishment (Frings and Kaminsky 2012). In some institutions, adolescents had to work on farms or in factories, but did not receive their wages. The wages were kept by the institutions (Runder Tisch Heimerziehung 2010).

6.3.5 From Interventionist Approaches Towards Working Together (1970–1990)

With the German student movement, including feminism and sexual liberation, in the late 1960s and 1970s discussions about the German past, state oppression, and democratic values arose. In the following years, they lead to a widening of participation of the public in democratic processes such as demonstrations. With the social changes in the 1960s and 1970s, the beliefs about child protection altered as well (Kindler and Borrmann 2012). The movement New Child Protection emphasized the importance of prevention of child maltreatment. Working together with families to protect children was strongly advocated. Feminists started to draw public attention to sexual violence against women, including sexual abuse of girls (Görgen et al. 2015). In contrast, based on the ideas of sexual liberation other movements publicly demanded impunity for sexual abuse if no physical violence was present (Görgen et al. 2015). In the 1970s, some non-governmental child protection organizations started working based on the concepts of New Child Protection. Especially, parenting support measures were developed. In the 1980s, these concepts began to affect the service provision on a more general level. The number of foster care placements instead of residential care placements rose (Hansbauer 2002). Additionally, the number of social workers employed by the state and non-governmental organizations increased drastically (Hansbauer 2002).

6.3.6 Denial of Child Maltreatment in the German Democratic Republic (1949–1989)

After World War II, the Eastern part of Germany was integrated as the German Democratic Republic ('East Germany') in the Soviet Block. Based on the ideas of Communism, a Socialist state was build. In agreement with Socialist ideology, child and youth welfare services were only considered necessary in the first phase of a Socialist regime as child maltreatment was seen as a problem of Capitalism (Bohler and Franzheld 2010; Gries 2002). The state used reports about child maltreatment in Western countries as propaganda against Capitalism (Gries 2002). The aim of child protection was to intervene to avoid "maladaptive" development of children towards Anti-Socialism (Bohler and Franzheld 2010; Helming et al. 1999). In order to silence any doubts about the achievements of the Socialist regime, child maltreatment was not discussed publicly even though a mandatory reporting system existed (Gries 2002). In scientific articles, the causes of maltreatment were solely attributed to personal problems of the parents and their Bourgeois values (Gries 2002). Youth welfare services were embedded in the educational system and provided by staff without professional training (Bohler and Franzheld 2010). The most common measure was placement in children's homes (Bohler and Franzheld 2010). Children living there were almost entirely isolated from the rest of society (Helming et al.

1999). This lead in many institutions to a system of rigid control and oppression of the children which included physical punishment as an educational principle and made children vulnerable to sexual abuse (Helming et al. 1999). Gries (2002) pointed out that the tremendous pressure and state instructed doping in the sports system as well as the exploitation of children for ideas of Socialism, e.g. pressuring them to take part in the governmental youth movement 'Free German Youth', should be considered child maltreatment as well.

6.3.7 When Is Working Together Not Enough? (1990–2010)

In 1990, East and West Germany were reunified, following the collapse of the Soviet Block. The year 1990/1991 is also considered a paradigm change in the child and youth welfare system. At that time, the new child and youth welfare law (Kinder- und Jugendhilfegesetz) came into effect. Child protection was now mainly conceptualized as the provision of support and collaboration with families instead of control and strict interventions. This introduced two thresholds: The first and lower one granted families in need of help the right to receive child and youth welfare services. The second one remained the threshold for intervention into family life, i.e. restriction of parental rights. The threshold for receiving support measures was set below the threshold for child endangerment to make sure that families have access to services to prevent child maltreatment. Overall, the new child and youth welfare law received very positive feedback (Kindler 2012; Kindler and Borrmann 2012) but there was some critique that the law did not state clear guidelines how local child and youth welfare authorities should handle cases of suspected child endangerment. This issue was widely discussed in society and politics. Some cases of children who died at the hands of their parents or caretakers while under the supervision of the Jugendamt were highly publicized in the media (e.g. "Laura-Jane" und "Kevin" in Bringewat 2001; Fegert et al. 2010 Bussmann 2005). In the following years, amendments were made to the law to protect children better. In addition, more preventive support services were established to provide early help for a broad range of families (BMFSFJ 2006).

Sexual abuse of girls by family members, particularly fathers, was widely discussed at the beginning of the 1990s (e.g. Kavemann and Lohstöter 1991). As in all other countries, it turned out to be difficult to substantiate intrafamilial child sexual abuse. In 1999 the German Federal Court of Justice ruled that criteria based content analysis (CBCA) of children's statements are valid enough to be admissible as evidence in court proceedings. In some cases, this makes substantiation of sexual abuse allegations easier (Köhnken 2004). However, due to some cases with suggestive interviewing of child witnesses (e.g. "Wormser Prozess") and thereby concerns about implanted false memories, strict methodological rules for CBCA were established. Overall, focus on children's well-being increased in the child protection discourse. This attitude led to the ratification of the United Nations Convention on the Rights of the Child (partially in 1992, fully in 2010), the law to banish violence against children in upbringing and education (in 2000), and changes in court proceedings prioritizing cases of child endangerment (in 2008).

6.3.8 Historic Abuse in Institutions (Since 2010)

In the most recent years, the importance of children's well-being and participation of children has continued to grow. In contrast to earlier attempts, which failed to gain public attention (Runder Tisch Heimerziehung 2010), sexual abuse of boys in boarding schools run by the Catholic Church (Hagenberg-Miliu 2014; Keupp et al. 2013; Obermayer and Stadler 2011) and those with progressive educational concepts (Dehmers 2011) was publicly discussed in 2010 (Fegert et al. 2015). Parts of the discussion of the so-called Sexual Abuse Scandal evolved not only around the perpetrators in boarding schools but also about the institutional dynamics that enabled them to abuse children for a long time. As a reaction to the Sexual Abuse Scandal, various measures were taken on federal and state level, including a rise in the funding of research in this area as well as establishing the Independent Commissioner for Questions Regarding Child Sexual Abuse.

The New Federal Child Protection Law came into effect in 2012. It further facilitated the exchange and cooperation in child protections and made quality standards for service providers in the field of child and youth welfare mandatory.

6.4 Basic Structures – Subsidiarity as Organizing Principle

The structures of the German welfare system are based on the principle of subsidiarity (lat.: subsidium: help, reserve). This principle, a kind of hierarchical ordering of solidarities, stems from Catholic theories of social organization in industrialized countries and has been introduced as a core principle of the German welfare state in the Weimar Republic (cf. Section, Historical Development of Concepts). Following this principle, the smallest unit of social organization has to provide help and support first. The next-larger unit only provides support if the smaller units of society are unable to provide the support themselves. Larger units respect the role and autonomy of smaller units. Therefore, help by the next-larger unit is provided in a way that enables smaller units to adapt. The principle of subsidiarity implies that non-governmental organizations are preferred over state organizations and that the smaller units are partly independent from the greater units. Following the principle of subsidiarity, the German child protection system is organized in such a way that first parents and families are in charge if children are in need or endangered. If they are willing to accept help, parents and families have the right to receive support while their autonomy is respected. Thus, they have rights to choose between services and participate in decision making. The state, the federal states and the municipalities, have the responsibility for providing structural conditions for child protection. Moreover, some statutory tasks (e.g. removal of custody) lie with state bodies. Municipalities coordinate, supervise, and finance child and youth welfare services. They have to provide services by themselves if no smaller social unit is available. States have rights and obligations as well, e.g. they finance family courts and decide on overarching organizational structures and procedures in child and youth welfare. Finally, the core principles are constituted in federal law.

For the sake of comparability, we have referred to the term "child protection system". However, we want to emphasize that no such term officially exists in the German welfare state. There is an interwoven structure between many different institutions with legal obligations to protect children from maltreatment and to offer help and support if they have been maltreated. But all of these institutions have broader roles and tasks in child and youth welfare. None is focused exclusively on child endangerment or child protection in the narrow sense. The different institutions and their responsibilities in the protection of children will be briefly outlined in this section.

6.4.1 Jugendämter – Key Institutions Within the Child and Youth Welfare System

The key institutions for child protection at the local level are the Jugendamt and the family court. There are 563 Jugendämter in total (Bundesarbeitsgemeinschaft der Bundesjugendämter 2015). Some obligations of the Jugendamt relate to activities and concepts in a broad or even extensive sense of child protection. These are for example early help programs, general parent support, youth social work, foster and residential care, as well as youth protection. The Jugendämter have to guarantee the provision of these but do not have to provide all these services themselves. They cooperate with child and youth welfare organizations, which are supported by the state but run by non-governmental organizations (freie Träger der Kinder- und Jugendhilfe). This cooperation between the state and non-governmental organizations has its roots in the first child and youth welfare law which was considered a compromise between the state and the Christian Churches (cf. Section, Historical Development of Concepts). The Jugendämter have to fund the services of the freie Träger and are responsible for ensuring that the demands of children and families are met (§§ 79, 80 SGB VIII). However, on a local level, the freie Träger take part in committees which decide on the structures of the child and youth organizations in that particular region. In 2014, 77.59% of the child and youth welfare institutions were freie Träger ($n = 25{,}521$; Statistisches Bundesamt 2015a). In total, 33.55% of the freie Träger are run by non-governmental institutions with a religious background ($n = 18{,}295$; Statistisches Bundesamt 2015a). Regarding child protection in a narrow sense, the Jugendamt has the sovereign duties to carry out investigations to determine whether a child is endangered (§ 8a SGB VIII) and to decide upon emergency placements of children (§ 42 SGB VIII). However, if parents do not agree with an emergency placement, the Jugendamt has to appeal to the family court, because only the family court can intervene in parental rights (§ 1666 I BGB).

6.4.2 *Family Courts – Legal Footing for Interventions into Parental Rights*

The 688 family courts are in charge of all matters concerning families, e.g. divorce and custody. However, this also includes proceedings regarding child endangerment (§ 1666 BGB). The family court can restrict or remove parental rights or make requirements to parents. In all matters concerning children, the family court has to put the children's well-being first and cases of (suspected) child endangerment have to be given priority. The family court and the Jugendamt ought to work conjointly to avert endangerment and support families. On the one hand, the Jugendamt has to appeal to the family court to intervene in parental rights (§ 8a II SGB VIII) and has the legal obligation to work with the family court in court proceedings. On the other hand, the court has to involve the Jugendamt in every proceeding about child endangerment. The family court can make requirements to the parents about the uptake of support measures. However, it cannot order the Jugendamt to provide certain services. In practice, the roles of the family court and the Jugendamt can lead to conflicts regarding the best decision about the well-being of the child (Münder et al. 2004). Although family courts are situated in every region, the procedures follow the federal law.

6.4.3 *The German Child Protection System – Complex and Flexible?*

The diversity of Jugendämter in each municipality and the variety of different institutions providing support and help result in varied services and policy approaches on a local level. This leads to flexible service provision based on the socio-demographic structure of the region that incorporates existing traditions. It might even lead to a higher adaptability of the system on a local level in case of an external crisis. Yet, changes in the child protection system take more time to reach practice if they are initiated top-down. Also for professionals from outside the child and youth welfare system as well as families and children, the complex structure of responsibilities is quite difficult to understand.

6.5 Framework of Child Protection

In Germany, everybody can report suspected child endangerment, but, except for the police, there is no mandatory reporting. During investigations (§ 8a I SGB VIII), social workers seek information about the family, including home-visits, and evaluate the situation of the child. This should be done conjointly together with other professionals. From an early point on, social workers are required to offer help and support to the family. At the end of an investigation, a decision is made about possible support measures and the need for an appeal to the family court.

In 2015, the Jugendämter carried out 129,485 investigations into child endangerment (97.17 per 10,000 children). In 31.90% of the investigations, it was decided on no further support or child protection action, in 33.35% on support but no child protection action needed, in 18.68% on latent child endangerment and in 16.07% on acute child endangerment (Statistisches Bundesamt 2016a).[1] In many aspects, the handling of cases of suspected child maltreatment and the provision of support services Germany is very similar to other European countries, but differences also emerge.

6.5.1 Professional Competency to Ensure Quality of Services

Since 2005, the legal framework provides some binding guidelines for carrying out investigations into child endangerment (cf. Table 6.1). Each Jugendamt may have guidelines that are more specific. However, social worker's professional discretion is stressed strongly in engaging with the family and decision making. Detailed guidelines restricting the decision-making scope are thought of as interfering with holistic approaches of social work, hindering acknowledgment of case dynamics, and interfering with professional autonomy (Biesel 2011; Bode and Turba 2014). A reluctance to use evidence-based approaches towards decision-making and interventions has been found in some studies (Jud et al. 2013). Moreover, there is no requirement by law or policy to use evidence-based practice (Kindler 2012). First professional training programs in social work started at the beginning of the twentieth century (Brumlik 2000). In contrast to the longstanding history of social work as a profession, there is a perceived need of social workers to justify their profession as necessary and important. This may lead to emphasizing the professional expertise and distinguishing the social work from other professional groups, in particular

[1] In German official statistics, it is differentiated between acute and latent endangerment. The first refers to an actual threat to the health and well-being of the child. The latter refers to an endangerment which is not as severe as acute endangerment, yet a risk for the development of the child is acknowledged.

Table 6.1 Legal guidelines for handling cases of child endangerment on federal level in Germany

Aspect of the investigation	Guideline on the federal level
Start of investigation	Weighty grounds to assume child endangerment
Collaboration	Involvement of at least two case workers
Emergency measures	In severe cases arrangement of emergency placement (for rights of the child during emergency placement see Table 6.2)
Working with family members	The inclusion of parents' and children's perspectives in the investigation (except if this leads to an endangerment of the child)
Home visit	If professionally necessary, the child has to be seen during a home visit
Support measures	If professionally necessary, support services have to be offered to the family
	Discussion of options for support with the parents; parents can choose comparable support measures.
	If parents are unwilling or unable to cooperate the Jugendamt can call upon the family court to intervene in parental rights

the health care system (Alberth and Bühler-Niederberger 2015). The need of a strict distinction may be further enforced by a huge difference in social status between health care professionals and social workers.

6.5.2 *Intertwining of Help and Protection*

All activities on child protection are based on the concept of intertwining of protection and support (Kindler 2012). Reasons for this connection are the strong value of the principle of subsidiarity emphasizing the need to help families to help themselves as well as a strong preventive orientation in child protection.

According to the broad definition of child protection, support measures are offered to families even before child maltreatment occurs on a voluntary basis. The threshold for the right of the parents to receive help and support is much lower than the threshold for involuntary state intervention due to child endangerment. Those support measures may still interfere largely into family life (e.g. out-of-home placement of children on a voluntary basis).

During investigations, support measures have to be offered at an early stage of the investigation by law. Social workers have to work together with the family and try to establish a good relationship with the parents, not only investigate the concerns. The concept of 'prevention first' can also be seen in other countries (Spratt et al. 2015) but is valued very much within the German child protection system. A strong tendency towards this principle was also demonstrated in internationally comparative research on decision making in child protection (Jergeby and Soydan 2002). The importance of 'offering help first' is also enforced by law as it poses an additional threshold for intervention into parental rights. If support measures have failed or are likely to fail, parental rights can be restricted (§ 1666a BGB).

Table 6.2 Planned support measures at the end of the investigation (2015)

	Total	Acute	Latent	Support only
General support (§§16–18 SGB VIII)	11.11	9.89	13.31	21.08
Mother/father-child assisted living (§19 SGB VIII)	0.38	1.26	0.51	0.23
Counseling on child rearing (§28 SGB VIII)	3.15	2.45	4.13	5.95
Outpatient or part time in- and outpatient support for child rearing (§§ 27, 29–32, 35 SGB VIII)	16.72	18.94	30.04	24.20
Placement outside home (§§ 27, 33–35 SGB VIII)	3.88	13.16	4.82	2.59
Integration support (§ 35a SGB VIII)	0.21	0.34	0.26	0.33
Emergency placement (§ 42 SGB VIII)	6.49	32.85	4.38	1.18
Child and adolescent psychiatry	1.14	2.16	1.91	1.31
Continue with already established support measures	13.36	16.56	20.28	20.50
Other support measure	8.21	9.13	19.51	9.24
No new support measures	10.42	7.88	11.98	20.74

Note. (Statistisches Bundesamt 2015b)

Most investigations end with voluntary support measures even in cases of acute and latent child endangerment. In deciding on support for the family, social workers should also consider help measures from other subsystems of the welfare system. Such are social welfare, debt counseling, assistance to find work, support in cases of disability or addiction, help to overcome social hardship and to avoid homelessness (Blüml 2006). Support measures are often provided by freie Träger. The frequencies of decisions about certain support measures at the end of the investigation are shown in Table 6.2.

6.5.3 *Family Service Orientation?*

The German child protection system has been characterized as family service oriented (Gilbert 1997; Gilbert et al. 2011) with four defining features: Understanding child maltreatment as family problem, responses oriented towards family needs, priority for working in partnership with families, and a high rate of voluntary arrangements in response to child maltreatment. However, there are still many cases in which the rights of parents do not remain unchallenged. In 2015, in 30.18% of cases of acute child endangerment, and in 12.08% of cases of latent child endangerment (Statistisches Bundesamt 2016a) the Jugendamt appealed to the family court. The family court can employ a range of involuntary measures to avert child endangerment: It may order the uptake of services offered by child and youth welfare or health care institutions (implementation order; § 1666 III (1) BGB). The court may also impose restraining orders and prohibit abusers from contacting the child (§ 1666 III (4) BGB). In addition, the court may make legal declarations in lieu of the parental custodian, or suspend or withdraw child custody in part or completely (§ 1666 III (5) (6) BGB). If parental custody is withdrawn wholly or in part, the court

Table 6.3 Children's and parents' rights in Germany

	Children's rights	Parents' rights
Child and youth welfare services	The right to participate in all decisions and be informed about procedures	The right to receive support measures
	The right to ask for help at the Jugendamt	The right to participate in planning services
	Receiving counseling without the knowledge of the parents	The right to choose between support measures
	The right to participate in planning services	
Investigations into child endangerment	The right to request emergency placement	Participation in the risk assessment (if not endangering the child)
	The right to receive counseling about support possibilities during emergency placement	The right to be informed immediately after emergency placement
	The right to inform somebody after emergency placement	
Family court proceedings	Child Well-being as the guiding principle	The right to be heard
	The right to be heard if the child is 14 years or older or if his or her wishes and attachment may be important	The right to terminate measures if the cause for the measure is no longer present
	The right to have a guardian (Verfahrensbeistand) during court proceedings	The right to have contact with the child
	The right to have contact with parents	

Note. Many laws build a legal framework for the rights of children. This overview only refers to those most closely linked to child protection procedures

appoints a guardian who decides on the appropriate support for the child. In 2015, the family court ruled a restriction or withdrawal of parental rights in 29,405 cases due to child endangerment (Statistisches Bundesamt 2016b). In most of these cases, the parents were required to take up a support measure (n = 8730) or the parental rights were partially restricted (n = 7818). But there is a high proportion of cases in which parental rights were withdrawn completely (n = 7.585; Statistisches Bundesamt 2016b).

In general, the German child protection system has not been considered to have a very strong children's rights orientation. Yet, in the last decades, more laws have been passed to strengthen the position of children within the society in general and also specifically in child protection (cf. Table 6.3 and Section, Historical Development of Concepts). During investigations into child endangerment and in court proceedings, children have the right to be heard and to participate in decision-making. In Germany, the right to have contact with birth parents and the value to grow up in a family are considered of great importance. The harm done by intervening into family life on a mandatory basis is viewed as a possible threat to children's well-being.

In sum, the threshold for a restriction of parental rights and removal of children from their family is high in Germany compared to other European countries. There is a strong belief that the relationship with the family of origin is crucial. A strong family orientation is as well an essential feature of other structures and services in the German welfare state such as the social security system (Mierendorff 2010). A strong family orientation may be further reinforced by mistrust in state interventions. The latter may be related to the German historic abuse of power of the state within the National Socialist Regime and the Democratic Republic of Germany. Contrarily, these do not lead to a reduced number of children in foster and residential care settings.

6.6 Relations to Other Systems

The child and youth welfare system is embedded in the larger context of the German welfare state and has connections to other social service systems. All three definitions of child protection as mentioned above can be found in these other systems as well.

6.6.1 Separation Between Criminal Prosecution and Support

As provision of help and support and establishing a good relationship with the family is considered crucial, there is a high barrier for passing on information from child and youth welfare system to the criminal justice system (Hagemann-White et al. 2010). With few exceptions professionals from the child and youth welfare system are not mandated to report child maltreatment to the criminal prosecution (§ 64 SGB VIII). However, the Jugendamt and the police work together on various occasions. For example, the Jugendamt has to be notified immediately by the police about suspected child endangerment. In 2015, 21.68% of reports of cases of child endangerment to the Jugendämter were made by the justice system (Statistisches Bundesamt 2016a). The police may intervene to avert danger to the child. They protect children and enforce an emergency placement in cases in which: (1) the legal guardians are untraceable, (2) the legal guardians do not want the child living in the household any longer, (3) living in the household may endanger the child, or (4) the child can give a plausible reason as to why he or she does not want to return to the home (PDV 382, 1997). The police have to inform the Jugendamt but can act on their own if they cannot reach the Jugendamt (PDV 382, 1997). In cases in which the protection of the child cannot be ensured otherwise, the Jugendamt has the right and obligation to report to the police (§ 8a IV SGB VIII). If concrete evidence that a child has been physically or sexually abused or neglected in a flagrant way are reported to the police, they have to investigate the case (§ 152 II STPO; principle of legality).

6.6.2 Challenges in Communication and Cooperation

Professionals from the educational system should report child endangerment to the Jugendamt and also have, as do health care professionals, the right to be counseled by a child protection expert (§ 8a SGB VIII). About 9.03% of the reports about child endangerment are made by professionals from schools, 3.42% by professionals from daycare (Statistisches Bundesamt 2016b). Professionals from the educational system are frequently contacted by the social workers of the Jugendamt during an investigation to provide information about the child, as they see the child almost every day. The health care system is involved in child protection concerning the detection of child endangerment as well as the treatment of maltreated children and parents with (mental) health problems. Early help programs often rely on the easy access of health care professionals to families with infants (Sann and Landua 2010). Health care professionals also provide help and support for maltreated children. About 6.43% of the reports of child endangerment are made from professionals working in the health care system (Statistisches Bundesamt 2016b).

The cooperation between educational system, health care system, and child and youth welfare system is considered challenging (Bertsch 2016; Fegert 2013–2014; Koch 2006; Zimmermann 2016) and insufficient cooperation has been identified as one key problem in serious case reviews (Fegert et al. 2010). Frequently highlighted difficulties are differing terminologies, conflicting professional principles, diverging structural conditions, insufficient role clarity, high expectation about the other professionals' abilities, and concerns about data privacy (Bertsch 2016; Fegert 2013–2014; Koch 2006; Zimmermann 2016). In some cases, conflicts regarding economic aspects occur (Bertsch 2016) as the health system is financed through health insurance companies and the child and youth welfare system by the state directly. For professionals from the educational system and the health system insufficient resources and a lack of transparency in the Jugendämter are also considered problematic (Bertsch 2016; Zimmermann 2016). The new child protection law from 2012 emphasizes the need for building networks. In practice, this is time intensive and difficult to manage as there are many different cooperation partners and networks, which have to be arranged on a local level (Bertsch 2016). This difficulty is reinforced by the diversity of the structures in every region, as it is necessary to agree on specific cooperation arrangements.

Since 2012, professionals in contact with children have the right to be anonymously counseled by a child protection expert if they assume a child to be endangered (§ 8a SGB VIII). First results from a study with a small sample showed only little changes in practice following the change of the law in 2012 (Bertsch 2015). Limited knowledge about their right to be counseled and time constraints were complicating the utilization of this possibility (Bertsch 2015).

6.7 Recent Challenges

Two main challenges of the German child protection system should be highlighted in this chapter.

6.7.1 Accountability of the System

In the most recent years, the focus of research was mainly in the recognition of child maltreatment, but not on the outcomes of help and support processes. Studies, which found positive effects, focused on the child and youth welfare system in general (Schmidt 2002a), but not on children who were endangered. The research specifically on child endangerment shows that sometimes interventions fail to protect children from harm in the long term (Bae and Kindler 2017), a high rate of mental health problems of children in out-of-home care (Kindler et al. 2011) and an increased risk for sexual (re)victimization (Allroggen et al. 2017). There is a shortage of outcome research on the child protection system regarding the effectiveness of intervention on the well-being and development of the child, which is connected to the nature and structures of the system itself. The family service orientation leads to more data collection on service provision than on individual outcomes of children (Jud et al. 2013) The freie Träger are run by various organizations and have very individual programs making it hard to collect data (Jud et al. 2013). Additionally, professional training of social workers is practice-oriented and does not include scientific methods (Jud et al. 2013). Moreover, there might be a reluctance to support state organized data collection due to the abuse of power by the state in the German history (AlEissa et al. 2009). First steps like a national database about the investigations into child abuse and neglect in 2012 are already accomplished, research regarding the effectiveness of early prevention measures (Taubner et al. 2013) and serious case reviews (Fegert et al. 2010) have been established, but further efforts have to be made to increase the accountability of the system (AlEissa et al. 2009; Jud et al. 2013, 2016).

6.7.2 Addressing Inequality and Discrimination

The public and the scientific discourse is also characterized by a lack of certain themes such as avoiding discrimination of minority groups (Jud et al. 2013; Kindler 2012) and families with a lower socioeconomic status. This is also linked to the topic of equal service provision to all children and families (Kindler 2012). Now, there is an overrepresentation of families with migration background and with low socioeconomic status receiving support measures compared to the general public. This fact might be due to actual need or accumulation of risk factors in these groups but could also be caused by a surveillance bias. Those two issues might become crucial in the next decades as the number of under-age refugees and economic disparity between poor and wealthy families increases. This is especially true as the lack of specific services for families with migration background was raised as a concern by the Committee on the Rights of the Child (2014) in Germany. The child protection system will have to adapt to this situation by finding ways to bridge between different cultures and providing support in cases of stigmatization and experiences of social disadvantages.

References

Alberth, L., & Bühler-Niederberger, D. (2015). Invisible children? Professional bricolage in child protection. *Children and Youth Services Review, 57*, 149–158. https://doi.org/10.1016/j.childyouth.2015.08.008.

AlEissa, M. A., Fluke, J. D., Gerbaka, B., Goldbeck, L., Gray, J., Hunter, N., et al. (2009). A commentary on national child maltreatment surveillance systems: Examples of progress. *Child Abuse & Neglect, 33*(11), 809–814. https://doi.org/10.1016/j.chiabu.2009.08.004.

Allroggen, M., Rau, T., Ohlert, J., & Fegert, J. M. (2017). Lifetime prevalence and incidence of sexual victimization of adolescents in institutional care. *Child Abuse & Neglect*. https://doi.org/10.1016/j.chiabu.2017.02.015.

Bae, H.-o., & Kindler, H. (2017). Child maltreatment re-notifications in Germany. Analysis of local case files. *Children and Youth Services Review*, 75, 42–49. https://doi.org/10.1016/j.childyouth.2017.02.012.

Baines, D., Cummins, N., & Schulze, M. S. (2010). Population and living standards, 1945–2000. In S. Broadberry & K. O'Rourke (Eds.), *The Cambridge economic history of modern Europe. Vol. 2: 1870 to the present* (pp. 390–419). Cambridge: Cambridge University Press.

Benz, W. (2009). Rassismus als Ideologie und Herrschaftspraxis (1933–1945). *Praxis der Kinderpsychologie und Kinderpsychiatrie, 58*, 491–503.

Bertsch, B. M. (2015). *Der erweiterte Beratungsauftrag für insoweit erfahrene Fachkräfte durch das Bundeskinderschutzgesetz: Beratung von Berufsgeheimnisträgern aus dem Gesundheitswesen.*

Bertsch, B. M. (2016). *Wirkungen des Bundeskinderschutzgesetzes – wissenschaftliche Grundlagen: Ergebnisbericht zu Erhebungen im Gesundheitswesen.*

Biesel, K. (2011). *Wenn Jugendämter scheitern: Zum Umgang mit Fehlern im Kinderschutz.* In K Biesel (Ed.), Soziale Organisationen und ihre Fehler. *Gesellschaft der Unterschiede: Vol. 4.* Bielefeld: transcript.

Blüml, H. (2006). Welche Angebote und Hilfen stehen dem ASD im Fall einer Beeinträchtigung oder Gefährdung des Kindeswohls zur Verfügung? In H. Kindler, S. Lillig, H. Blüml, T. Meysen, & A. Werner (Eds.), *Handbuch Kindeswohlgefährdung nach §1666 BGB und Allgemeiner Sozialer Dienst (ASD).* München: DJI Abt. Familie.

BMFSFJ (2006). *Frühe Hilfen für Eltern und Kinder und soziale Frühwarnsysteme: Aktionsprogramm des Bundesministeriums für Familie, Senioren, Frauen und Jugend zum Schutz von Kleinkindern, zur Früherkennung von Risiken und Gefährdungen und zur Implementierung effektiver Hilfesysteme.* Berlin: BMFSFJ.

Bode, I., & Turba, H. (2014). *Organisierter Kinderschutz in Deutschland: Strukturdynamiken und Modernisierungsparadoxien*. Wiesbaden: Springer VS. https://doi.org/10.1007/978-3-658-03354-5.

Bohler, K. F., & Franzheld, T. (2010). *Kinder- und Jugendhilfe vor und nach dem Systemwechsel*. Bundeszentrale für politische Bildung.

Bracher, K. D., Sauer, W., & Schulz, G. (1960). *Die nationalsozialistische Machtergreifung*. Opladen: Westdeutscher Verlag.

Bringewat, P. (2001). *Tod eines Kindes: Soziale Arbeit und strafrechtliche Risiken* (2. Aufl.). Baden-Baden: Nomos-Verl.-Ges.

Brumlik, M. (2000). Soziale Arbeit. Funktionale Erfordernisse, ideologische Selbstmißverständnisse und vergessene Traditionen. In D. Benner & H.-E. Tenorth (Eds.), *Zeitschrift für Pädagogik. Bildungsprozesse und Erziehungsverhältnisse im 20. Jahrhundert* (pp. 186–211). Weinheim: Beltz Juventa.

Bussmann, K.-D. (2005). *Report über die Auswirkungen des Gesetzes zur Ächtung der Gewalt in der Erziehung*. Berlin.

Chamberlain, S. (1998). *Adolf Hitler, die deutsche Mutter und ihr erstes Kind: Über zwei NS-Erziehungsbücher, Reihe "Edition Psychosozial"* (2nd ed.). Giessen: Psychosozial-Verlag.

Committee on the Rights of the Child. (2014). *Concluding observations on the combined third and fourth periodic reports of Germany. Hg. v.* United Nations.

Cox, M. E. (2013). War, blockades, and hunger: Nutritional deprivation of German children 1914–1924. *University of Oxford Discussion Papers in Economic and Social History*, No. 110.

Dahl, M. (2001). Aussonderung und Vernichtung-Der Umgang mit "lebensunwerten" Kindern während des Dritten Reiches und die Rolle der Kinder-und Jugendpsychiatrie. *Praxis der Kinderpsychologie und Kinderpsychiatrie, 50*, 170–191.

Dehmers, J. (2011). *Wie laut soll ich denn noch schreien? Die Odenwaldschule und der sexuelle Missbrauch* (1. Aufl.). Reinbek bei Hamburg: Rowohlt.

Demm, E. (2001). Deutschlands Kinder im Ersten Weltkrieg: Zwischen Progaganda und Sozialfürsorge. *Militärgeschichtliche Zeitschrift, 60*, 51–98.

Dickinson, E. R. (1996). *The politics of German Child Welfare from the empire to the Federal Republic*. Harvard: Harvard University Press.

Dickinson, E. R. (2002). 'Until the Stubborn Will is Broken': Crisis and reform in Prussian Reformatory Education, 1900—34. *European History Quarterly, 32*(2), 161–206.

Elder, S. (2014). A right to beat a child? Corporal punishment and the law in Wilhelmine Germany. *Central European History, 47*(01), 54–75. https://doi.org/10.1017/S0008938914000624.

Fegert, J. M. (2013–2014). Bedingungen, Prinzipien und Herausforderungen interdisziplinärer Kooperation im Kinderschutz. *IzKK-Nachrichten: Konstruktiv kooperieren im Kinderschutz*, 4–9.

Fegert, J. M., Ziegenhain, U., & Fangerau, H. (2010). *Problematische Kinderschutzverläufe: Mediale Skandalisierung, fachliche Fehleranalyse und Strategien zur Verbesserung des Kinderschutzes. Studien und Praxishilfen zum Kinderschutz*. Weinheim: Juventa-Verl.

Fegert, J. M., Böhm, B., Rassenhofer, M., & Witte, S. (2015). Reaktionen auf die Missbrauchsfälle in der katholischen Kirche in Deutschland. *Nervenheilkunde, 34*(7), 501–513.

Frings, B., & Kaminsky, U. (2012). *Gehorsam, Ordnung, Religion: Konfessionelle Heimerziehung 1945–1975*. Münster: Aschendorff.

Gilbert, N. (1997). *Combatting child abuse: International perspectives and trends*. New York: Oxford University Press.

Gilbert, N., Parton, N., & Skivenes, M. (2011). Changing patterns of response and emerging trends. In N. Gilbert, N. Parton, & M. Skivenes (Eds.), *Child protection systems: International trends and orientations* (pp. 243–258). New York: Oxford University Press.

Görgen, A., Griemmert, M., & Kessler, S. (2015). Sexueller Missbrauch und Kinderschutz -: Perspektiven im Wandel. In J. M. Fegert (Ed.), *Sexueller Missbrauch von Kindern und Jugendlichen. Ein Handbuch zur Prävention und Intervention für Fachkräfte im medizinischen, psychotherapeutischen und pädagogischen Bereich* (pp. 27–40). Berlin: Springer.

Gries, S. (2002). *Kindesmisshandlung in der DDR: Kinder unter dem Einfluss traditionell-autoritärer und totalitärer Erziehungsleitbilder*. Zugl.: Bochum, Univ., Diss., 2001. *Studien zur DDR-Gesellschaft: Vol. 9*. Münster: Lit.

Hagemann-White, C., Römkens, R., & Meysen, T. (2010). *Feasibility study to assess the possibilities, opportunities and needs to standardise national legislation on violence against women, violence against children and sexual orientation violence*.

Hagenberg-Miliu, E.-C. (2014). *Unheiliger Berg: Das Bonner Aloisiuskolleg der Jesuiten und die Aufarbeitung des Missbrauchsskandals*. Stuttgart: Kohlhammer.

Hansbauer, P. (2002). Large-scale changes in the German residential care system during the 1980s. *European Journal of Social Work, 5*(1), 21–29. https://doi.org/10.1080/714052982.

Heberer, P. (2011). *Children during the holocaust*. Lanhan: AltaMira Press.

Helming, E., Schattner, H., & Blüml, H. (1999). *Handbuch Sozialpädagogische Familienhilfe* (3., überarb. Aufl.). *Schriftenreihe des Bundesministeriums für Familie, Senioren, Frauen und Jugend: Vol. 182*. Stuttgart u.a.: Kohlhammer.

Jacobi, J. (2014). Versorgte und unversorgte Kinder. In M. Baader, F. Eßer, & W. Schröer (Hrsg.), *Kindheiten in der Moderne. Eine Geschichte der Sorge* (pp. 21–41). Frankfurt/New York: Campus.

Jergeby, U., & Soydan, H. (2002). Assessment processes in social work practice when children are at risk: A comparative cross-national vignette study. *Journal of Social Work Research and Evaluation, 3*(2), 127–144.

Jud, A., Fluke, J., Alink, L. R. A., Allan, K., Fallon, B., Kindler, H., et al. (2013). On the nature and scope of reported child maltreatment in high-income countries: Opportunities for improving the evidence base. *Paediatrics and International Child Health, 33*(4), 207–215. https://doi.org/10.1179/2046905513Y.0000000092.

Jud, A., Fegert, J. M., & Finkelhor, D. (2016). On the incidence and prevalence of child maltreatment: A research agenda. *Child and Adolescent Psychiatry and Mental Health, 10*, 17. https://doi.org/10.1186/s13034-016-0105-8.

Kavemann, B., & Lohstöter, I. (1991). *Väter als Täter: Sexuelle Gewalt gegen Mädchen; "Erinnerungen sind wie eine Zeitbombe"* (Orig.-ausg., 46. – 50. Tsd). *Rororo: 5250: rororo aktuell: rororo Frauen*. Reinbek bei Hamburg: Rowohlt.

Keupp, H., Straus, F., Mosser, P., Gmür, W., & Hackenschmied, G. (2013). *Sexueller Missbrauch, psychische und körperliche Gewalt im Internat der Benediktinerabtei Ettal: Individuelle Folgen und organisatorisch-strukturelle Hintergründe*. München.

Kindler, H. (2012). *Qualitätsindikatoren für den Kinderschutz in Deutschland: Analyse der nationalen und internationalen Diskussion – Vorschläge für Qualitätsindikatoren*. München/Köln.

Kindler, H., & Borrmann, S. (2012). Prominent facets of child protection in Germany. In J. Hämäläinen, B. Littlechild, O. Chytil, M. Sramatá, & E. Jovelin (Eds.), *ERIS monographs: Volume 2. Evolution of child protection and child welfare policies in selected European countries* (pp. 161–179). Ostrava: University of Ostrava—ERIS; Albert Publisher.

Kindler, H., Helming, E., Meysen, T., Jurczyk, K. (Hg). (2011). *Handbuch Pflegekinderhilfe* (2. Aufl.). München: Deutsches Jugendinstitut.

Koch, E. (2006). Was zeichnet die Zusammenarbeit mit kinder- und jugendpsychiatrischen Diensten und Insitutionen im Zusammenhang mit Kindeswohlgefährdung aus? In H. Kindler, S. Lillig, H. Blüml, T. Meysen, & A. Werner (Eds.), *Handbuch Kindeswohlgefährdung nach §1666 BGB und Allgemeiner Sozialer Dienst (ASD)*. München: DJI Abt. Familie.

Köhnken, G. (2004). Statement validity analysis and the 'detection of the truth'. In P. A. Granhag & L. Strömwall (Eds.), *The detection of deception in forensic contexts* (pp. 41–63). Cambridge: Cambridge University Press.

Kölch, M. (2002). *Theorie und Praxis der Kinder- und Jugendpsychiatrie in Berlin 1920–1935. Die Diagnose "Psychopathie" im Spannungsfeld von Psychiatrie, Individualpsychologie und Politik*. Dissertation. Berlin: Freie Universität Berlin.

Lewy, G. (2000). *The Nazi persecution ot the Gypsies*. Oxford: Oxford University Press.
Lhotzky, S. (1994). Karl Wilker's Lindenhof. *Journal of Emotional and Behavioral Problems*, 3(2), 53–55.
Mierendorff, J. (2010). *Kindheit und Wohlfahrtsstaat: Entstehung, Wandel und Kontinuität des Musters moderner Kindheit. Kindheiten Neue Folge*. Weinheim: Juventa-Verl.
Mitscherlich, A, Mitscherlich, M. (1998). *Die Unfähigkeit zu trauern. Grundlagen kollektiven Verhaltens,* Serie Piper (Vol. 168, 15. Aufl.). München: Piper.
Münder, J., Mutke, B., & Schone, R. (2004). *Kindeswohl zwischen Jugendhilfe und Justiz. Professionelles Handeln in Kindeswohlverfahren*. Weinheim: Juventa.
Obermayer, B., & Stadler, R. (2011). *Bruder, was hast du getan? Kloster Ettal; die Täter, die Opfer, das System* (1. Aufl.). Köln: Kiepenheuer & Witsch.
Peukert, D. J. (1986). *Grenzen der Sozialdisziplinierung: Aufstieg und Krise der deutschen Jugendfursorge von 1878 bis 1932*. Köln: Bund-Verlag.
Richter, J. (2011). *"Gute Kinder schlechter Eltern". Familienleben, Jugendfürsorge und Sorgerechtsentzug in Hamburg, 1884–1914*. Wiesbaden: VS Verlag.
Runder Tisch Heimerziehung. (2010). *Runder Tisch – Heimerziehung in den 50er und 60er Jahren: Abschlussbericht*.
Sachße, C., & Tennstedt, F. (1992). *Der Wohlfahrtsstaat im Nationalsozialismus*. Stuttgart: Kohlhammer.
Sann, A., & Landua, D. (2010). Systeme Früher Hilfen: Gemeinsam geht's besser! *Bundesgesundheitsblatt – Gesundheitsforschung – Gesundheitsschutz, 53*(10), 1018–1028. https://doi.org/10.1007/s00103-010-1124-x.
Schmid, H., & Meysen, T. (Eds.). (2006). *Handbuch Kindeswohlgefährdung nach § 1666 BGB und Allgemeiner Sozialer Dienst (ASD): Was ist unter Kindeswohlgefährdung zu verstehen?* München.
Schmidt, M. H. (2002a). *Neues für die Jugendhilfe? Ergebnisse der Jugendhilfe-Effekte-Studie*. March: Verl. für das Studium der Sozialen Arbeit.
Schmidt, H. (2002b). *Gefährliche und gefährdete Mädchen. Weibliche Devianz und die Anfänge der Zwangs- und Fürsorgeerziehung*. Opladen: Leske + Budrich.
Spratt, T., Nett, J., Bromfield, L., Hietamäki, J., Kindler, H., & Ponnert, L. (2015). Child protection in Europe: Development of an international cross-comparison model to inform national policies and practices. *British Journal of Social Work, 45*(5), 1508–1525. https://doi.org/10.1093/bjsw/bcu109.
Statistisches Bundesamt. (2015a). *Statistiken der Kinder- und Jugendhilfe: Einrichtungen und tätige Personen (ohne Tageseinrichtungen für Kinder) 2014*. https://www.destatis.de/
Statistisches Bundesamt. (2015b). *Statistiken der Kinder- und Jugendhilfe: Gefährdungseinschätzungen nach § 8a Absatz 1 SGB VIII 2014*. Wiesbaden.
Statistisches Bundesamt. (2016a). *Statistiken der Kinder- und Jugendhilfe: Gefährdungseinschätzungen nach § 8a Absatz 1 SGB VIII 2015*. Wiesbaden.
Statistisches Bundesamt. (2016b): *Pflegschaften, Vormundschaften, BeistandschaftenPflegeerlaubnis, Sorgerechtsentzug, Sorgeerklärungen – 2015. Statistisches Bundesamt*. Wiesbaden.
Stolleis, M. (2013). *Origins of the German welfare state*. Berlin: Springer.
Taubner, S., Munder, T., Unger, A., & Wolter, S. (2013). Zur Wirksamkeit präventiver Früher Hilfen in Deutschland – ein systematisches Review und eine Metaanalyse. *Praxis der Kinderpsychologie und Kinderpsychiatrie, 62*(8), 598–619. https://doi.org/10.13109/prkk.2013.62.8.598.
Uhlendorff, U. (2003). *Geschichte des Jugendamtes: Entwicklungslinien der öffentlichen Jugendhilfe 1871–1929*. Univ., Habil.-Schr.--Kassel, 2001 (1. Aufl.). *Beltz-Votum: Vol. 2*. Weinheim: Beltz.
Vliet, V. V. (2013). *Caritas im Zeitalter der" Volkspflege"*. Dissertation. München: Ludwigs-Maximilians-Universität.

Wapler, F. (2015). *Kinderrechte und Kindeswohl: Eine Untersuchung zum Status des Kindes im Öffentlichen Recht* (Vol. 240). Tübingen: Mohr Siebeck.
WHO. (2017). *World health statisics 2017*.
Winkler, H. A., & Sager, A. (2006). *Germany: The long road west* (Vol. 1, pp. 1789–1933). Oxford: Oxford University Press.
Winkler, H. A., & Sager, A. (2007). *Germany: The long road west* (Vol. 2, pp. 1933–1990). Oxford: Oxford University Press.
Zimmermann, J. (2016). Das Bundeskinderschutzgesetz aus Schulperspektive. *Sozial Extra, 40*(5), 42–45. https://doi.org/10.1007/s12054-016-0083-3.

Susanne Witte, PhD. Susanne is a family psychologist and has received her PhD at the Ludwig Maximilian University of Munich. Currently she is working at the German Youth Institute, located in Munich, as well as at the Department of Child and Adolescent Psychiatry and Psychotherapy of the University Hospital Ulm. She is conducting studies covering a broad range of topics regarding child maltreatment. Her specific research interests are sibling relationships in the context of child maltreatment, training professionals to prevent child maltreatment, and international comparisons of child protections activities.

Laura Sophia Miehlbradt, M.A. Laura studied sociology, psychology, and social work research. She is research assistant at the German Youth Institute in Munich, Germany. She is especially interested in the interrelation of state and privacy in the context of social work and family research, and welfare state theories.

Eric van Santen (PhD) is senior researcher at the German Youth Institute in Munich, Germany, Department "Youth and Youth Welfare". He studied human resource management in The Hague (Netherlands), sociology in Munich (Germany) and got his PhD at the FU Berlin (Germany). He is strongly empirically orientated and specialized in inter institutional cooperation, volunteering, child and youth welfare institutions, regional disparities in (foster) care utilization, foster care careers, and disruption of foster care placements. He was involved in the evaluation of the new German Child Protection law.

Heinz Kindler, PhD, developmental and legal psychologist, received his PhD in 2001 at the University of Regensburg. In 2013 he became lead of the Division on Family Services and Child Protection at the German Youth Institute in Munich. Major research projects are on risk assessment in child protection, children in foster or adoptive families, prevention of sexual abuse, and quality development in child protection services.

Chapter 7
Child Protection and Welfare Systems in Ireland: Continuities and Discontinuities of the Present

Kenneth Burns and Caroline McGregor

7.1 Introduction

> We must do better for children and families. It will take time for us to create this new reality out of the rubble of a system that has been crumbling for decades, but this report is a major step on the road (Fitzgerald, 2012 cited in McGregor 2014, p. 772).

In 2012, several moments occurred that could arguable by defined as pivotal for the child protection and welfare system in Ireland. In no particular order of importance, the following developments mark key changes in the child welfare system that happened in that year. Firstly, the *Report of the Task Force on the Child and Family Support Agency* was published (Department of Children and Youth Affairs 2012). This set the blueprint for the establishment of the new Child and Family Agency (also known as Tusla) in Ireland as a separate independent State authority responsible for child protection and family support services. Up until then, child protection and welfare services were part of an overall health and social service delivery system under the governance of the Health Service Executive (HSE) (Skehill 2004). In 2012, standards for child protection and welfare were launched by the Health Information Quality Authority (HIQA). In the same year, a new statutory body called the Health and Social Care Professionals Council (known as CORU), began regulating professionals and had registered its first profession – social work – marking a new regulatory phase in social work in Ireland. A constitutional referendum was also held in 2012 referred to as the Children's Rights Referendum and resulted in a new sub-article 42A on children's rights being inserted in the constitution to bring Irish law and policy into line with the United Nations

K. Burns (✉)
University College Cork, Cork, Ireland
e-mail: k.burns@ucc.ie

C. McGregor
National University of Ireland, Galway, Ireland
e-mail: caroline.mcgregor@nuigalway.ie

L. Merkel-Holguin et al. (eds.), *National Systems of Child Protection*, Child Maltreatment 8, https://doi.org/10.1007/978-3-319-93348-1_7

Convention on the Rights of the Child (1989). The new Article 42A also made greater provision for child protection decision-making, opening up the option to use adoption as a care option for those in medium to long-term state care, which had not previously been possible except in exceptional circumstances (see McCaughren and McGregor 2017; Burns et al. 2017a).

There are a number of publications that examine the history and development of the Irish child welfare and protection system prior to 2012 (see, for example, Buckley et al. 1997; Ferguson and O'Reilly 2001; Skehill 2004, Lynch and Burns 2008; Burns and Lynch 2012; Buckley and Burns 2015). This chapter does not re-examine content already covered by these publications. Instead, we have structured this chapter around 2012 as an important year in time, drawing broadly from the ideas of a history of the present approach. This implies that the history we tell is one that helps to illuminate the present best. It is an approach that considers key moments in time and space that went before and after the key moment of 2012. The intention of this approach is to use history to inform a critical understanding and problematization of the present (Dean 1994; Foucault 1977; Skehill 2007).

The chapter beings with a brief mapping of the child protection and welfare system, followed by a concise commentary on key historical events to provide a context for the developments in 2012. This is followed by a review of select developments and key themes in child protection and welfare in Ireland from 2012 to 2017. Our decision to focus on select developments avoids 'skimming' over themes, but it has meant that other developments such as the introduction of a limited mandatory reporting system at the end of 2017, placing our child protection guidelines on a statutory footing, changes to the adoption system, a critical examination of the experiences of children in Ireland's 'direct provision' service for families seeking asylum (see Christie 2010; Horgan and Ní Raghallaigh 2017), the development of Tusla's Prevention, Partnership and Family Support (PPFS) programme, among other developments, are not addressed. The chapter will conclude by returning to reflect on 2012 as a catalyst year for change and we argue that getting to a point where we consider our child protection and welfare system to be good enough, we suggest, is the first step needed in this direction. It is too early to be definitive as to whether the changes begun in that year have made the system better for the protection and welfare of children in Ireland. One could be overly-negative and point out all that needs to be done with the system and what could have been done differently; but one also has to be hopeful and recognise the renewed energy, investment and policy focus brought to the child protection and welfare system between 2012 and 2017. The best chance of this 'better' does indeed lie in this present and its near future.

A Brief History of the Present of Child Protection and Welfare in Ireland

Table 7.1 provides a brief overview of the structures of the child protection and welfare system in Ireland back to 1862. These structures are important as they provide a platform to analyse the role of the Irish State in the governance and delivery of child protection and welfare services in Ireland, and seeds of some of the current challenges still faced in the present day are evident in these structures. In line with a history of the present approach (see Skehill 2007), we identify some key

Table 7.1 Overview of child protection and welfare systems in Ireland, 1862–2012

Period	Governance of child welfare	Main child protection law	Main forms of alternative care	Family support services	Minister responsible/ governance model
2012-present	Tusla: Independent Child and Family Welfare Agency	Child Care Act 1991 (as amended)	Foster Care (one third kinship)	Integrated in Tusla/ partnerships with community and voluntary organisations	Minister for Children and Youth Affairs/ directly accountable to minister
1970–2012	Integrated Health and Welfare	Children Act 1908	Institutional care with some foster care (called boarded out)	Mostly third sector/voluntary/ community with some statutory provisions	Minister for Health/junior minister for Health and Children/ Minister for Children and Youth Affairs
1921/2–1970	County Governance-Health Authorities	Children Act 1908	Institutional care with some foster care (called boarded out)	Almost exclusively third sector/voluntary/ community with limited statutory provisions	Minister for Local Government and Public Health/minister for Health/ Minister for Education
1862–1920/1	Great Britain/ United Kingdom Governance	Children's Charter, Children Act 1908	Institutional care /Foster care developing	Almost exclusively third sector/voluntary/ community with limited statutory provisions	Minister for Local Government

developments in 2012 that are significant as we look back to some key moments and events in the past that help to illuminate their significance and relevance in the present.

In 2012, the *Report of the Task Force on the Child and Family Support Agency* led to the establishment of a new dedicated agency called Tusla. The Child and Family Agency (also known as Tusla, a neologism meaning new day from two Irish words Tús and lá) was established in 2014 in response to long-held criticisms that children's services in Ireland were marginalised within a larger health system where hospitals consumed most of the resources and management time. This is the first time that child welfare was governed through an independent authority. Before this, it was one small part of the health and social services and governed by the Health Service Executive (HSE), whose primary focus and attention was on the hospital sector. Before the HSE, Health Boards shared the governance of health and social services across 11 regions. Since the Health Act 1970, which established Ireland's modern health and welfare system, child welfare and protection jostled for space, recognition, resources, and some would say understanding, in a largely medically-dominated system (see Whyte 1980 and Hensey 1972 for a consideration of the medical and social system; see Harvey 2007, Skehill 2003, 2004 and McGregor 2014 for specific considerations of the development of statutory social work in child protection). While it is commonly and correctly stated that the State system did not develop substantially until after 1970 and that it was mostly private, philanthropic and/or religiously-oriented services prior to this, Ireland has had a statutory child welfare obligation for more than 150 years. Skehill (2004) contends that there has been a continuous line of State involvement in child welfare that is traced back to the foundation of the foster care system (originally called Boarding Out) for children in the State workhouses in 1862. Predecessors to social workers, called Inspectors of Boarded out Children, have managed a fostering system in Ireland since 1902 and in the mid-twentieth century, it was mostly public health nurses and social workers who operated in this space. A non-denominational voluntary organisation – the Irish Society for Prevention of Cruelty to Children (ISPCC) – also played a significant role up to 1970 (Buckley 2013). As the welfare state developed after 1970, child protection became the primary domain of statutory social work and this remains the case up to the present day. The Health Boards established under the Health Act 1970, were subsumed into a new large, all-encompassing health and social service body called the Health Service Executive in 2005.

Guidance relating to the identification and response to child abuse and neglect was developed from the late 1970s onwards culminating in the Children First 1999 guidelines, becoming Ireland's first *comprehensive* national policy and guidance on child protection and welfare. These guidelines were updated in 2011 and 2017 (Department of Children and Youth Affairs 2011, 2017), and were placed on a statutory basis at the end of 2017 in light of new legislation relating to mandatory reporting. In 2011, a child protection and welfare practice handbook was launched (HSE 2011). In addition to the development of guidance for practice, the Irish State incrementally introduced other key elements of the system during the 2000s. For example, a new Ombudsman for Children post was established in 2004; an independent Special Rapporteur for Child Protection was appointed in 2006 and the first full senior Minister for Children and Youth Affairs was appointed in 2011. As detailed in the next section, during this period, a new system of standard-setting and inspection of child welfare and protection was also developed.

The second moment identified in the introduction in 2012 was the increased regulation of child protection by the Health Information and Quality Authority (HIQA) and the social work profession by the Health and Social Care Professionals Council (CORU). While there were systems of accreditation for social work education and systems of review and standard setting in child protection in the past, this new level of regulation marked a particular change in regime. The child protection system by this time had become organised around a National Child Care Information System and the introduction of a 'Business Process System' that was in development for a number of years (Health Service Executive 2002). Critics would argue these developments marked the emergence of a period of managerialism, proceduralization and bureaucratisation of services that was previously a common feature in the United Kingdom (UK) systems (see, for example, Garrett and Conneely 2015). The emergence of a discourse of managerialism in Irish child protection is to some extent reminiscent of a wider global trend influenced by neo-liberalism and risk society (see Parton 2014). It might also be attributed, in its timing, to events that had taken place around this period. For example, in 2010 a major child abuse inquiry occurred in Roscommon (Gibbons et al. 2010) which led to a number of recommendations for change at both organisational, policy and court level, as well as for social work practice and management levels (see recommendations, pp. 83–93).

While inquiries into the role of the State in protecting children from harm within their home have had a significant impact on the Irish child protection and welfare system (see, for example, Buckley and O'Nolan 2013), it has been the revelations of historical abuse of children in certain Irish Institutions that have caused the greatest political attention and public debates in more recent years. In 2009, the *Commission to Inquire into Child Abuse Report* (Ryan 2009) reported its massive five-volume tome showing extensive and systematic abuse of children in industrial schools, which were the main form of institutional care for children in Ireland up to 1970. The Ryan report, and the subsequent 'implementation' plan produced by the Department of Children and Youth Affairs to reform child protection services, is likely to have been a major catalyst for change that manifested in the establishment of the new Agency and the holding of a children's rights referendum (Kilkelly 2012). McGregor (2014) suggests that the findings from this Commission highlight the learning for the present of a lack of regulation and accountability that enabled such extensive abuse and neglect to go unchecked for so long (see O'Sullivan 2009, Buckley and McGregor 2018 and Buckley and Burns 2015 who offer further analysis of institutional care, during the early and mid-twentieth century).

Another strand of historical and contemporary revelations related to abuse of children by the clergy in communities (see, for example, Murphy 2009) which together with the significant Ryan report based on the work of the *Commission to Inquire into Child Abuse*, has resulted in the once perceived altruistic role of the Church in child care services being represented through irrefutable evidence as a source of deliberate and damaging harm for many children (Ryan 2009). These reports emphasise the harm and danger caused by a lack of regulation and accountability of institutions and government departments in the past. In other words, because of the close and mutually reliant relationship between the statutory and voluntary, mostly the religious social and education sectors in Ireland historically, there was a high level of trust and a low level of accountability demonstrated. This highlights the importance, in the present, of the need for a critical and balanced engagement with processes of regulation and accountability that challenges the negative effects of over-proceduralisation such as too much focus on bureaucracy and diversion of time from direct practice, while at the same time ensuring sufficient levels of accountability for those responsible for child protection, welfare and family support.

The third event in 2012 that we identify as a key moment is the children's rights referendum. In reviewing the development of social and child welfare policies towards a children's rights ethos, the first explicit evidence of a discourse of children's rights in policy can be found in the *National Children's Strategy* in 2000 which included for the first-time consultations with children through the education system. One could argue that prior to this, the discourse of child protection was a welfarist and paternalistic one. Looking back from 1970 and prior to the development of a coherent statutory system, the discourses can be associated with moralisation and normalisation mostly within a socio-spiritual frame (Skehill 2004; see also Skehill 1999, 2000). With regard to constitutional reform, between 1993 and 2012, a number of attempts were made to have a referendum on the Irish constitution to change Articles 41 and 42 (see Lynch and Burns 2012). A call for constitutional reform to give greater rights to children and to strengthen the powers of the State to intervene to protect all children irrespective of the marital status of the parents, was first made explicitly by Judge Catherine McGuinness in the *Kilkenny Incest Investigation* report (McGuinness 1993) and over the next 20 years, various committees and drafts of the proposed amendment were developed. A Constitution Review Group was established in 1996. The UN Committee on Rights of Child called for constitutional reform in its response to Ireland's submission in 1998 and again in 2006 and in the following year, 2007, the Joint Oireachtas Committee on the Constitutional Amendment on Children was established and they produced the wording for a new Article 42A. As McCaughren and McGregor (2017) argue:

> The momentum for the need for reform was reinforced in light of the Ryan Report on the Commission to Inquire into Child Abuse in 2009 which brought to the fore the issue of children's rights and cemented commitment to work towards reform (Ryan 2009) … the Roscommon Child Abuse Inquiry 2010 served as a reminder of the problem related to the former position of children before the amendment was passed in 2015 when it came to balancing the (imprescriptible and inalienable) rights of parents (2017: 4).

This look back from 2012 from the platform of three important events/moments gives a sense of the present through reference to the past. However, for the international reader, the story might still be somewhat sketchy. For those interested in reading more about the history of child protection and welfare in Ireland, the following sources are recommended. Buckley (2013) provides an in-depth recent history of the ISPCC, the main civil society organisation involved in child protection in Ireland up to 1970. Original reports relating to the development of the statutory child welfare system in 1970 provide an insight into a key moment of change (Kennedy Report 1970; Task Force on Child Care Services 1980). For developments during the 1980s and 1990s the work of authors such as Robbie Gilligan, Valerie O'Brien, Ruth Torode, Harry Ferguson and Helen Buckley examine issues relating to child welfare and protection in Ireland during and leading up to those moments in time (see Skehill 2004 for a detailed review of literature and authors for this period). Devaney and McGregor (2016) provide another more current and useful thematic and sequential review of the history also, with a particular focus on the relationship between child protection and family support in Ireland.

This section concludes with a brief summary of Buckley and Burns' mapping of seminal development in child protection and social work from 1970 to 2013, which will help us to crystallise the key practice issues and policies relevant for the present day. Firstly, they explain how social work was developing in parallel with, and as part of, the child protection system that was emerging during 1970. Like most histories of this period, the final *Task Force on Child Care Services* in 1974 is identified as signifying a key moment for system change away from institutional care (see also the Kennedy Report 1970) towards family-based care and preventative and community-based approaches to families in need. It was during this period that statutory social work 'took over' from the voluntary and philanthropic management of most child protection and when formal State child protection system as we know it now was developed. Buckley and Burns helpfully remind readers that this role was not necessarily resisted, but indeed was welcomed in social work as an opportunity to develop its identity and expertise (see also Skehill 2004).

Another key moment for Buckley and Burns, as found in most historical accounts, is the publication of the Child Care Act 1991. This was a seminal reform period for many European countries who were also updating their child protection and welfare laws: Norway's Child Welfare Act in 1992; England's Children Act in 1989; Sweden's Care of Young Persons Act in 1990; and Germany's Child and Youth Welfare Law in 1990 (Burns et al. 2017a). The Child Care Act 1991 in Ireland repealed the Children Act 1908 and its various amendments during the twentieth century. It extended the potential for intervention from evidence of harm, to evidence of significant risk of harm or abuse. Buckley and Burns explain how this led to the increased regulation of child protection. Another 'moment' is the first big inquiry in Ireland into why the State did not intervene in a case of incest – the Kilkenny Incest Investigation (McGuinness 1993). They outline how this was a watershed moment, not just for social work, but for the general public and system as a whole with the 'revelation' that children could be harmed in their own home by family members. The analytical approach of the McGuiness report is particularly important: at this point in abuse inquiries, far more emphasis was put on system culpability rather than on individual professional responsibility. The two authors capture the complexity of developments during the decade of the 1990s. On the one hand, principles of prevention, inclusion, early intervention, engagement with children and early intervention gained greater ground in policy. On the other hand, from 1996, the question of mandatory reporting is placed on the reform agenda for Irish child protection. It is only now that a system of mandatory reporting for designated professionals and mandated persons (see Government of Ireland 2015) was implemented in December 2017. At the time of writing, media reports based on documents obtained under the Freedom of Information act highlighted how the Child and Family Agency resisted the introduction of mandatory reporting, fearing that its introduction will overwhelm a service that is already struggling to address existing waiting lists (RTÉ 2017).

Post 2008, three weights came down on the system in the form of: the Ryan Report (2009) exposing extensive abuse of children in institutions in the past; the Roscommon child abuse inquiry (Gibbons et al. 2010) that exposed negligence and failure to protect six children from neglect, physical and sexual abuse; and the economic recession and austerity policy measures which created new poor families in Ireland experiencing poverty, discrimination, exclusion and health problems. The authors follow on from this summary of the history to consider the hope for future development of the system post-2012, as we do here again in this chapter a few years later. Buckley and Burns conclude this history to ask if there is a sense of *déjà vu* with the hope of the (last) Task Force in 1974, given that it was the 'front door of child protection' that remained very much the focus in the run up to 2012. The Task Force on the New Child and Family Agency in 2012 had a major challenge to consider a new avenue and a wider range of doors and entry points for support and protection of children in need and at risk. The low turnout rate for the Children's Referendum and modest gains for children's rights made in the Children's Referendum in 2012 left advocates in little doubt that the quest for 'better' was still many steps away from the aspiration to do 'good enough'.

In sum, in 2012, we can see a number of important continuities and discontinuities within the child welfare and protection system in Ireland that were significant to that moment. The main discontinuities or major shifts in the system are identified as: 1970 – a move from mostly voluntary to a statutory child welfare system; 1991 – introduction of legislation to repeal the Children Act 1908 and the enactment of greater powers for risk management and prevention of neglect and abuse; 1993 – the first major inquiry into how the child welfare system had failed a child; 1999 – the culmination of a decade of revelation of historical abuse of children in institutions in particular, a redefining of the history of child care in Institutions and under the care of religious orders, and the publication of a major overhaul of the key child protection policy document (Children First); 2000 – the emergence of a notable children's rights discourse in policy and 2012 as the year a number of events came together to define our most recent key moment of change, which, as explained in the next section, was the establishment of a new national State-led Child and Family Agency. The main continuities to note are an ongoing quest for change and improvement since the first moment identified in 1970 and the protracted nature of that change up to the present. Throughout the period of change, a lack of resources has persisted as another continuity leading to a constraint to progression. The pull towards risk and crisis management continuously prevents the achievement of implementation of the principles of prevention, early intervention and family support laid down in principle since the 1980 Task Force and legislated for since the Child Care Act 1991. The question to consider now is whether, almost 50 years on, the context, appetite for and investment in change is to be realised in the biggest structural change to the context of child welfare services since the development of Community Care under the Health Act in 1970.

Building a New System, Whilst Simultaneously Addressing the Past, 2012–2017

Following on from our consideration of some key moments in the past that inform the present, this section provides a commentary on the development of the child welfare system since 2012. We examine what we consider to be five contemporary defining features of the Irish child protection and welfare system. Firstly, we examine the establishment of Tusla, the Child and Family Agency and the strengths and weaknesses of this Agency. In this, we summarise related policy and legislative developments in Ireland at this moment in time. Secondly, we examine the introduction and implementation during 2017–2018 of Signs of Safety® as Ireland's new national approach to child protection practice. Thirdly, we present data on child protection and welfare in Ireland which will give the reader a sense of the Irish model, particular in terms of the profile of children in Ireland, the profile of presenting issues for children referred to Tusla and the thresholds to enter the system, including the thresholds for reception into State care. Fourthly, we examine the high retention, low turnover rates for social workers in child protection and welfare in Ireland over the last decade. Finally, we focus on the fact that while there has been extensive focus on building a new child protection system, there is also simultaneously strong pressure on government – largely from civil society organisations – to address historical (retrospective) issues associated with the care and protection of children. Underpinning these changes, some major law reforms have led to profound changes to the system since 2012. These include the introduction of the Children and Family Relationships Act 2015, which extended the scope of guardianship, the Adoption Amendment Act 2017 which makes provision for the adoption of children from State care in certain circumstances and the Government of Ireland 2015 which makes provision for mandatory reporting of concerns about child welfare in Ireland for the first time.

7.1.1 Establishment of Tusla, the Child and Family Agency

While the initial aim of the Agency was to consolidate all other child and family services within the Health Services Executive, it presently only incorporates child protection and welfare school attendance, family support and domestic and sexual violence. Although intended to be included, public health visiting (community nursing), child and adolescent mental health and psychological services currently remain within the HSE due to a number of reasons, including: a concern about resourcing and pace of change in the development of the new Agency and an assertion of their own 'best fit' with other services remaining in the HSE (e.g. general hospital and adult mental health services).

As articulated in the *Report of the Task Force on the Child and Family Support Agency* in 2012, the principles of what came to be called the Child and Family Agency (Tusla), were articulated within a broad family support ethos. Supported by philanthropic investment, a new programme of Parenting, Prevention and Family Support (PPFS) was launched to complement the existing services of the Agency that included mainly child protection and welfare intake, assessment and intervention services, alternative care services (foster care and residential care) and education and welfare services. Education and welfare services were newly incorporated from the Department of Education into the new Agency. An assessment framework and thresholds guidance framework was used to inform the nature and level of intervention. Hardiker's 4 level model is used as a guide to differentiating levels of need and intervention from Level 1 (Universal services) to Level 2 (Some unmet need),

Level 3 (significant unmet need and/or risk of harm) and Level 4 (high level/acute need and /or risk/harm) (see Hardiker et al. 1991).

Five strands of development are involved in the PPFS programme and a comprehensive process of external evaluation of each package has been in place since 2014 led by the UNESCO Child and Family Research Centre, NUI Galway. The first strand relates to commissioning of services and the development of a Market Position Statement which is the guidance for how the public sector service Tusla will commission services from outside of its own provision. This position statement rationalises the process of commissioning of child and family services from the voluntary and community sector (Shaw and Canavan 2017). The second strand relates to the extended development of the parenting support services of Tusla. The establishment of an online Parenting 24/7 service has been one of the significant developments (Connolly and Devaney 2017). The third relates to the development of a participation programme for enhancing child participation which has already developed training and practice within the Agency significantly and in line with the new Article 42A in the constitution concerned with listening to and taking account of the voice of the child (McGreal and Kennan 2017). The fourth strand of PPFS relates to public awareness of parenting and family support services which is informing the Agency's communication strategy (McGregor and Nic Gabhainn 2016). The final, and arguably the most significant strand of the programme is the introduction of new practice model based on the principles of early intervention and prevention. This model is called 'Meitheal', which is an old Irish word 'that describes how neighbours would come together to assist in the saving of crops or other tasks' (Tusla, Child and Family Agency 2015, p. 1). 'Meitheal', in the context of Tusla's work, means a new practice model based on learning from international best practice in relation to early intervention and draws from work in the UK, for example, in relation to the use of the My World Triangle. Meitheal is a partnership model that requires full agreement and engagement with parents and young people/children. It is based on the principle that the child should be at the centre of services and is designed on the basis of inter-agency and inter-disciplinary co-operation. Significantly, the lead practitioner is appointed on the basis of their relationship with the family, rather than their disciplinary background. Meitheal is a service offered to families to prevent them coming into contact with the child protection and welfare services. Meitheal is a targeted early intervention and preventative service for families who present with a level of need or risk (usually Level 2 or 3) that does not meet the threshold for child protection and welfare intervention. Meitheal can be initiated through a parental or professional referral. Also, when families' cases are being closed with child protection and welfare, they can also be referred to Meitheal as a 'step down' process. The practice model evaluation is already showing positive outcomes for families and practitioners (see Cassidy et al. 2016), but it is too early to report on its overall impact and interaction with the child protection system which has also just recently introduced a new model for practice (Signs of Safety, see next section).

Collectively, the introduction of the PPFS programme is indicative of a discursive and organisational shift in the orientation of child welfare services towards prevention, early intervention and family support (see Devaney and McGregor 2016; Cassidy et al. 2016). However, the challenge of how this practice model fits with the child protection intake, assessment and intervention system is something that is still being worked through and worked out in terms of balancing the emphasis on support at levels 1 and 2 alongside responding to the high levels of referrals and needs for intervention at levels 3 and 4.

7.1.2 *Signs of Safety Model as Ireland's New National Approach to Practice*

The Signs of Safety model is an internationally recognised approach to child protection developed by Steve Edwards and Andrew Turnell in the 1980s in Australia. It is currently being implemented in Ireland as a new national standardised approach to practice. All child protection social workers in Ireland during 2017/2018 were trained in the model by Andrew Turnell and colleagues (Holland 2017, p. 1). It is the recognised practice model incorporated into the Tusla *Child Protection and Welfare Strategy 2017–2022* launched in May 2017. Called 'Creating Effective Safety', the strategy reiterates the principles contained within Children First (Department of Children and Youth Affairs 2017), the primary one being that 'the safety and welfare of children is everyone's responsibility'. It sets out six strategic objectives.

Firstly, to implement a National Model-Signs of Safety. Signs of Safety has been implemented in countries including New Zealand, Japan, Europe, Canada, and Cambodia, and is generally recognised as a leading participative model of child protection case work although it has been subject, to date, to limited systematic external evaluation. Turnell and Murphy (2017) in the fourth edition of their briefing paper for the model summarise the three core principles of Signs of Safety as: Working relationships; 'Munro's Maxim: thinking critically, fostering a stance of inquiry' and 'landing grand aspirations in everyday practice'. Together, they show critical learning from past inquiries and recent reports such as Munro's impactful review of child protection in England in 2011 (Munro 2011). The second strategic objective for Tusla is to develop clear thresholds and responsive pathways. To achieve this, it states that there will be 'an increased level of analysis and judgement to be promoted to improve consistency in determining the appropriate response pathway for children and families ensuring they receive a proportionate and timely response'. The third strategy is to create and embed a system-wide learning environment. The fourth relates to developing proactive relationships with partners that includes internal and external stakeholders, children, families and their extended networks. The fifth refers to 'empowering our people' to help staff to make more 'risk–sensible' decisions and 'work in a more participative way with children and families'. This will include organisational reform to support the new national approach to practice and the development of career pathways for all staff. The final objective, no. 6, is to have defined, measurable outcomes. The strategy makes a commitment that meaningful measures will be developed that will allow Tusla to assess how successfully they are outcomes for children and families, for staff and for the organisation.

Launching the strategy, CEO Fred McBride announced that:

> 'The creation of Tusla in 2014 represented a fundamental shift in the provision of family support, child protection, educational welfare and alternative care services. Since the Agency's establishment, we have led the most comprehensive reform of these services in Ireland and our new *Child Protection and Welfare Strategy 2017–2022* is a hugely important step in this journey' (Tusla, Child and Family Agency 2017a).

This reform process is something we will observe with interest in the coming years. To contextualise further the climate and potential of such reform, the following section provides current statistics on children and child protection in Ireland.

7.1.3 Statistical Data on Children and Child Protection and Welfare in Ireland

Ireland has a relatively young population compared to many other European countries, with 1,190,478 children (aged 0–17) in a total population of 4,757,976 (26%) in 2016 (Central Statistics Office 2017). 331,515 of these children were aged between 0 and 4 years, 548,693 were aged between 5 and 12 years and 310,270 aged between 13 and 17 years.

In 2015, the Child and Family Agency received new 43,596 referrals and there were 26,655 cases open to social work departments (Tusla, Child and Family Agency 2017a, b, c). The Child and Family Agency is the only body authorised to receive children into state care under the Child Care Act 1991. Ireland operates a high threshold for the reception of children into State care relative to other jurisdictions, due to a provision in our constitution which stipulates that State interventions into the family domain must only be exercised in exceptional circumstances (see Burns et al. 2017b). At the end of 2016, there were 6,258 children in statutory care which is a 16% rise on the numbers in care at the end of 2006 (Tusla, Child and Family Agency 2017b). However, the total number of children in care per 1,000 at the end of 2016 was 5.3, which is virtually unchanged since 2011 (5.35). This figure would be at the lower end of child in care per 1,000 and be closer to the United Kingdom and the United States, but under half the rate you would find in Switzerland, Norway or Finland (Burns et al. 2017a). Sixty-five percent of children in State care live in general foster care, 27% live in foster care with relatives, 5% live in residential care and 2% live in accommodation categorised as 'other' (Tusla, Child and Family Agency 2017c). Of the children that come into state care, two-thirds enter through the voluntary care pathway and one third of children come into care through care order applications made to the District Court (Tusla, Child and Family Agency 2016). The voluntary care system is managed by Child and Family Agency social workers, with virtually no independent supervision and there are no time-limits on how long a child care be signed into voluntary care, except that voluntary care must

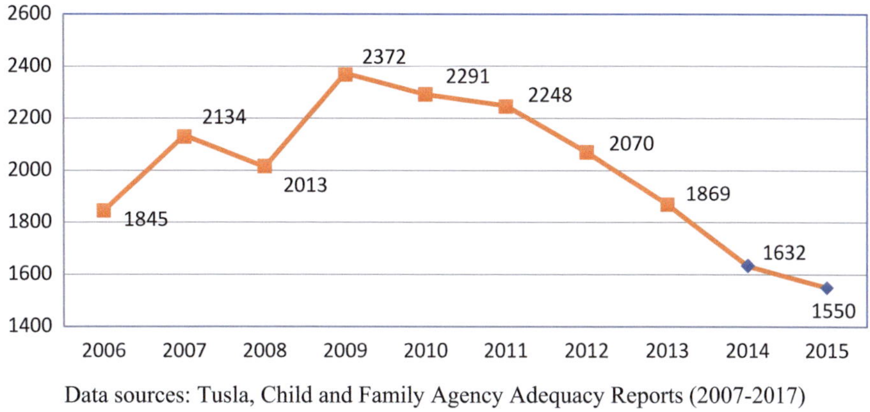

Fig. 7.1 Admissions of children into state care by year, 2006–2015. (Data sources: Tusla, Child and Family Agency Adequacy Reports (2007–2017))

end before their 18th birthday. The District Court in Ireland, except for the Dublin Metropolitan District, is a single judge, non-specialist general court of limited and local jurisdiction that also deals with civil and criminal cases, alcohol licensing, domestic violence, maintenance and custody. Fig. 7.1 illustrates the peak in admissions of children to State care in 2009 and admission have been falling year on year since, with a 31% reduction in admissions in the last 5 years:

While the total numbers of children in care at year end has increased 16% in the last decade, there is no obvious explanation as to why admissions of children into State care have fallen so sharply, particularly given the very large increase in the numbers of children being referred to the Child and Family Agency for abuse or welfare reasons. On the one hand, the Child and Family Agency could argue that prevention and family support services are leading to the reduction, but this explanation is unconvincing as the investment in these new services has not been extensive to date, nor has there been sufficient time up to now to evaluate their impact. On the other hand, the reduction could indicate that the system is at capacity with significant numbers of children awaiting assessment due to years of austerity. Furthermore, it may also mean that thresholds in the courts for care orders have increased or are being more strictly enforced by judges, which may have resulted in social workers bringing fewer cases to court. This is a development that requires more in-depth research and is beyond the scope of this chapter (see the work of the Child Care Law Reporting Project for more background on this point).

Whatever the reasoning, one factor that is evident is that there have been inadequate numbers of social workers employed within the system to respond to demand. At the end of December 2016, the Child and Family Agency had 1,458 whole time equivalent social work posts working on 25,034 open cases,[1] of which 19,621 chil-

[1] 'Open cases include cases held on intake, allocated and unallocated child welfare and protection children in care cases' (Tusla, Child and Family Agency 2016, p. 2).

dren had an allocated social worker and 5,413 children (22%) were awaiting allocation. This means that cases will have been assessed via an Intake system, but no worker allocated to follow up with more detailed assessment and intervention. Worryingly, 801 of these cases awaiting allocation were considered high priority cases. Included in the 25,034 open cases were 6,258 children who at the end of December 2016 were in state care, 7% (n = 453) of whom did not have an allocated social worker (Tusla, Child and Family Agency 2017a). In the November 2017 budget, the government has attempted to address this issue by allocating 300 new posts to the Child and Family Agency.

7.1.4 High Retention Rates for Child Welfare and Protection Social Workers

For the last decade, retention rates for Irish child protection and welfare workers has been relatively high, leading to a stable workforce with high levels of experience and expertise. Retention data for 2014 indicated an 8% turnover rate (6.63% excluding retirements) for social work staff in Tusla, although this figure likely conceals a few teams where turnover is high and recruitment is challenging. Also, this data is for all social workers in Tusla, and not child protection only. This low turnover rate for Ireland is in stark contrast to reports of low retention/high turnover from other countries such as the United States, with reports of turnover rates of between 30% and 40% and less than a two-year tenure length (Lizano and Mor Barak 2015). The dominant narratives (see, for example, Ferguson 2011; McFadden et al. 2017; Truter et al. 2017) in this literature about retention and turnover in child protection and welfare are, that: child protection and welfare work is intellectually and emotional demanding labour; at times highly stressful labour; child protection and welfare is at the 'hard' edge of State intrusion into private family life involving the social sanctioned use of 'controlling' and 'surveillance' activities by professionals; stakes are high in terms of potential harm to children and young people with high levels of responsibilities for those who undertake this work; conflict and disagreements are a feature of this work, and it is high visibility work in terms of public/media scrutiny and criticism when there are perceived errors. For these reasons, the dominant narrative suggests that workers don't stay long in this work, with short tenure rates reported. Furthermore, because of high turnover, this is work undertaken, mostly, by newly-qualified workers as it is the sector with the most vacancies and newly-qualified workers perceive [whether this is borne out by the evidence is open to debate] that they must 'prove' themselves in a hard sector of social work before moving on to their preferred area of practice (see Burns 2011).

However, there is also a lesser-reported retention narrative, whereby: social workers describe this work as meaningful with very good levels of job satisfaction; it is professionally stimulating work that is rarely 'boring'; the work is demanding, but this facilitates high levels of skill use and problem-solving; social workers' experience high levels of autonomy, which they value highly; there are strong levels of peer support; immediate management are knowledgeable and supportive, even if the volume of work militates against these managers providing 'balanced' supervision [i.e. not 'case-management' supervision]; there is a cohort of social workers who want to continue working in this sector and are not seeking to leave even if there are suitable job alternatives, and are willing to continue despite not receiving essential required personal, supervision and organisational supports (Burns et al. 2017). The high retention/low turnover rates in Ireland has meant that there are workers on some child protection and welfare teams who have practiced for between 5 and 30 years, with concomitant high levels of expertise, meaning this sector in Ireland has had a strong mix of novice, experienced and expert workers. These experienced workers are not always visible in the research literature.

It is difficult to know for sure why Ireland's retention rates have been so high, although there are some likely reasons. Unlike some other countries, Ireland has not de-professionalised child protection and welfare: to work in this area, you must have a social work degree with either a 4-year undergraduate bachelor of social work (BSW) or have a Masters in social work (MSW, 5 years in university). The salary rates for this work are good with an entry salary point for professionally qualified social work grade of €39,819, with a high point of scale of €57,889 (correct at April 2017), with opportunities for promotion to senior practitioner grades and management posts. The State has not abrogated its responsibility for child protection work to other sectors and social workers working for the State have access to what would be considered internationally as excellent pension entitlements, tenure, sick leave arrangements and they have an entitlement to 29 days annual leave a year. High retention rates between 2008 and 2015 were also likely to be a by-product of a severe economic recession, whereby job alternatives were in short supply as there was a significant reduction in funding for civil society organisations and there was an employment embargo in most State agencies. This may have resulted in some workers feeling 'stuck' in their post and/or appreciative of the 'safe-haven' a public tenured job provided in a precarious job market, particularly given that some of their partners lost their jobs in the recession. However, recent data from a soon to be published qualitative longitudinal study of retention in this sector found that over three-quarters of the social workers in this small sample stayed because this work was their career preference, they found the work meaningful, job alternatives were not a significant factor and they are committed to this work as their 'career preference' (see Burns et al. 2017). Even in times of strong job opportunities, the social work sector in Ireland is smaller than other similar sized countries; child protection and welfare is the largest employer and therefore job alternatives are always going to be somewhat limited which will contribute to higher retention. At the time of writing, the workforce situation in Ireland is rapidly changing with recruitment restarted and a growth in posts in most areas of social work, a loosening of the public employment embargo which further increases job opportunities. In this new context, the recruitment of sufficiently qualified staff and also issues with the retention of social workers in some child protection teams, has, once again, become a feature of the sector.

7.1.5 Dealing with the Past: Retrospective Disclosures, Institutional Abuse and Church – State Relations

While there is significant contemporary focus on building a new child protection system, there continues to be a moral imperative and pressure from advocacy groups in Ireland to deal with retrospective disclosures of child abuse. This involves listening to the experiences of those who were abused in institutions and those who were harmed in their family homes and local communities. In this regard, the *Commission to Inquire into Child Abuse Report* (Ryan 2009; see also, Powell and Scanlon 2015), discussed earlier, was a watershed moment for Ireland in addressing institutional abuse of children and young people in the period 1940 to present. However, this inquiry is but one chapter in the ongoing process of recognising, hearing from and seeking redress, for those who were harmed by these 'care' systems.

There is an ongoing Commission (2015–2018) led by Judge Yvonne Murphy investigating the experiences of mothers and babies who resided in Mother and Baby homes in Ireland between 1922 and 1998 (see Murphy 2017). Mother and baby homes were religious run institutions for unmarried women and their children, at a time in Ireland when having a child outside of wedlock was a significant social stigma for the parents and their families. Pregnant women lived in these homes, gave birth to their children there, reared their children there and were paid miniscule amounts of money for their labour in laundries. The Commission is undertaking its work against the backdrop of excavations of a site on the grounds of a former mother and baby home in Tuam which operated from 1925 to 1961, where in March 2017, it was confirmed that the bodies of up to 800 infants and children under the age of 3 were found in an underground chamber.

Garrett (2017, p. 370) argues that while this Commission is to be welcomed, that we should guard against the emerging narrative surrounding the mother and baby homes which may 'be seeking to relegate the issue to one entirely residing in Ireland's troubled past'. He illuminates this point by identifying contemporary troubling practices associated with the treatment of 'unmarried mothers' in Ireland. Evidence of the changing nature of the relationship between Church and State away from that which existed in the period of the mother and baby homes, was played out in a battle in 2017 over the ownership of the new national maternity hospital. The state was seeking to build a new national maternity hospital on the grounds of the St. Vincent's hospital, which is owned by the Sisters of Charity. The state proposed to grant full ownership to the Sisters of Charity after it was built, as it was on their private hospital campus. There were vociferous debates about the appropriateness of this arrangement in a modern, secular Ireland. This debate was also held against the backdrop of strong lobbies to reform Ireland's restrictive abortion laws and the need to separate the Church from medical decisions. While religious orders had extricated themselves from the provision of care homes for children and mother and baby homes largely by the 1990s, some religious orders continue to be leading providers of private hospital care and education. In modern, democratic secular states, decisions in maternity hospitals on the care and welfare of parents and babies, and more widely on reproductive rights, need to be made on the basis of prevailing legislation and social policy, rather than on a Catholic ethos. While this debate is largely outside the scope of this chapter, it may be significant to note for international readers that 96% of Irish primary schools are owned by, under the patronage of and run by the Catholic Church, with faith formation a core part of daily class time (see Collahan et al. 2012). The UN Committee on the Rights of the Child (UNCRC) in their most recent report on Ireland (2016), noted their concern about the lack of non-denominational places in schools and that schools were legally permitted to discriminate in their admissions policies on the basis of a child's religion.

A further strand to dealing with the past is the recent establishment of new teams within Tusla to deal with the retrospective disclosures by adults of abuse when they were children. This abuse may have been perpetrated by clergy members in the community, within care institutions, or by members of their family or members of the wider community. The organisation *One in Four* was established in 2003 to provide professional support to, and advocacy on behalf of, victims of childhood sexual abuse in Ireland. In the Dáil (Irish Parliament) in May 2017 the Minister for Children and Youth Affairs reported that Tusla, during March 2017, had 1,895 cases of historical abuse on record, most of which related to sexual abuse. Seven hundred and fifty-four of these cases were awaiting allocation (Zappone 2017). As these teams are new there is very little available data to examine this work. Mooney (2017) argues that this area of social policy and legislation which is still in a nascent form in Ireland, is concerning for three main reasons. Firstly, services need to develop to help those who were abused as children to tell their story, to be heard and taken seriously, and to take further appropriate actions. At the moment, these processes are under-developed. Secondly, once these stories are heard and assessed, there may be further implications for other yet to be identified children in the present day. Thirdly, perpetrators of past abuse continue to live in communities and have yet to be held to account. Furthermore, other adults who may have been abused as children by the same perpetrator, are yet to be identified.

7.2 Concluding Comments

At the beginning of this chapter, we quoted former Minister Fitzgerald, a social worker by training, at the beginning of her tenure saying that Ireland must do better for children and families. This chapter has documented the extensive steps taken by Ireland to create a new system out of the "rubble". It is evident from the content of the chapter thus far that the Irish child welfare and protection system in Ireland is undergoing substantial changes and development at this present moment in time. We used the idea of history of the present to identify 2012 as a key moment that has triggered the current pace of change and reform for reasons summariesed above. We have outlined a number of important developments that are underway that cannot yet be evaluated or assessed in terms of their impact and outcomes. The most significant points to note about the Irish child protection and welfare system in Ireland at present are as follows.

Firstly, it is a mixed economy of service with a strong state-lead, combined with a historically continuous reliance on the voluntary, community and third sector service providers to deliver support and prevention services in particular. Discontinuous with the past, private providers are also now gaining space especially in the field of alternative care residential services and to a lesser extent, foster care services.

Secondly, the new child and family welfare agency, Tusla, has been explicitly constructed as a deliberate break with the past which was characterised by a strong subsidiary relationship with Catholic Church provided services and a reactive crisis-driven approach to child protection and welfare. Tusla's PPFS initiative and the adoption of the Signs of Safety model, based on a strengths-based approach to practice, are two indicators of a strong motivation and intentional reorientation and redirection of child protection and welfare policy in line with the principles of prevention, family support and early intervention. This conceptual leap will take time to become embedded. There remains gaps between what has traditionally been seen as the 'child protection' and the 'family support' aspect of the service. Tusla's *Child Protection and Welfare Strategy 2017–2022* mentions family support briefly and makes no reference to the relationship between family support and the 'step down' model of Meitheal. This is indicative of a point in time where contradictions and probably differences of standpoint exist regarding how to reconcile demand for intervention at all levels of need and their prioritisation. Both the message that 'child protection is everyone's business' and the message that 'all intervention requires a family support practice orientation' are acknowledged, but not necessarily aligned as yet. This is part of the project for those involved in the development of policy, practice and education over the coming years.

Thirdly, with the success of the 2012 referendum, Ireland's child welfare and protection is being pulled more in line with the UN Convention of the Rights of the Child and recommendations made specifically to Ireland over the years about its attention to children's rights, participation, religious freedom and family independence. Constitutional reform and associated legislative changes have stimulated the potential for children's rights-based practice and many mechanisms to realise this shift have now been put in place. The challenge for achieving this change in approach seems to lie across many domains from micro to macro levels. These include: issues of resourcing and allocation of social workers to children in care; conceptual coherence across the system and support for this at all levels; inevitability of differences in practice and implementation at regional levels and a nagging doubt about political will and transformational practice relating to services for children and families in light of the evidence of inaction about chronic circumstances in which some families and children live in Ireland presently. Children who are in direct provision and children who are homeless with their families are two particular categories of great concern. The widening of adoption options of children in state care poses a challenge in that on the one hand, it offers the potential for greater rights to permanence and security for children, but on the other hand, it also poses a significant threat to the sanctity of the family of origin and family ties.

Fourthly, the relationship between the 'past' and 'present' is very significant in Ireland at the moment for many reasons. Post-Ryan report, ongoing issues continue to emerge around the fallout from the disclosures of abuse within institutions and the generally passive and often resistant response from the Irish Catholic church leaders regarding the same (the orders have significant unpaid bills owed to the State from the redress system, despite owning significant assets). The ongoing inadequacy of policy to deal with retrospective disclosure of abuse keeps history firmly within the present for many victims: survivors and advocates are lobbying for changes within a system that arguably re-traumatises individuals through historically inadequate responses to their disclosures and the fact that many survivors are on a waiting list for services now that they are adults. The internationalisation of children's rights and global concern about religious extremism and discrimination has also forced Irish policy makers to consider critically the implications and significance of the explicit preferential position given to the Catholic Church within the Irish education system. What seemed like a logical and cosy arrangement 50 years ago is now identified by the UN Committee on the Rights of the Child as a form of discrimination because of the predominance of Catholic Schools in Ireland and limited choice for children to be educated in a secular non–denominational context unless living in a city, near to the growing but still very marginal Educate together system or have the means to be able to pay private tuition.

And finally, despite what seem like more challenges than opportunities above, you have a workforce that are highly qualified, motivated and valued by virtue of position and salary. While grave problems exist in relation to lack of adequate resources and time to do the work that should and must be done with children and families, the potential for change and motivation for improvement is evident also. In the present moment, a discontinuity with the past is the level of political and public awareness about child welfare and protection issues in Ireland. An unprecedented level of change in terms of structures, laws, policies and new practice models is underway. The considerable resources and political energy invested in the system in recent years, has led to improvement in living standards for children in Ireland in the last two decades, although there is much work yet to be done (see UNICEF 2017; Department of Children and Youth Affairs 2014, 2016). This period of transition offers unique opportunities for review, reflection, research and evaluation to intensely and carefully consider the question of how we can do child protection and welfare work better and more effectively into the future. The answer to this remains speculative, but an approach that embraces the underpinning principle of the new Agency's practice – that the child should be at the centre – suggests the potential for a welcome and necessary discontinuity from the past in Ireland with regard to the attention paid to, and responsibility taken for, the care and welfare of children, young people and their families.

References

Buckley, S. A. (2013). *The cruelty man: Child welfare, the NSPCC and the state in Ireland*. Manchester: Manchester University Press.

Buckley, H., & Burns, K. (2015). Child welfare and protection in Ireland: Déjà vu all over again. In A. Christie, B. Featherstone, S. Quin, & T. Walsh (Eds.), *Social work in Ireland: Continuities and changes* (pp. 51–70). Basingstoke: Palgrave/Macmillan.

Buckley, H., & O'Nolan, C. (2013). *An examination of the recommendations into events in families, implemented by state services and impact on practice*. Dublin: Department of Child and Youth Affairs.

Buckley, H., Skehill, C., & O'Sullivan, E. (1997). *Child protection practices in Ireland: A case study*. Dublin: Oak Tree Press.

Buckley, S. A., & McGregor, C. (2018). Interrogating institutionalisation and child welfare: The Irish case, 1939–1991. *European Journal of Social Work*. https://doi.org/10.1080/13691457.2018.143.

Burns, K. (2011). 'Career preference', 'transients' and 'converts': A study of social workers' retention in child protection and welfare. *British Journal of Social Work, 41*, 520–538.

Burns, K., & Lynch, D. (2012). Politics, democracy and protecting children. In D. Lynch & K. Burns (Eds.), *Children's rights and child protection: critical times, critical issues in Ireland*. Manchester: Manchester University Press.

Burns, K., Christie, A., & O'Sullivan, S. (2017, May 19). *What can we learn about retention from social workers with 10–30 years' experience of child protection work?* Dublin: Department of Children and Youth Affairs Seminar.

Burns, K., Pösö, T., & Skivenes, M. (2017a). Removals of children by the child welfare system – Variations and differences across countries. In K. Burns, T. Pöso, & M. Skivenes (Eds.), *Child welfare removals by the state: A cross-country analysis of decision-making systems* (pp. 146–173). New York: Oxford University Press.

Burns, K., O'Mahony, C., Shore, C., & Parkes, A. (2017b). Child removal decision-making systems in Ireland: Law, policy and practice. In K. Burns, T. Pöso, & M. Skivenes (Eds.), *Child welfare removals by the state: A cross-country analysis of decision-making systems* (pp. 146–173). New York: Oxford University Press.

Cassidy, A., Devaney, C., McGregor, C., & Landy, F. (2016). Interfacing informal and formal help systems: Historical pathways to the Meitheal model. *Administration, 64*(2), 137–155.

Central Statistics Office. (2017). *Census of population 2016*. Cork: Central Statistics Office. Retrieved from http://www.cso.ie/en/releasesandpublications/ep/p-cpr/censusofpopulation2016-preliminaryresults/. Accessed 1 Apr 2017.

Child Care Law Reporting Project. (2012–2017). https://www.childlawproject.ie

Christie, A. (2010). Whiteness and the politics of 'race' within child protection guidelines in Ireland. *European Journal of Social Work, 13*(2), 199–215.

Collahan, J., Hussey, C., & Kilfeather, F. (2012). *The forum on patronage and pluralism in the primary sector report of the forum's advisory group*. Dublin: Department of Education and Skills.

Connolly, N., & Devaney, C. (2017). Parenting support: Policy and practice in the Irish context. *Child Care in Practice, 24*, 15. https://doi.org/10.1080/13575279.2016.1264365.

Dean, M. (1994). *Critical and effective histories: Foucault's methods and historical sociology*. London: Routledge.

Department of Children and Youth Affairs. (2011). *Children first: National guidance for the protection and welfare of children*. Dublin: Government Publications.

Department of Children and Youth Affairs. (2012). *Report of the Task Force on the Child and Family Support Agency*. Dublin: Government Publications.

Department of Children and Youth Affairs. (2014). *Better outcomes, brighter future: The national policy framework for children and young people, 2014–2020*. Dublin: Government Publications.

Department of Children and Youth Affairs. (2016). *State of the nation's children: Ireland 2016*. Dublin: Department of Children and Youth Affairs.

Devaney, C., & McGregor, C. (2016, December 16). Child protection and family support practice in Ireland: A contribution to present debates from a historical perspective. *Child and Family Social Work*. https://doi.org/10.1111/cfs.12342.

Devaney, C., McGregor, C., & Cassidy, A. (2017). Early implementation of a family-centred practice model in child welfare: Findings from an Irish case study. *Practice, 29*, 331. https://doi.org/10.1080/09503153.2017.1339786.

Ferguson, H. (2011). *Child protection practice*. New York: Palgrave Macmillan.

Ferguson, H., & O'Reilly, M. (2001). *Keeping children safe: Child abuse, child protection and the promotion of welfare*. Dublin: A&A Farmar.

Foucault, M. (1977). *Discipline and punish*. Harmondsworth: Penguin.

Garrett, P. M. (2017). Excavating the past: Mother and baby homes in the Republic of Ireland. *British Journal of Social Work, 47*(2), 358–374.

Garrett, P. M., & Conneely, E. (2015). Social workers and social justice during a period of intensive neoliberalization: A preliminary investigation from the Republic of Ireland. *Journal of Progressive Human Services, 26*(2), 125–147.

Gibbons, N., Lunny, L., Harrison, J., & O'Neill. (2010). *The Roscommon child care case*. Dublin: Health Service Executive.

Government of Ireland. (2015). *Children first act*. Dublin: The Stationary Office.

Hardiker, P., Exton. K., et al. (1991). *Policies and perspectives in preventive child care*. Aldershot: Avebury.

Harvey, B. (2007). *Evolution of the health services and health policy in Ireland*. Dublin: Combat Poverty Agency.

Health Service Executive. (2002). *National child care information: Final report on options for systems development and implementation*. Dublin: Health Service Executive.

Health Service Executive. (2011). *Child protection and welfare practice handbook*. Dublin: Health Service Executive.

Hensey, B. (1972). *The health services in Ireland*. Dublin: Institute of Public Administration.

Holland, K. (2017, June 26). Social workers 'retrained' to manage risk instead of remove it. *The Irish Times*.

Horgan, D., & Ní Raghallaigh, M. (2017). The social care needs of unaccompanied minors: The Irish experience. *European Journal of Social Work,* Advanced online edition, https://doi.org/10.1080/13691457.2017.1357018.

Kennedy, E. (1970). *Reformatory and industrial schools system report 1970 chaired by District Justice Eileen Kennedy*. Dublin: Stationery Office.

Kilkelly, U. (2012). Children's rights in child protection: Identifying the bottom line in critical times. In *Children's rights and child protection: Critical times, critical issues*. Manchester: Manchester University Press.

Lizano, E. L., & Mor Barak, M. (2015). Job burnout and affective wellbeing: A longitudinal study of burnout and job satisfaction among public child welfare workers. *Children and Youth Services Review, 55*, 18–28.

Lynch, D., & Burns, K. (2008). Introduction: Contexts, themes and directions in Irish child protection and welfare social work. In K. Burns & D. Lynch (Eds.), *Child protection and welfare social work: Contemporary themes and practice perspectives*. Dublin: A&A Farmar.

Lynch, D., & Burns, K. (2012). *Children's rights and child protection: Critical times, critical issues in Ireland*. Manchester: Manchester University Press.

McCaughren S., & McGregor C. (2017). Reimagining adoption in Ireland – A viable option for children in care? *Child Care in Practice*: 1–16, Advance internet edition, https://doi.org/10.1080/13575279.2017.1319799.

McFadden, P., Mallet, J., & Leiter, M. (2017). Extending the two-process model of burnout in child protection workers: The role of resilience in mediating burnout via organizational factors of control, values, fairness, reward, workload, and community relationships. *Stress and Health*. Advance online edition, *34*, 1–12. DOI: https://doi.org/10.1002/smi.2763.

McGreal, B., & Kennan, D. (2017). *The perspectives of educational welfare officers on children and young people's participation in decision-making, prior to the implementation of the programme for prevention, partnership and family support*. Galway, The UNESCO Child and Family Research Centre, National University of Ireland, Galway.

McGregor, C. (2014). Why is history important at moments of transition? The case of 'transformation' of Irish child welfare via the new Child and Family Agency. *European Journal of Social Work, 17*(5), 771–783.

McGregor, C., & Nic Gabhainn, S. (2016). Public awareness of parenting, prevention and family support services: Population survey baseline report, The UNESCO Child and Family Research Centre, Galway: National University of Ireland, Galway.

McGuinness, C. (1993). *Report of the Kilkenny incest investigation*. Dublin: Government Publications.

Mooney, J. (2017). Adult disclosures of childhood sexual abuse and section 3 of the child care act 1991: Past offences, current risk. *Child Care in Practice*: 1–13, Advanced internet access, https://doi.org/10.1080/13575279.2017.1347145.

Munro, E. (2011). *Munro review of child protection: Final report – A child-centred system*. London: Department of Education.

Murphy, J. Y. (2009). *Report into the Catholic archdioceses of Dublin*. Dublin: Department of Justice Commission of Investigation.

Murphy, Y. (2017). *Commission on mother and baby homes: Second interim report*. Dublin: Mother and Baby Homes Commission of Investigation.

O'Sullivan, E. (2009). Residential child welfare in Ireland, 1965–2008: An outline of policy, legislation and practice: A paper prepared for the Commission to Inquire into Child Abuse, *Commission to Inquire into Child Abuse*. Retrieved from http://www.childabusecommission.com/rpt/04-04.php. Accessed 27 Feb 2014.

Parton, N. (2014). *The politics of child protection. Contemporary developments and future directions*. Basingstoke: Macmillan Palgrave.

Powell, F., & Scanlon, M. (2015). *Dark secrets of childhood: Media power, child abuse and public scandals*. Bristol: Policy Press.

RTÉ. (2017). Tusla opposed to mandatory reporting of abuse concerns. *RTÉ News*. Retrieved September 20, 2017 from https://www.rte.ie/news/2017/0903/901937-tusla/

Ryan, S. (2009). *Commission to Inquire into Child Abuse Report (Volumes I – V)*. Dublin: Stationery Office.

Shaw, A., & Canavan, J. (2017). *Introducing commissioning in Ireland: Establishing a baseline*. Galway: The UNESCO Child and Family Research Centre, National University of Ireland, Galway.

Skehill, C. (1999). *The nature of social work in Ireland: A historical perspective*. New York: Edwin Mellen Press.

Skehill, C. (2000). Notes on the history of social work: An examination of the transition from philanthropy to professional social work in Ireland. *Research in Social Work Practice, 10*(6), 688–704.

Skehill, C. (2003). Social work in the Republic of Ireland: A history of the present. *Journal of Social Work, 3*(2), 141–159.

Skehill, C. (2004). *History of the present of child protection and welfare social work in Ireland*. New York: Edwin Mellen Press.

Skehill, C. (2007). Researching the history of social work: Exposition of a history of the present approach. *European Journal of Social Work, 10*(4), 449–463.

The Kennedy Report. (1970). *Reformatory and school system report*. Dublin: Stationery Office.

The Task Force on Child Care Services. (1980). *Final report to the minister for health*. Dublin: Stationery Office.

Truter, E., Fouché, A., & Theron, L. (2017). The resilience of child protection social workers: Are they at risk and if so, how do they adjust? A systematic meta-synthesis. *British Journal of Social Work, 47*, 846–863.

Turnell, A., & Murphy, T. (2017). *Signs of safety: Comprehensive briefing document.* Signs of Safety.
Tusla, Child and Family Agency. (2007–2017). *Review of adequacy reports*. Retrieved from http://www.tusla.ie/publications/review-of-adequacyreports. Accessed 1 Apr 2017.
Tusla, Child and Family Agency. (2013b). *Guidance for the implementation of an area based approach to prevention, partnership and family support.* Dublin: Tusla, Child and Family Agency. Retrieved from http://www.childandfamilyresearch.ie/publications/policy-practice. Accessed 5 Feb 2014.
Tusla, Child and Family Agency. (2015). *Meitheal. A national practice model for all agencies working with children, young people and their families.* Retrieved from http://www.tusla.ie/services/family-community-support/guidance-documents. Accessed 10 Sept 2017.
Tusla, Child and Family Agency. (2016). *Review of the adequacy of child care and family support services available 2014.* Retrieved from http://www.tusla.ie/publications/review-of-adequacy-reports. Accessed 10 Nov 2016.
Tusla, Child and Family Agency. (2017a). *Child protection and welfare strategy 2017–2022.* Retrieved http://www.tusla.ie/uploads/content/Tusla_Child_Protection_and_Welfare_Strategy.pdf. Accessed 20 Sept 2017.
Tusla, Child and Family Agency. (2017b). *Integrated performance and activity report quarter 4 2016.* Tusla, Child and Family Agency Quality Assurance Directorate. Retrieved from http://www.tusla.ie/uploads/content/Q4_2016_Integrated_Performance_and_Activity_Report_Final_V2_Table_8_Amended_08Mar2017.pdf. Accessed 15 April 2017.
Tusla, Child and Family Agency. (2017c). *Monthly performance and activity data, January 2017.* Retrieved from http://www.tusla.ie/uploads/content/Monthly_Performance__Activity_Dashboard_Jan_2017.pdf. Accessed 15 April 2017.
UNESCO Child and Family Research Centre. (2017). *Development and mainstreaming*. Galway: NUI, Galway. Retrieved from http://www.childandfamilyresearch.ie/cfrc/mainstream. Accessed 6 July 2017.
UNICEF. (2017). *Innocenti report card 14 – building the future: Children and sustainable development goals in rich countries.* Retrieved from https://www.unicef-irc.org/publications/pdf/RC14_eng.pdf. Accessed 20 Sept 2017.
Whyte, J. H. (1980). *Church and State in Modern Ireland 1923–1979.* Dublin: Gill and Macmillan.
Zappone, K. (2017). *Dáil Debates, 11th May 2017.* Dublin: Houses of the Oireachtas. http://oireachtasdebates.oireachtas.ie/Debates%20Authoring/DebatesWebPack.nsf/takes/dail2017051100025?opendocument&highlight=tusla. Accessed 6 July 2017.

Kenneth Burns is a college lecturer and Deputy Director of the Master of Social Work course at University College Cork, Ireland. He has worked as a social worker and social work team leader in child protection and welfare and continues to support practice in this area. Kenneth is the Principal Investigator for an inter-disciplinary research group on child care proceedings, a longitudinal study on social workers' retention in child protection and joint coordinator of a five-country European Commission Directorate-General for Justice and Consumers action grant (IDEA project). Kenneth is co-editor of an eight-country cross-country analysis of child welfare removals published by Oxford University Press in 2017. Kenneth is a joint institutional Principal Investigator on a European Commission Horizon 2020 study on Responsible Research and Innovation called EnRRICH (2015–2017) and a researcher on a European Research Council consolidator project called DISCRETION. Kenneth was twice awarded the President's Award for Excellence in Teaching and is the Principal Investigator for a research group that was awarded the University College Cork Research Team of the Year Award.

Caroline McGregor is Professor at the School of Political Science and Sociology with lead responsibility for the discipline of social work. She is also a Senior Research Fellow at the UNESCO Child and Family Research Centre. Formerly Dr. Caroline Skehill from Queen's University, Caroline's research has been mainly in relation to history of social work in Ireland and Europe and research into the nature and form of child protection and welfare social work. She also has a particular interest in child protection practice and policy; history of the present methodologies, socio-legal studies and young people in and leaving care. Her current work is focused on: outcomes for young people leaving care, public awareness of child protection and welfare, family support services and policy and cultural competence in social work.

Chapter 8
The Israeli Child Protection System

Ruth Gottfried and Asher Ben-Arieh

Acronyms

EBP:	Evidence Based Practices
ELI:	Association for Child Protection
IMLSASS:	Israel Ministry of Labor, Social Affairs and Social Services
IMLW:	Israel Ministry of Labor and Welfare
IMW:	Israel Ministry of Welfare
IMWSS:	Israel Ministry of Welfare and Social Services
INCC:	Israel National Council for the Child
PIEC:	Planning, Intervention, and Evaluation Committee
SSD:	Social Services Department
SWAL:	Social Worker to the Adoption Law
SWCP:	Social Worker to Court Proceedings
SWYL:	Social Worker to the Youth Law
SWDL:	Social Worker to the Disabilities Law (i.e., social worker for the law of protection of people with developmental and mental disabilities)

8.1 Introduction

Israel is a relatively small country located in the Middle East, with a particularly high level of immigration and a multicultural and diverse population, which comprised around 8.67 million Israeli citizens and permanent residents on the eve of Israel's 69th Independence Day in 2017 (Central Bureau of Statistics 2017a;

R. Gottfried (✉)
The David Yellin Academic College of Education, Jerusalem, Israel
e-mail: ruthgottfried@dyellin.ac.il

A. Ben-Arieh
The Haruv Institute and the Paul Baerwald School of Social Work and Social Welfare,
The Hebrew University of Jerusalem, Jerusalem, Israel
e-mail: benarieh@huji.ac.il

L. Merkel-Holguin et al. (eds.), *National Systems of Child Protection*,
Child Maltreatment 8, https://doi.org/10.1007/978-3-319-93348-1_8

Weiss et al. 2003). Data published by the Israeli Central Bureau of Statistics (2017b) for the 2016 United Nations Universal Children's Day, also showed that by the end of 2015 there were nearly 2.77 million Israeli children aged 0–17, comprising 33.0% of the Israeli population. Of these, 70.0% were Jewish, 23.0% Muslim, 1.5% Christian, 1.6% Druze and 3.0% with unspecified religion. Moreover, in 2015 34.7% of Israeli children (i.e., 19.8% Jewish, 65.6% non-Jewish) were living in families with incomes below the poverty threshold (INCC 2016). Comparatively, approximately two out of three Jewish Ultra-Orthodox children were living below the poverty line in 2015 (61.5%; INCC 2016). Correspondingly, the United Nations Children's Fund (UNICEF 2016) reported that Israel has the highest level of child poverty of the world's 41 most developed countries. Given the strong correlation between poverty and higher rates of child maltreatment (Nadan et al. 2015; Pelton 2015), the current chapter should be read bearing the above in mind; while also taking into account that in the last three decades there has been an approximate fourfold increase in the percentage of Israeli children living below the poverty threshold (8.1% in 1980 to 30.0% in 2015; INCC 2016).

Further, in 2015, 443,548 Israeli children were known to social services, of which 365,981 were children at risk (i.e., 16.0% due to poverty, income and/or employment difficulties). Of these, 43,971 (i.e., comprising a rate of around 16 per 1000 children) were new referrals to designated child protection officers titled 'Social Workers to the Youth (Care and Supervision) Law' (SWYL; Dolev et al. 2008a; Faber and Slotsky 2007; INCC 2016). The new referrals to SWYL were due to neglect (33.5%), physical abuse (26.1%), sexual abuse (11.0%), emotional abuse (6.5%), diagnosis, treatment and psychiatric hospitalization (3.7%), involvement in criminal activities (2.0%), suicide attempts (2.0%), addictions (1.0%) and other (14.2%); with 92.7% of investigated referrals found to be truthful (i.e., substantiated; INCC 2016).

The past two decades have seen a growing literature comparing child protection systems worldwide. This has provided for an ongoing process of critical reflection and learning; as well as opportunities for identifying different ways of looking at familiar policy and day-to-day practice dilemmas (Gilbert et al. 2011; Stafford et al. 2011). Understanding how decisions involving alleged maltreatment are influenced by a country's context may also be an incentive for changes in national policies and practices (Baistow 2010; Benbenishty et al. 2015). Compared to international research on child protective systems, however, Israeli research in this field is comparably young and underdeveloped (e.g., Benbenishty and Chen 2003; Osmo and Benbenishty 2004). Correspondingly, child maltreatment only began to be perceived in Israel as a national health concern in the late 1980's (Tzimrin 1983; Kadman 1992). Likewise, scientific interest in child protection service practitioners' decision-making processes only began to develop in Israel in the early 2000's (e.g., Davidson-Arad and Benbenishty 2008, 2010, 2016; Enosh and Bayer-Topilsky 2014; Gold et al. 2001). Further, to the best of our knowledge, this chapter is the first time Israel's national child protection system is included in an international comparative analysis of child protective systems.

The current international literature on child protective systems identifies three broad orientations in the systems designed to protect children. These frameworks include: (1) a child protection orientation; (2) a family service orientation; and (3) a child-focused orientation (Gilbert et al. 2011). Gilbert et al. further suggest that countries' child protective systems should be viewed in the context of the above three dimensional framework. As such, the present 2018 snapshot of the Israeli child protection system can be broadly characterized as closest to a child protection orientation, striving toward a family service orientation (i.e., wherein child protection is addressed in the context of wider family services and support); while also including child-focused orientation building blocks. The latter, in line with the 'Sabra Generation' in lieu of the 'Pioneer Generation' ideology of creating a new non-Diaspora Israeli society, based on children whose formative years coincided with the formative years of the establishment of the State of Israel (Almog 2000). The '360 degrees – Israeli National Program for Children and Youth at Risk' (hereinafter: the 'National Program') discussed below, complimentarily broadens the Israeli approach to child protection through the prioritization of prevention and early intervention (Szabo-Lael and Zadka 2015).

Furthermore, Israel's social welfare system includes universal health care, from infancy to old age; with services including, but not limited to: a general child allowance, free education, and health promotion and prevention care centers titled 'Tipat Halav' (i.e., 'Drop of Milk' in Hebrew) for women during pregnancy and infants and children from birth to early childhood (e.g., Rosen et al. 2015). The Israeli national health expenditure also compares favorably with that of other developed countries (Bloomberg's Global Health Index 2017; i.e., statistics compiled from the World Health Organization (WHO), the United Nations Population Division and the World Bank). Additionally, the 1995 'Israeli National Insurance Law' provides for a standardized basket of medical services, including hospitalization; with the medical services supplied via the country's four comprehensive health funds (Tasher et al. 2016). Moreover, between 2012–2018, the 'Israeli Ministry of Labor, Social Affairs and Social Services' (IMLSASS) net budget will have increased by approximately 55.0%; with the IMLSASS 2018 expenditure for children at-risk estimated at 21.0% of the overall net budget (IMLSASS 2017a).

Note that unless otherwise specified, the term 'children' herein, refers to both children and youth under 18 years of age; with the term 'children at risk' officially used in the Israeli context to describe all children who live in adverse familial and/or environmental situations/circumstances, including familial economic difficulties which hinder their rights as prescribed to them by the 'United Nations Convention on the Rights of the Child' (INCC 2016; United Nations 1989). More specifically, the term 'at risk' also includes children: (1) suffering from behavioral and/or intellectual disorders, (2) harming themselves or others; and/or (3) in adverse life circumstances/crises due, for instance, to high-intensity divorce disputes, unemployment, immigration, illness, and/or death of one or both parents (IMLSASS 2017b). Further, the 'Israel Ministry of Labor, Social Affairs and Social Services' (IMLSASS) has had different names over the years. These include the 'Israel

Ministry of Welfare and Social Services' (IMWSS), the 'Israel Ministry of Labor and Welfare' (IMLW), and the 'Israel Ministry of Welfare' (IMW). Throughout the chapter, excluding references, IMLSASS will be the term used, even though the official title of this Ministry has changed over time.

Likewise, there are several types of Child Protection Officers in Israel. These include 'Social Workers to the Youth Law' (SWYLs), primarily referred to in this chapter; 'Social Workers to Court Proceedings' (SWCPs), who interact with the courts on a variety of issues relating to minors welfare and safety; 'Social Workers to the Adoption Law' (SWALs), who supervise adoption proceedings; and 'Social Workers to the Law for the Protection of People with Developmental and Mental Disabilities' (hereinafter: 'Social Workers to the Disabilities Law'; SWDLs) who, alongside their additional duties, mirror those of SWYLs – as pertaining to at-risk children suffering from developmental and mental disabilities (IMWSS 2014b; Stalker and McArthur 2012). Note also that the ongoing Israeli-Palestinian conflict's impact on children's rights, child protection, and child welfare in all areas administered by Israel and for all populations residing therein – is beyond the scope of the present chapter (e.g., Ben-Arieh et al. 2006; Harel-Fisch et al. 2016; Saltzman et al. 2017; United Nations 1989).

8.2 Historical Development of Social Services and Child Protection in Israel

The Israeli social service system was founded in 1931 by an executive body of the Jewish community, the 'National Council', under the British Mandate for Palestine (e.g., Raz 2010). The first non-academic formal training course for social workers opened therein in 1934; with the 'Israeli Association of Social Workers' established shortly after, in 1937 (Spiro et al. 1998). Following the establishment of the State of Israel in 1948, the first university-based school of social work opened at the Hebrew University in Jerusalem in 1958 (Spiro 2001). The year 1958 likewise marked the legislation of the 'Social Welfare Law', mandating all municipalities and local authorities in Israel to maintain a Social Service Department (SSD; Welfare Services Law, 1958). An additional law, the 1960 'Youth (Care and Supervision) Law' (hereinafter: the 'Youth Law'), enabled the transfer of the responsibility of child protection to child divisions of local authority SSDs, who gradually, as of the early seventies, began qualifying social workers to apply said law (Alfandari 2015). The field of social work has since undergone a constant process of change, growth and professionalization (Gal and Weiss-Gal 2011; Weiss et al. 2004); with a total of eleven schools of social work currently offering social work degrees in universities and colleges across the country (Azaiza et al. 2015; Makaros and Weiss-Gal 2014).

Dramatic changes have likewise taken place with regard to how maltreated children are perceived and responded to in Israel. As leading non-governmental nonprofit organizations, the 'Association for Child Protection' (ELI), founded in 1979; and the 'Israel National Council for the Child' (INCC), founded in 1980, both played a significant role in the above mentioned process of change (Ajzenstadt and Cavaglion 2004; Tzimrin 1983, 2007). The INCC was likewise the driving force in the creation of and advocacy for the 1989 Israeli 'Law for the Prevention of Abuse of Minors and Helpless/Defenseless Persons' (hereinafter: the 'Mandatory Reporting Law'). This legislative process was accelerated following the tragic death, in 1989, of a three-year-old Israeli girl who had suffered serious and continuous maltreatment, including head injuries, burns and sexual abuse perpetrated by her uncle. Notwithstanding the severity of the abuse, the professionals in contact with the family, neighbors as well as family members, refrained from reporting the abuse even though they had more than reasonable grounds to suspect it (Kadman 1992).

The mandatory reporting legislation was monumental. Not only did it make reporting child abuse and neglect mandatory, but it also classified child maltreatment for the first time in the Israeli criminal code (Kadman 1992). That is, until the late 1980's, child maltreatment, as a public health concern, was neither explicit in Israeli society nor manifest in Israeli legislation (Faber 2009; Kadman 1992, 2010). The sturdiness of Jewish values, treasuring the 'Jewish Mother' as one who would never harm her child, have been cited as reasons for this almost complete lack of awareness (Ajzenstadt and Cavaglion 2004; Rosenfeld and Kedem 1999). Relatedly, Ajzenstadt and Cavaglion argue that the late 1980s should not be taken as an abrupt chronological decisive moment. They point out that the realization that child maltreatment was a social rather than a private condition was a gradual process of gestation and maturation within Israeli society, beginning as early as the 1960s.

An additional relevant landmark includes the 1996 'Social Workers Law', which formalized the field's achievements, regulated the level of training required for the profession, and strengthened social workers' proprietorship in various fields of activity; including child protection service positions in local Social Service Departments (SSDs) (Auslander 2000; Doron et al. 2008; Spiro et al. 1998). To date, there are more than 270 SSDs located throughout Israel. These are supervised by the 'Service for Children and Youth' within the 'Israeli Ministry of Labor, Social Affairs and Social Services' (IMLSASS), which is the governmental authority responsible for securing the safety and well-being of children at risk. This service is likewise in charge of national child protection policymaking, development of interventions for at-risk children and their families, as well as workforce professional qualifications and development (Gorbatov and Ben-Simhon 2011; Zeira 2004). The establishment, in 1998, of the 'Joint Distribution Committee-Ashalim' (JDC-Ashalim) strategic partnership between JDC-Israel, the Government of Israel and the Jewish Federation of New-York is another relevant landmark. JDC-Ashalim was created to address the challenges of development, accessibility and assimilation of solutions, knowledge and services for children at risk and their families, as well as for the professionals who work with them (JDC-Ashalim 2016; Ben Rabi et al. 2008).

Practice in the Social Service Departments (SSDs), including child protection services, comprise the main social services provided in Israel. The SSDs workforce is broadly divided between: (1) generalist social workers, also referred to as community/family social workers, who deal with a wide array of community needs such as working with residents to enhance community resilience; and (2) specialist social workers, appointed by the Minister of 'Labor, Social Affairs and Social Services' to carry out various investigation and intervention child protection responsibilities (Bar-On 2012). Although not all part of the SSDs, additional child protection roles, include: (3) 'Child Investigators', who deal with the investigation and testimony in court of children (i.e., younger than age 14), who are direct victims, witnesses or alleged offenders of violence – via the 1955 'Evidence Amendment Law (Child Protection)'. These specially trained social work investigators are employed within the 'Israeli Ministry of Labor, Social Affairs and Social Services' (IMLSASS) 'Child Investigations and Special Investigations Unit' (i.e., 'Special Investigators' are designated social workers specifically trained to collect evidence from children with intellectual disabilities); and (4) 'Youth Investigators', who are specially trained police officers employed within the 'Investigations Unit' of the 'Investigations and Intelligence Division' of the Israeli police force. These professionals investigate youth (i.e., aged 14 and older), who are direct victims, witnesses of crime, or are alleged juvenile offenders. Added child protective roles include: (5) hospital based child protection teams, established in all hospitals in accordance with the 'Israeli Ministry of Health's' 1985 guidelines (Benbenishty et al. 2014; Ben Natan et al. 2012). These multidisciplinary teams, usually comprise a pediatrician, nurse, psychiatrist, and social worker, and are primarily responsible for the mandatory reporting of hospitalized children for whom there is a reasonable cause to suspect maltreatment; and (6) The 'Shefi Psychological Counseling Service', which provides psychological services and educational counseling services within the 'Israeli Ministry of Education'. For illustration, this service develops and implements, ministerial interventions following severe maltreatment cases published in the media (Shefi Psychological Counseling Service 2017).[1]

Further, thirteen 'Emergency Centers' currently operate throughout Israel to serve maltreated children (i.e., younger than age 14) in intra-familial cases (Freed et al. 2010). These multidisciplinary (e.g., clinical psychologists, social workers, creative arts therapists, teachers) centers serve as comprehensive, protective, diagnostic, short-term therapeutic and long-term planning systems, which generally operate via 2 units: (1) an internal unit for children in situations of serious intra-familial danger; and (2) a consulting-external unit for children (i.e., who have not been removed from their home) and their families. In accordance with the 2008 'Assistance to Minors who are Victims of Sex Offenses or Violence Law', Israel through its' eight 'Child Advocacy Centers', also provides an initial investigative response for maltreated children (i.e., younger than age 18); as well as for sexually abusive minors (i.e., younger than age 12; Cohen 2005). These centers focus on protection, diagnosis, investigation and decision-making, and efficiently serve to prevent unnecessary bureaucratic procedures involving a large number of interviews and examinations in various locations and over a lengthier period of time. This efficiency is achieved by the centers' multi-professional teams, which include:

[1] See Davidov, Sigad, Lev-Wiesel and Eisikovits (Davidov et al. 2017) for an overview of the four key occupational groups involved in child maltreatment work in Israel (i.e., mental health professionals, law enforcement agents, medical personnel and educators).

designated child protection officers, doctors, child investigators (i.e., specially trained social workers) and youth investigators (i.e., specially trained police officers); with each center also accompanied by an attorney from the district attorney's office (IMLSASS 2017c). Additionaly, there are currently 13 governmental funded centers for the clinical treatment of sexually abused children, spread throughout the country (e.g., Bnai Zion Medical Center 2017).

8.2.1 Main Governmental Commissions

Several main governmental commissions have been established over the years to examine the topic of children at risk in Israel. These include: (1) the 'Prime Minister's Commission' (i.e., the 'Katz Commission'), appointed in 1971 to examine the global topic of poor and excluded populations and particularly children at risk. The commission placed the issue of at-risk children on the public agenda and contributed to the development of relevant formal and informal governmental and non-governmental organizations, programs and services; as well as to the provision of more resources allocated for the treatment of children at risk. The issues, however, of child abuse in general and child sexual abuse in particular were not specifically dealt with and remained silenced in the commission's final report (Prime Minister's Commission 1973; Schmid 2007); (2) the 'Rotlevi Commission', appointed in 1997 to conduct a comprehensive examination of Israeli law on the subjects of children's rights, legal status and welfare, in light of the 'United Nations Convention on the Rights of the Child' (United Nations 1989; Israel Ministry of Justice; IMJ 2003); (3) the 'Gilat Commission', appointed in 2002 to examine the topics of out-of-home placements, visitation rights, adoption, and the functioning of the child protection service 'Decision Committees' – renamed, following the commission's final report: 'Planning, Intervention and Evaluation Committees' (i.e., hereinafter: PIECs; IMLW 2002); and (4) the 'Schmid Commission', appointed in 2003 to review the topics of childhood maltreatment and children suffering from other forms of social and economic distress. Among this commission's main recommendations were: placing the well-being of children at the top of the governments' agenda, allocating appropriate budgets for that purpose, and implementing the 'National Program' described below. The commission also reported that most of the Israeli child protection system's resources were targeted toward identification, investigation, and intervention, rather than prevention efforts (Government of Israel Resolution No. 1007, November 16, 2003; Schmid 2007; State of Israel 2006).

Two additional main commissions were established following the 2008 disappearance and murder of a four-year old immigrant girl by her grandfather and mother, who were living in a common law relationship. The tragic case of the young girl whose body was found inside a suitcase at the bottom of the 'Yarkon' River in Tel Aviv, dominated Israeli media headlines. The case gave rise to much public soul searching over how a child could disappear for months without anyone noticing, and heightened public awareness regarding the need to report suspected cases of maltreatment. The two subsequent commissions were: (5) the 'Vinter Commission', and (6) the 'Silman Commission'. The former was appointed in 2009 to evaluate maltreated minors in serious danger, as well as to delineate a safety net to protect such children within the community. Among the main foci of this commission were: analyzing tragic cases in which children were killed by their parents, discussing ways to create cooperation between various authorities to locate children in danger, examining the current legal situation regarding the sharing of information between professionals; and establishing synchronization between the networks of public agencies and professionals responsible for identifying children in immediate danger (State of Israel 2010). The 'Silman Commission' was appointed in 2013 to examine topics such as children of parents in situations of high-intensity conflict due to separation and/or divorce, children in out-of-home placements, and policies for protecting social workers (IMWSS 2014a). The latter topic was included, considering the growing verbal and physical violence and online shaming and bullying, that is being directed towards designated and generalist social workers in Israel (e.g., Ben-Arieh 2016). Recommendations by the 'Silman Commission' also focused on the need to develop and implement training for child protective social workers on the topic of multiculturalism and characteristics of immigrant and minority societies (IMWSS 2014a).

8.2.2 360 Degrees – The Israeli National Program for Children and Youth at Risk

Based on the successful implementation of a pilot program initiated in 11 Social Service Departments (SSDs) in 2003, titled 'Community 2000', and the ensuing 2004 larger scaled 'Facing the Community' policy, the Israeli government established an inter-ministerial committee. This committee was officially headed by the chief executive officer of the 'Israeli Ministry of Labor, Social Affairs and Social Services' (IMLSASS), responsible for carrying out the 'Schmid Commission' recommendations as pertaining to the 'National Program' (Dolev et al. 2007, 2008b; Szabo-Lael and Zadka 2015). The 'National Program' reform began in 2007 in 72 local authorities from the lowest socioeconomic clusters throughout Israel. This extensive reform in the area of community services for children at risk, is designed for children (i.e., younger than age 18) and young adults with special needs (i.e., up to age 21).

Headed by an inter-ministerial committee and associated directorate, the 'National Program' includes representatives from the following Israeli Ministries: Labor, Social Affairs and Social Services (IMLSASS), Education, Health, Immigrant Absorption, and Public Security. Additional partners include the 'Center for Local Government' and the 'Joint Distribution Committee-Ashalim' (JDC-Ashalim). Via a flexible and multi-year budget allocation, the 'National Program' enables local authorities to assess their needs and transfer resources, previously intended solely for out-of-home placements, for developing services within the community for children at risk, including children exiting out-of-home placements. The program thereby enables local authorities to choose applicable programs for their community's specific needs, relevant to different age groups (i.e., preschoolers, children aged 6–11, adolescents, and all age groups younger than 18). Noteworthy as well, in this respect, is that many 'National Program' services are implemented within universal settings that serve all children in the community (e.g., schools, preschools), thereby decreasing the preceived stigma associated with receiving them (IMLSASS 2017d; Szabo-Lael and Zadka 2015).

As such, the 'National Program' focuses broadly on family services and support, preferring quality care within the community to out-of-home placements; and emphasizing families' responsibility towards their children. Further, the 'National Program' emphasizes early childhood via the 'New Beginnings' component of the program (Sikron-Vazan and Ben-Rabi 2016); as well as special populations of children at risk, including immigrant, Bedouin, Arab and Jewish Ultra-Orthodox minors (IMLSASS 2017d; Szabo-Lael and Zadka 2015). Relatedly, Ben-Arieh (2010a, b) reported that: (1) Arab children are disadvantaged compared to their Jewish peers as pertaining to local public expenditures on education and welfare, (2) both 'Social Workers to the Youth Law' (SWYLs) and generalist social workers are less available in Arab localities, and (3) social service allocation is limited in Jewish localities characterized by a high percentage of the Ultra-Orthodox. Moreover, social services for the Bedouin population are extremely under-developed, especially in the widely scattered, small communities in the Southern part of Israel (Ben Rabi et al. 2009).

Sample findings concerning the 'National Program' are described below. In 2004, 68.0% of the 'Israeli Ministry of Labor, Social Affairs and Social Services' (IMLSASS) budget for children at risk was designated for out-of-home services, while community-based services, for the majority of at-risk children, were only allocated the remaining 32.0% (IMWSS 2014a; Schmid et al. 2008). By 2015, 53% and 47% of this budget, was allocated to out-of-home and community-based services, respectively (Bar 2017). For the years 2009–2011, 156,024 children at risk were identified in the localities where the 'National Program' was implemented, totaling 16.0% of all the children in these localities (Szabo-Lael and Zadka 2015). By the year 2014, the 'National Program' serviced approximately two-thirds of Israel's children in 170 Social Service Departments (SSDs) across the country; with additional local authorities slated to join the program in the course of upcoming years (Dolev et al. 2007, 2008b; Dolev, Ben-Rabi, Szabo-Lael & Tilkin, 2007). Of note is that the above data are not limited to maltreated children, but rather pertain to children at risk in general.

8.3 The Child Protection Legislative Framework

The existing laws for child protection social work practice are numerous and complex; and they are further complicated by a plethora of often-inconsistent regulations and ordinances (Doron 2012; IMWSS 2010; Shnit 1998). This situation arose, primarily as many of the Israeli welfare laws were legislated in response to pressing social needs and public opinion pressures, without adequate preliminary arrangements. Thereby, a legal framework of social service provision was created that has been characterized as patchy and inconsistent (Shnit 1998; IMWSS 2010). Furthermore, the Israeli legal framework for child protection mainly comprises protective rather than granting legislation. The former involves laws that describe the need to protect children's welfare; whereas the latter involves laws that define rights to receive particular services as well as the binding legal basis to receive said services (Hovav 2007; Shnit 1998). Outlined below is the definition of child maltreatment in section 368C of the 'Israeli Penal Code' (1977); as well as the two main laws under which 'Social Workers to the Youth Law' (SWYLs) work in Israel: (1) the 'Youth Law' (1960), encompassing the 'Prevention of Family Violence Law' (1991) and the 'Prevention of Stalking Law' (2001); and (2) section 368D of the 'Israeli Penal Code' (1977), referred to as the 'Mandatory Reporting Law' (1989).[2]

8.3.1 Child Maltreatment in the Israeli Penal Code

Section 368C of the 'Israeli Penal Code' (1977) refers to maltreatment as an act of commission and/or omission/non-prevention of physical, mental and/or sexual abuse perpetrated against a minor or defenseless/helpless individual (i.e., defined as persons who because of age, illness, disability, or for any other reason, are unable to provide for their livelihood, health and welfare). Section 368C further states that perpetrators of maltreatment who are not in a position of responsibility towards the abused and/or neglected child shall be liable to 7 years of imprisonment, whereas offenders who are in a position of responsibility will be liable to 9 years of imprisonment. As for neglect/non-prevention, relevant sections include 361–363 of the 'Israeli Penal Code' (1977), and section 323. The latter section states that a caregiver responsible for a child who is a member of his/her household is obligated to prevent abuse, bodily injury or any other harm to the child's health and wellbeing; and if not fulfilling said duties will be considered responsible for causing such consequences to the child (Fugatz 2007).

Extreme cases in which children have died as a result of abuse and/or neglect are included in the 'Israeli Penal Code' (1977) in chapter 10 (e.g., sections 337 and 340); with succeeding sections (345–355) detailing, among other topics, the extent to which Israeli law broadly protects against the existence of sexual offenses perpetrated within the family. Relatedly, in 1995, the 1991 'Criminal Procedure Law' was first amended to enable the courts to request a 'Victim Report' as pertaining to victims of sexual offenses (Levin-Iger and Levi 2007). To date, this includes reports relating to victims of sexual offenses or severe violence resulting in murder (section 187). Note also that the 'Victim Report', written by a district welfare officer, is introduced in court as evidence prior to determining a perpetrator's punishment. This report serves as a mirror, reflecting the mental, physical, familial, and social state of the victim (i.e., if the offense resulted in murder, the 'Victim Report' refers to one or more members of the child's family members).

[2] See Ben-Arieh and Kimhi (2007) for a review of additional social service laws and children's rights relevant to this chapter.

8.3.2 The Youth (Care and Supervision) Law

The Israeli multi-sectional 'Youth Law' (1960), described here in brief, is designed to protect children in need who are in circumstances or situations that require the intervention of a designated social worker and/or a Juvenile Court to ensure their safety, welfare and wellbeing. The term 'children in need' therein specifies that: (1) there is no responsible caregiver for the minor, (2) the responsible caregiver for the minor is unable to care for or is neglecting the minor, (3) the minor committed a criminal act and was not brought before justice, (4) the minor was found wandering, begging, or street vending, (5) the minor is exposed to negative influence, or permanently resides in a place where illegal activities take place, (6) the minor's physical or mental welfare is or may be in danger; and/or (7) the minor was born with a drug deficiency syndrome (i.e., withdrawal syndrome). Note, as well, that the term 'children in need' is encompassed within the related term 'children at risk' described above in the introduction section.

Although 'Social Workers to the Youth Law' (SWYLs) are social workers in their training and therapeutic orientation, under the 'Youth Law' (1960), they act as legal agents with expansive authority (Gal and Schilli-Jerichower 2017). SWYLs are therein authorized to impose emergency measures in extreme situations, including, for example, directing a minor to inform his/her parents that he/she tested positively for HIV. Further, under this law, SWLYs may immediately remove a minor in need of protection from his/her home even without the consent of the minor's parents or a judicial decision. The law does not detail however the way in which designated social workers should exercise said authority; and these interventions are regulated through internal guidelines (i.e., for more details see the 'Decision Making in Child Protection' section below). Further, the 'Youth Law' (1960) authorizes the Juvenile Courts to issue all orders necessary for the care and protection of minors in need, including but not limited to, instructing a minor to take a psychiatric examination, receive treatment or be hospitalized; and permanently removing a minor from his/her parents' custody against the parents' wishes. The latter action, described in more detail in the section focusing on adoption below, is taken only in the most urgent cases, and conditional that all other possibilities were exhausted.

The 'Prevention of Family Violence Law' (1991) and the 'Prevention of Stalking Law' (2001), referred to in section 3A of the 'Youth law' (1960), also enable the Juvenile Courts to protect minors by issuing restraining orders preventing adult family members or other adults from endangering them (i.e., including within the family home). Relatedly, 'Social Workers to Court Proceedings' (SWCPs) may make recommendations to Family or Religious Courts with respect to parents' custody disputes over minors in divorce cases, and can request these courts to issue protective orders against violent family members that endanger minors safety and wellbeing (Prevention of Domestic Violence Law, 1991; IMWSS 2014c). Regarding the Religious Courts, these comprise the Jewish Rabbinical Court, the Muslim Sharia Court, and the Christian or Druze Religious Courts, all of which receive judicial authority from the state of Israel (Enosh et al. 2016).

8.3.3 The Law for the Prevention of Abuse of Minors and Helpless/Defenseless Persons

The 'Israeli Penal Code' (1977), encompassing the 'Mandatory Reporting Law' (1989), places all adult citizens under the obligation to report, as soon as possible, any knowledge of, or probable cause to suspect, recent cases of maltreatment inflicted upon a child. The punishment for not reporting is up to 3 months imprisonment. The law likewise mandates professionals, including those with confidential information, to report any suspected offenses that come to their attention during their professional practice. These include police officers, doctors, nurses, educational staff (e.g., teachers, counselors), psychologists, social workers, social services workers, clergy, criminologists, para-medical professionals (e.g., occupational therapists, expressive arts therapists); as well as directors and staff members of relevant educational or therapeutic/health care institutions (e.g., residential homes, medical centers). The above mandated professionals are required to report not only recent cases, but also suspected offenses perpetrated anytime in the past. Lawyer–client privileged information is exempt from this requirement.

An additional differentiation delineated in the 'Mandatory Reporting Law' (1989), between the general public of adult citizens and professionals, is that stricter sanctions for failure to report apply to the latter, who may be sentenced to prison for up to 6 months. A six month sentence likewise applies to caregivers (e.g., adoptive parents, foster parents, a parent's current or divorced spouse), and other adult family members, or other adult persons in a position of responsibility, trust or power with respect to the minor, who fail to report. This includes reporting suspected offenses, recent or otherwise, whereby the offense was perpetrated by another adult family member, or other individual above the age of 18 who is responsible for the minor; or by a family member younger than age 18 who is suspected of perpetrating a sexual offense against another minor within the family. The enumerated offenses listed within the law include any act of abuse/assault that endangers the life or health of a minor, including neglect, abandonment; and offenses associated with prostitution, obscenity, and human trafficking.

The Israeli 'Mandatory Reporting Law' (1989) specifies that reports of alleged maltreatment must be reported either to the police or to a designated social worker; and also establishes the actions that the police or said social worker must carry out following the receipt of such a report (See Fig. 8.1 for a schematic flowchart of the Israeli child protective system). In cases when a 'Social Worker to the Youth Law' (SWYL) is the first to receive a report, the SWYL is obligated to forward the report to the police, along with a recommendation to act or not in connection with the report. This procedure is followed unless granted temporary or permanent permission not to do so by one of the designated 'Israel Ministry of Justice' (IMJ) 'Exemption Committees' established in this regard in each of Israel's six districts. Exemption applications may be warranted, for example, due to SWYLs request to complete a therapeutic procedure or gather additional information, or the child's life being perceived to be in danger if the report is immediately forwarded to the police. Members of the 'Exemption Committee' include a representative of the District Attorney as

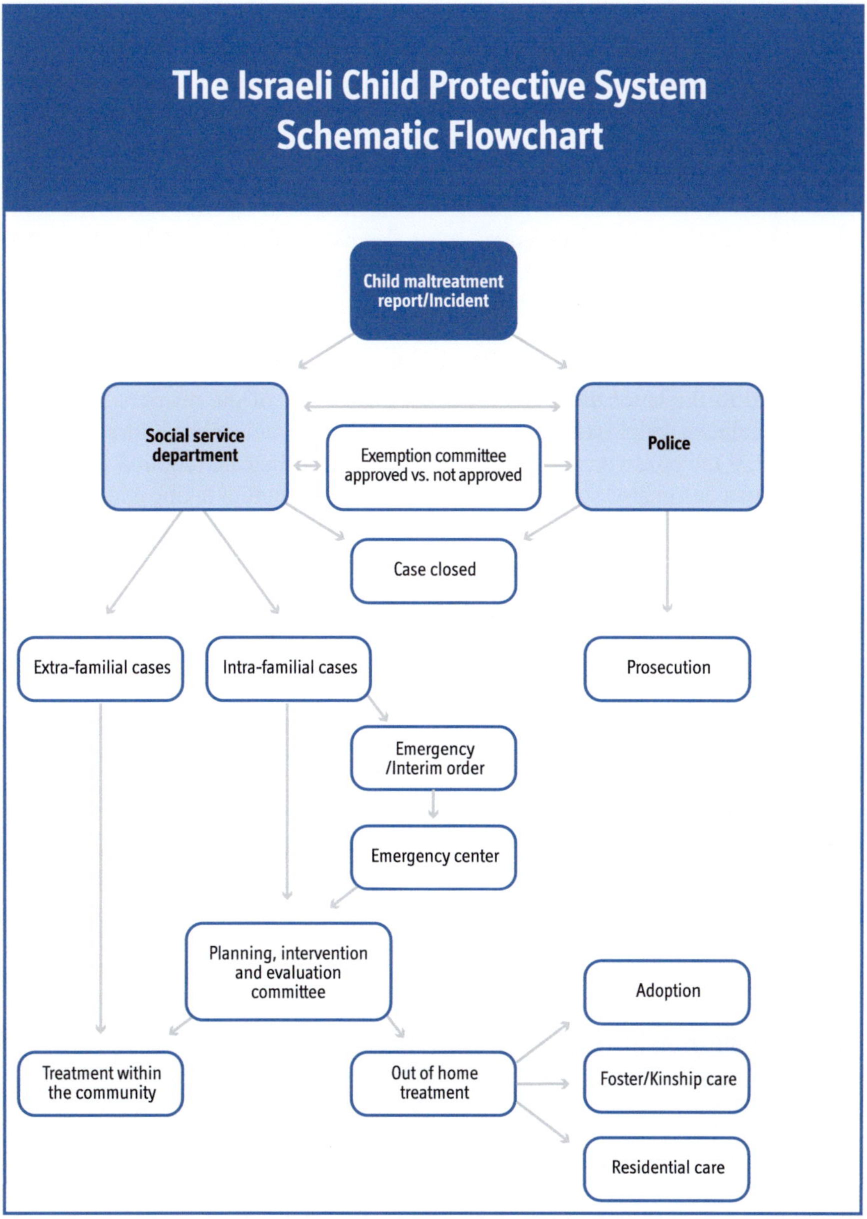

Fig. 8.1 Schematic flowchart describing the Israeli child protective system

chairman, a police officer with the rank of superintendent or higher, and a social worker appointed by law to the specified district. Note, however, that there are no laws or written guidelines concerning 'Exemption Committees' modes of operation.

Further, though 'Exemption Committee' discussions are held in confidential closed-door hearings, if a committee does not approve the exemption application, then the 'Social Worker to the Youth Law' (SWYL) is obliged to report the incident to the police. In such cases, the information that had been brought before the committee may not remain confidential from the police (Faber and Slotsky 2007; Nachmani-Rot 2010). Over the years, requests by SWYLs to 'Exemption Committees' have increased significantly (e.g., 20 such requests were made in 1995, with 9 requests accepted; while more than 1669 requests were made in 2015, with 1552 accepted; INCC 2016). Several limitations should be noted, however, with regard to the latter data. For example, that in one of the districts examined, requests included helpless/defenseless individuals and not only children. On the other hand, if the police are the first to receive a report, they are required to forward the report to a designated social worker for consultation before taking action, unless immediate action is called for. While determining the urgency of an investigation, the police consider such factors as the seriousness of the offense, the victim's need for immediate medical attention, the urgency entailed in locating the suspected perpetrator; and concerns pertaining to possible obstruction of justice or elimination of evidence (Berkovitz 2007). Thereafter, the police are required to forward the report to a designated social worker for collaborative consultation.

Data on the sources of child protection referrals to both child protective officers and the police in Israel are lacking. The dramatic rise in reporting rates to 'Social Workers to the Youth Law' (SWYLs) since the legislation of the 'Mandatory Reporting Law' (1989) clearly shows, however, that this law has greatly increased public awareness regarding child maltreatment in Israel (Kadman 2010). This is demonstrated, for illustration, by twice the number of referrals to SWYLs in 2015 compared to 1997 (i.e., 43,971 vs. 21,765, respectively; INCC 2016).[3] Of note is that to date there have been extremely few prosecutions for failure to report (Kadman 2010).

8.4 Decision Making in Child Protection

A review pertaining to decision making within the Israeli child protection system is now presented. This section reviews the topics of substantiations and responses, 'Planning, Intervention and Evaluation Committees' (PIECs), out-of-home care and adoption.

[3] For added reading, see: (1) Shapira (2010) and Tzimerman et al. (2010), on policy and practice controversies concerning the Israeli mandatory reporting legislation; (2) Shmueli (2010), on Jewish law and Israeli law pertaining to the Israeli mandatory reporting system; (3) English et al. (2015), on the need to pay more attention to emotional maltreatment in child welfare; and (4) Goldstein and Laor (2007), on intercultural aspects relating to the obligation to report, as referring to immigrants from the former Soviet Union, Ethiopia, and the Israeli Jewish Ultra-Orthodox and Arab societies.

8.4.1 Substantiations and Responses

Within Social Service Departments (SSDs), initial assessments regarding child maltreatment reports are evaluated by designated social workers. Cases lacking evidence that meet the legal standards for child maltreatment are closed without forwarding them to the police; with no formal requirement for registration (Faber and Slotsky 2007). Such reports, however, are often forwarded to community/family social workers for voluntary treatment. As outlined by Faber and Slotsky (2007), reports determined to indicate the likelihood of child maltreatment are either initially brought before an 'Exemption Committee', when deemed necessary, as detailed above in the 'Mandatory Reporting Law' section, or immediately forwarded to the police for consultation. In inevitable situations, intra-familial cases may also be initially dealt with via an 'Emergency Order' or Juvenile Court 'Interim Order', as detailed below in the section on out-of-home placements. Following a SSD investigation, intra-familial cases are brought before a 'Planning, Intervention and Evaluation Committee' (PIEC) for intervention decisions (Oppenheim-Weller et al. 2017). When a child and his/her parents agree to collaborate, interventions are given voluntarily. However, in cases when a child or his/her parents refuse support, coercive legislation, in the child's best interests, may also be applicable in acute situations, as a worst case scenario (Faber and Slotsky 2007). The latter, taking into consideration parents' rights to raise their children in privacy and autonomy in accordance with the basic 1992 'Law of Human Dignity and Liberty'. In extra-familial cases, following the SSD investigation, voluntary or coercive treatment within the community may be recommended.

8.4.2 Contemporary Reform: The Planning, Intervention and Evaluation Committees

For the past two decades, harsh political and public debates in Israel have dealt with improving the child protection system decision-making practice. At the heart of these debates were the 'Decision Committees' (IMLW 1995), special child protection committees so named until 2002 (IMLW 2002) and renamed 'Planning, Intervention and Evaluation Committees' (PIECs) following the 'Gilat Commissions' final report. The transition to the PIEC format is commonly also linked to the first and only nationwide empirical study focusing on the 'Decision Committees', by Dolev et al. (2001). Sample recommendations by the 'Gilat Commission' specified that in the PIECs: (1) discussions should include children and their parents, (2) families should be given the opportunity to present an alternative treatment plan, (3) children and parents should be entitled to legal representation; and (4) committee proceedings should be made transparent through accessible meeting protocols (IMLW 2002). These recommendations are taken into account, though not embedded into the practice of the PIECs.

'Planning, Intervention and Evaluation Committees' (PIECs) comprise inter-organizational and multi-disciplinary teams that discuss, assess and thoroughly evaluate risks, possible family preservation options, and alternative care solutions in intra-familial cases for at-risk children in need of intensive interventions, in particular out-of-home placements. The PIECs are likewise in charge of carrying out systematic documentation of practice and following-up on implementation outcomes. Further, preferably, PIECs should be comprised of the child whose case is being discussed, his/her parents, a 'Social Worker to the Youth Law' (SWYL), a community/family social worker, and representatives of the local educational, mental-health and/or other services relevant to the discussion (e.g., 'Social Workers to the Adoption Law' (SWALs) participate in relevant PIEC discussions concerning children aged 6 or younger; Alfandari 2015, 2017; Oppenheim-Weller et al. 2017). See the 'Critical Analysis of the Challenges of the System' section below, for further information regarding children and parent's participation in PIECs.

As mentioned, the 'Planning, Intervention and Evaluation Committees' (PIECs) do not operate through specific legislation but rather according to internal guidelines, which comprise a decision-making innovative framework and supplementary user's guide (IMWSS, 2004a, b, 2008, 2009). As outlined in the implementation team's decisions paper (IMWSS 2004b), the PIEC reform includes a mandatory duty to ascertain and give weight to children's wishes and opinions (i.e., according to their age and maturity) in the decision making process. The framework also sets forth the following stages which the PIECs should adhere to: introduction, information sharing, information analysis, systematic discussion of solution alternatives, formulating a detailed intervention plan, clearing reservations, deciding on a follow-up scheme, and ratification of the intervention plan. For a critical analysis of the PIEC contempory reform, see Alfandari (2015, 2016, 2017) and Oppenheim-Weller et al. (2017).[4]

8.4.3 *Out-of-Home Placements*

In situations that undermine at-risk children's ability to exercise their basic rights to security, protection and dignity according to the 'United Nations Convention on the Rights of the Child' (United Nations 1989), the 'Israeli Ministry of Labor, Social Affairs and Social Services' (IMLSASS) offers varied responses, including out-of-home placements. In the Israeli context, these include IMLSASS supervised residential care (e.g., educational, rehabilitative, therapeutic, residential care as an alternative to psychiatric hospitalization, or post-psychiatric hospitalization residential care), foster care, kinship care (i.e., only a very small portion of foster care in Israel is kinship placements), adoption and short-term emergency services (Dolev et al. 2009;

[4]Further related studies focusing on decision-making in child protection in Israel include Benbenishty et al. (2015), Davidson-Arad and Benbenishty (2010), Enosh and Bayer-Topilsky (2014), and Levin et al. (2016).

IMWSS 2014a). Placement of at-risk children in need of protection in out-of-home care by the Israeli child protection system generally follows either a 'Planning, Intervention and Evaluation Committee' (PIEC) decision, or alternatively a Juvenile Court order. Temporary or permanent removal is considered only in unavoidable situations where all other community-based alternatives have been exhausted (Faber and Slotsky 2007).[5]

In accordance with the 'Youth Law' (1960), following the approval of a provincial designated supervisor, 'Social Workers to the Youth Law' (SWYLs) may also issue an 'Emergency Order' in very high-risk intra-familial situations, as a means of ensuring that minors in-need receive care that cannot be delayed. This latter order enables SWYLs to remove a minor from home for a maximum of 7 days in extreme cases (i.e., signifying both immediate danger to the child; and parental refusal to cooperate). A request for a court order is submitted in retrospect following the immediate removal of the child from his/her home (Faber and Slotsky 2007). SWYLs may also request assistance in enforcing said order, from the police, hospital based child protection teams, child advocacy centers and/or emergency foster care. An 'Interim Order' obtained through the Juvenile Courts is an additional emergency measure enabling SWYLs to remove a minor in-need from his/her home with the aim of ensuring the minor's safety while his/her situation is being assessed. This order also applies to intra-familial cases, and is applicable for a period of up to 30 days, with the option of extending it for an additional period of up to 3 months (Faber and Slotsky 2007). SWYLs must be convinced, however, based on the information at their disposal, that such immediate protection is necessary. In 2015, for example, a total of 578 children were placed in emergency centers in Israel. Of these, 78.5% were placed in various follow-up out-of-home frameworks, and 21.5% were reunited with their families (INCC 2016). Once a child has been removed from home, either by an emergency measure or following a 'Planning, Intervention and Evaluation Committee' (PIEC) or Juvenile Court decision for temporary placement, efforts aimed at the reunification of the minor with his/her family take place (e.g., family therapy, parent education/treatment, home visitations, and financial/housing assistance; IMLSASS 2017e).

For the full breadth of the topic of children residing out-of-home in Israel, authoritative out-of-home placement (i.e., by court order or under the 'shadow of the law') of adolescents in situations of delinquency and social deviation is likewise noteworthy. The latter, as provided by the 'Youth Protection Authority Rehabilitation Services Division' within the 'Israeli Ministry of Labor, Social Affairs and Social Services' (IMLSASS; e.g., between 2002 and 2015, the number of cases in said authority's care increased from 1297 to 1815; INCC 2016). Further, the 'Youth Protection Authority's' hostel system is likewise relevant. These relatively small frameworks, located in residential buildings within the community, are intended for up to 16 adolescents who are continually monitored, yet lead a relatively independent lifestyle. The decision to reside out-of-home may alternatively be made voluntarily, as in the

[5]The topic of partial privatization and its effects on child protective out-of-home services is not reviewed herein due to space limitations (e.g., Sorek et al. 2014).

'Youth Villages' supervised by the 'Division for Rural Education, Boarding Schools and Immigrant Youth' within the Israeli Ministry of Education (Kashty et al. 2008). See Dolev et al. (2009) for a review of the historical-cultural roots of the development of residential care in Israel, including the role of said facilities following the Holocaust and the mass immigration wave of 1950; and as associated with the collectivist Zionist ideology and the 'Kibbutz' collective community movement.

8.4.4 Adoption

The governmental 'Service for the Child' in the 'Israeli Ministry of Labor, Social Affairs and Social Services' (IMLSASSs) 'Department of Social and Personal Services' – heads the topic of adoption in Israel by virtue of the 1981 'Child Adoption Act'. Within the framework of child protection, note that in intra-familial cases when various previous placement options have failed to secure a child's well-being, and parents are deemed incompetent with no likelihood of changing in the foreseeable future (i.e., despite reasonable assistance and financial aid provided by welfare authorities; Ben-David 2011, 2015, 2016; Gal 2015), 'Social Workers to the Youth Law' (SWYLs) may recommend non-consensual adoption proceedings in the child's best interests. These complex adoption cases are initiated at the end of an evaluating process aimed at determining whether a child is at high risk of abuse, neglect, or endangerment within his/her family of origin, and if the parents are competent or not of assuming their parenting responsibilities. According to the 1981 Israeli 'Child Adoption Act', a child can be declared eligible for non-consensual adoption if the state establishes one of the adoption causes delineated by the Act, the most common being lack of parental capacity (Ben-David 2011; Budd 2005). Official legal records cite a total of 261 such non-consensual adoption decisions (i.e., usually due to severe child maltreatment), between the years 1960 and 2012, representing all non-consensual adoption decisions during that time period (Ben-David 2016). Further, the number of Israeli children adopted following the 'Service for the Childs' recommendation, has steadily decreased between the years 1995 and 2015 from 215 to 115, respectively (i.e., not including children adopted by same-sex families and intercountry and kinship adoption cases; INCC 2016).

8.5 Critical Analysis of the Challenges of the System

The challenges described below are by no means comprehensive, but rather highlight a number of selected issues. High-priority essential steps are urgently needed to meet these challenges, for the best interests of children, families and communities in Israel.

8.5.1 Strengthening Children's and Parents' Participation

The national reform of child protection practice in Israel includes the aim of strengthening children's and parents' participation in intervention decisions carried out in 'Planning, Intervention and Evaluation Committees' (PIECs; Kosher et al. 2016). These formal committees, alongside the Juvenile Courts, are the two key authorities involved in child protection intervention decisions in Israel (Alfandari 2017). Alfandari's qualitative study (N = 21 case studies) revealed however that child participation is still a rare occurrence in PIECs, that children have little impact on said committees decisions; and that social workers rarely convey to PIECs, the views of children who do not attend the meetings. Similarly, Oppenheim-Weller et al. (2017) report that children's opinions have little influence on PIECs ultimate decisions. The latter comprises a quantitative study of 80 PIEC coordinators from Social Service Departments (SSDs) throughout Israel. The restorative child protection practice of children participating as active partners in decision making processes that impact their realities, rather than as addendum and occasional guests, has thereby yet to be fully implemented in Israel (Gal 2015; Kilkelly and Donnelly 2011; McCafferty 2017). Findings by Oppenheim-Weller et al. indicate, as well, that at-risk children are more likely to be involved in PIECs when child protection social workers prepare parents prior to their participation in the committee meetings, and when professionals who are more senior are assigned to coordinate PIEC cases. Oppenheim-Weller et al. also report that PIEC coordinators consider the participation of parents in PIEC discussions important. This follows Benbenishty et al. (2015) and Davidson-Arad and Benbenishty (2008), who recommended that more weight be given to parents' wishes by Israeli child protective professionals.

Factors found to be linked with the failure to give greater precedence to children's views within 'Planning, Intervention and Evaluation Committees' (PIECs) include the national reform of child protection practice in Israel being ill fitted to Social Service Departments (SDDs) organizational working environment and culture, as well as unreasonable and intensive caseloads of over 100 families per child protection social worker (e.g., Fryer et al. 1988; Itzick and Kagan 2017). Added cited factors include professionals' lack of time and communication skills with both children and parents, as well as directives regarding practice priorities and differences in personal judgments of PIEC coordinators. Variances in implementation of guidelines in SSDs due in part to the lack of grounding of the guidelines in legislation is yet another adversely impacting factor (Alfandari 2016, 2017). Moreover, Alfandari (2015, 2017) reports that not all PIECs adhere to the 'Israeli Ministry of Labor, Social Affairs and Social Services' (IMLSASS) decision-making framework and supplementary user's guide; and often create adaptations, shorter versions, or do not use the framework at all. Thereby, adversely affected are the reform's overall therapeutic target of formulating effective and tailor-made intervention plans that take, alongside parents' views and wishes, children's needs and preferences into account – in accordance with Article 12 of the 'United Nations Convention on the Rights of the Child' (United Nations 1989).[6]

8.5.2 *Obtaining Increased Resources*

Sample main gaps in the protection of children in Israel, demonstrating the pressing need for increased resources, include the lack of resources (i.e., both budgetary and service wise) for serving families following the placement of a child in out-of-home care; and the need to strengthen the relationship between children in out-of-home care and their parents (i.e., when this is in the best interests of the children; Dinisman et al. 2013). As a direct result, treatment has been and currently still is mostly focused on children and not on the family unit or on parental capacities. As reported also by the 'Silman Commission' (IMWSS 2014a) this is a systemic flaw that leads to two main problems: (1) the chances of children returning to live with their parents is undermined, and (2) families' additional children are placed at risk, seeing as they may be subject to the same maladaptive caregiving behaviors. Moreover, achieving increased resources is crucial considering the ongoing acute shortage of community-based solutions, emergency responses, and out-of-home care options designed for at-risk children with special needs (IMWSS 2014a). This shortage continues notwithstanding findings and recommendations by Hershkowitz et al. (2007), based on their representative Israeli study of forensic statements made by alleged child victims (i.e., N = 40,430, 3–14 year old alleged victims of sexual and physical abuse, over a 7 year period; i.e., 1998 to 2004). Hershkowitz et al. found that Israeli children with disabilities were at a heightened risk compared to their typically developed peers, to: (1) be abused by parent figures, (2) experience physical abuse resulting in body injury, (3) experience serious sexual offenses, and (4) delay disclosure or fail to report abuse when questioned.[7]

An additional example in need of upgrade, is the allocation of resources for developing a system of ongoing prevention and treatment for child protection service professionals themselves, focusing on the 'Cost of Caring' associated with this field of work (e.g., secondary traumatic stress, compassion fatigue; Dagan et al. 2016; Gottfried 2017). Relatedly, as treatment of at-risk and maltreated children is provided, alongside social workers, by additional professionals such as creative arts therapists, these practitioners should likewise receive ongoing 'Cost

[6] For a relevant analysis of the challenges in implementing Article 12 of the 'United Nations Convention on the Rights of the Child' (United Nations 1989) in child protection decision-making social work practice; as well as recommended practical solutions, see McCafferty (2017).

[7] For additional related findings see Jones et al. (2012) and Taylor et al. (2016).

of Caring' prevention trainings, as well as respectable employment conditions and wages. Note that in Israel, the creative arts therapies are a significant component of the countries' mental healthcare system (Schwartz 2014).

8.5.3 Increasing Foster Care Frameworks

A better balance between residential and foster care is warranted in Israel. For the 2013–2014 school year, for example, a total of 10,570 children were placed by the Israeli child protection system in out-of-home care: 70.7% in residential care, 21.7% in foster care, 3.5% in foster care following the child's psychiatric hospitalization, 3.4% in emergency centers, and 0.7% in therapeutic communities (IMWSS 2014a; INCC 2016; Sulimani-Aidan and Benbenishty 2011). Accordingly, strengthening foster care frameworks in general and kinship care in particular is called for by promoting foster care legislation, recruiting more foster families, and providing that financial support for kinship care be comparable to regular foster care (i.e., this support includes financial maintenance to cover foster children's ongoing expenses and rebates for special expenses; IMWSS 2014a). Concomitantly continuing to strengthen and develop community services and reduce their cost, at least to a level equal to that of out-of-home placements, may also encourage families to use more community services (IMWSS 2014a).

8.5.4 Moving Towards a Family Service Orientation

The strong relationship between the law and social work practice in Israel in the field of child protection is an additional pertinent issue to be highlighted herein, as this dual role policy influences professional practice in numerous ways. On the one hand, it grants social workers an exclusive occupational monopoly and powerful authority. On the other, it emphasizes judicial decisions, exposes 'Social Workers to the Youth Law' (SWYLs) to harsh public criticism over alleged misuse of power, and creates high expectations for these professionals to protect and provide unlimited solutions (Doron 2012; Shnit 1998; Vismonsky 2016; Weiss et al. (2004). Moreover, SWYLs need to balance the inherent contradictions arising at different stages of their work as they are both in charge of children at risk receiving treatment, and at times also responsible for imposing said treatment. Ongoing investment in training programs, post-qualification programs, alongside continuing professional guidance imparting both therapeutic and legislative knowledge and skills, are thereby important in this regard (Alfandari 2015; Ofek 2009). Notwithstanding, Pelton (2015) has advocated for a radical restructuring of the child welfare system from an investigative, coercive, policing, child removal system to a more proactive and prevention-oriented system.

He describes the potential benefits of implementing this alternative policy in the United States, instead of the present dual role policy of many current worldwide child protective systems.

8.5.5 Updating the Public Agenda

Public awareness campaigns are vital for the promotion of child protective system social workers' status in Israel. This is because these professionals are subject to an increasing amount of violence by service users, the media and social network bullying and shaming; particularly following alleged omissions in certain cases (Vismonsky 2016). The above is relevant as public attitudes toward child protection practitioners and social service agencies are highly influential as sources of legitimacy and support for the field of child protection[8] (e.g., Krugman 1996; Schmid and Benbenishty 2011). Moreover, improving public attitudes is necessary, considering the need for increased numbers of child protection social workers, and the improvement of their employment conditions and salaries (e.g., Abu-Bader 2000; Kagan 2016). In addition, the Israeli public's sentiments regarding how effectively the issue of at-risk children and child maltreatment, in particular, are being addressed have a major impact on policies and subsequent resource allocation. Continuing to upgrade the status of community/family social workers within the child protective system, including a required internship of treatment of at-risk children, is also relevant (IMWSS 2014a). Moreover, as the scope and severity of child poverty in Israel presents a major challenge to the Israeli child protection system, updating the public agenda to significantly reduce poverty levels among children in Israel is also extremely important (Ben-Arieh and Gal 1998).

8.5.6 Increasing Multidisciplinary Training and Practice

Israeli social workers are the primary profession in child protection service positions in local Social Service Departments (SSDs). Davidov et al. (2016), stress, however, in their qualitative study of 40 in-depth interviews with Israeli child abuse professionals (i.e., law enforcement agents, educators, mental health, and medical personnel), that work with maltreated children is cross-disciplinary by nature (e.g., Bross et al. 1988). International literature demonstrates that practitioners in this field often encounter confusing and conflicting professional viewpoints; besides which they experience the ever-changing social dynamics as complex, ambiguous and potentially leading to inter-professional information blocking (Bross et al. 2000; Chiesa and Bross 2014). This situation may unfortunately arise in lieu of cross-disciplinary

[8] See Schmid and Benbenishty (2011) who focus on the implications for policy of public attitudes toward child maltreatment in Israel.

cooperation and communication, mutually integral input and information sharing. As the need to work in a cross-disciplinary manner is crucial, Davidov et al. propose an alternative professionalization model (i.e., the 'Craftsmen's Framework') for bridging conflicting professional viewpoints. This framework involves, for example, child abuse practitioners acquiring basic knowledge of intervention protocols in parallel core professional domains related to their occupational focus, including medicine, law enforcement, mental health, and education. The above example is valuable, considering that the 'Vinter Commissions' recommendations (i.e., mentioned above in the 'Main Governmental Commissions' section), have not yet been implemented; and there continues to be a lack of coordination and synchronization between the various relevant public authorities in Israel (State of Israel 2010).

Further, the use of evidence-based practices (EBP), though widespread in the field of social work elsewhere (e.g., Aarons et al. 2011), is still very limited in the child welfare therapeutic discourse in Israel (e.g., Zeira 2014). Moreover, child welfare organizations do not customarily offer or require their staff to use EBP. David and Schiff (2015) describe an evidence based Israeli pilot study focusing on the implementation of 'Child-Parent Psychotherapy' for traumatized children and their families. They discuss the implications of importing new evidence based interventions considering the different Israeli dissemination system and professional culture. Implementing systematic evaluation as part of EBP to support the welfare of children is extensively recommended as well. Thereby, advancing EBP in direct child welfare therapeutic practice in Israel, along with its systematic evaluation, comprises an additional important challenge.[9]

8.5.7 *Working in a Multicultural Society*

Developing and carrying out added training for child protection practitioners on the subject of multiculturalism and the characteristics of different groups within the population is yet another relevant issue for discussion (IMWSS 2014a). By way of illustration, Wahle et al. (2017) offer their perspectives on risk and protection of young Israeli children originally from Ethiopia, stating that understanding marginalized children's experiences is crucial for creating culturally competent prevention and intervention programs. Further, the Jewish Ultra-Orthodox community in Israel has set up an independent network of organizations to complement child protection services (Shapiro 1997). Buchbinder and Shoob (2013) discuss to what extent these organizations cooperate with 'Social Workers to the Youth Law' (SWYLs). Cooperation is essential, but is not always achieved, considering that the SWYLs are often perceived as threatening to this community's values. It is thereby important to implement steps to improve this needed cooperation. Moreover, as discussed by Sulimani-Aidan and Benbenishty (2013), protective services also need to better

[9] See Zeira (2014) for associated facilitators and barriers that such practices would entail as pertaining to organizational, cultural and social work direct practice climates in Israel.

understand the dynamics of maltreatment in Arab localities. It is important, according to these authors, to learn from Arab child protection professionals how they understand child maltreatment and reporting patterns, so that the true needs of children in this group can be identified and met.[10] Paramount, as well, is enhanced understanding of the Israeli–Palestinian political conflict's impact on child protection practice in Israel as discussed, for example, by Baum (2007).

Applying cultural competence to child protection practice in Israel involves not only gaining knowledge of essentialist and homogenic cultural characteristics, but also: (1) knowledge on intra-cultural diversity, (2) awareness of the continuum of acceptable and unacceptable caregiving behaviors within each particular culture, (3) understanding the impact of other crucial contextual factors besides culture; such as the intersectionality of migration, poverty, and minority status; and (4) giving priority to a strength-based rather than a deficiency-based approach (Korbin and Spilsbury 1999; Nadan 2016; Nadan et al. 2015). As Israel is a multicultural and diverse society with varied socio-cultural sub-groups, added training in this field, and the subsequent transition to more heterogenic and divergent rather than uniform services is called for.

8.6 Summary and Main Conclusions

The present chapter comprises the first-time inclusion of Israel's child protection system in an internationally comparative survey of such systems. The comprehensive overview and bibliography presented herein are therefore designed to provide an in-depth introduction to the Israeli system. Accordingly, the chapter begins by referring to the high level of poverty among Israeli children and the strong positive correlation between poverty and rates of child maltreatment. It then describes the historical development of the Israeli child protective system, associated legal framework, relevant governmental commissions, and prevention-oriented 'National Program'. Further presented are the topics of substantiations and responses, 'Planning, Intervention and Evaluation Committees' (PIECs), out-of-home placements, adoption; and selected current challenges facing the system.

Originally based on a child-focused orientation (i.e., in line with the 'Children of the Dream' in lieu of the 'Generation of the Desert' ideology; Rosenfeld and Kedem 1999), the Israeli child protection system, can be presently characterized as closest to a child protection orientation; while striving towards a family service orientation (Gilbert et al. 2011). The latter, via such initiatives as the 'Planning, Intervention and Evaluation Committee' (PIEC) reform and the 'National Program' (Oppenheim-Weller et al. 2017; Szabo-Lael and Zadka 2015), which advocate and promote both children's and parents' empowerment and participation; and point to the importance the Israeli child protection system attaches to working cooperatively with families. Additional fundamentally profound positive developments concern how Israeli law

[10] For further reading see Ben-Arieh's (2010a, b) findings on the pronounced inequalities between Arab and Jewish municipal localities' social service expenditures.

and child protection practice have perceived and responded to the 'United Nation's Convention on the Rights of the Child' in general (United Nations 1989), and to child maltreatment in particular (Kadman 1992, 2010).

Summarizing, child protection legislation and comprehensive professional knowledge are currently well-established in Israel. However, the system unfortunately still has large gaps between available and desirable child protection services. Foremost is the lack of widespread recognition of the scope and severity of child maltreatment as an urgent social and public-health national concern (e.g., Lev-Wiesel et al. 2016). This lack is due in part to the: (1) intensification of individualistic conceptions and decline in social solidarity (e.g., Boas et al. 2016), (2) public vacillations across the continuum of child safety versus family preservation values (e.g., Fluke et al. 2016), (3) limited public awareness campaigns; and (4) serious ongoing budgetary constraints.

Considering that children represent the country's future, national as well as local authorities need to mobilize increased budgetary and service resources to deal with the demanding challenges facing the child protective system (Ben-Arieh 2010b; Ben-Arieh and Kimhi 2007). Inadequate resources for child protection in Israel have created a dissonance between the existing advanced legislation and the available protective services. Moreover, to date, the outcomes of the Israeli child protective system are not sufficiently monitored to assess their effectiveness. Policy, practice and research professionals, as well as public stakeholders for improving the current child protection system should thereby actively engage in serious dialogues and political lobbying regarding these critical issues.

References

Aarons, G. A., Hurlburt, M., & Horwitz, S. M. (2011). Advancing a conceptual model of evidence-based practice implementation in public service sectors. *Administration and Policy in Mental Health and Mental Health Services Research, 38*(1), 4–23.

Abu-Bader, S. H. (2000). Work satisfaction, burnout, and turnover among social workers in Israel: A causal diagram. *International Journal of Social Welfare, 9*(3), 191–200.

Ajzenstadt, M., & Cavaglion, G. (2004). Sociological perspectives on the origins of the child abuse legislation in Israel. *Israel Law Review, 37*(1), 169–196.

Alfandari, R. (2015). *An evaluation of child protection reform in Israel*. Ph.D. dissertation. London School of Economics.

Alfandari, R. (2016). Partnership with parents in child protection: A systems approach to evaluate reformative developments in Israel. *British Journal of Social Work, 47*(4), 1061–1077.

Alfandari, R. (2017). Evaluation of a national reform in the Israeli child protection practice designed to improve children's participation in decision-making. *Child & Family Social Work, 22*(S2), 54–62.

Almog, O. (2000). *The Sabra: The creation of the new Jew*. Berkeley: University of California Press.

Auslander, G. (2000). Social work research and evaluation in Israel. *Journal of Social Work Research and Evaluation, 1*(1), 17–34.

Azaiza, F., Soffer, M., & Taubman, D. (2015). Social work education in Israel. *Social Sciences, 76*(1), 75–94.

Baistow, K. (2010). Cross-national research: What can we learn from inter-country comparisons? *Social Work in Europe, 7*, 8–13.
Bar-On, A. (2012). *Between specialist and generalist: Case management of individuals and family*. Jerusalem: IMWSS (Hebrew).
Baum, N. (2007). Social work practice in conflict-ridden areas: Cultural sensitivity is not enough. *British Journal of Social Work, 37*(5), 873–891.
Bar, I. (2017). *Out-of-home welfare frameworks for children and youth: Budgeting method and costs estimates*. The Knesset, Research and Information Center, Budget Supervision Department (Hebrew). Retrieved from https://www.fkn.org.il/webfiles/fck/files/123.pdf
Ben Natan, M., Faour, C., Naamhah, S., Grinberg, K., & Klein-Kremer, A. (2012). Factors affecting medical and nursing staff reporting of child abuse. *International Nursing Review, 59*(3), 331–337.
Ben Rabi, D., Dolev, T., Cohen-Navot, M., Amiel, S., Kahan-Strawczynski, P., & Rivkin, D. (2008). *Ashalim celebrates a decade of activity – Accomplishments and future challenges*. Jerusalem: The Myers-JDC-Brookdale Institute.
Ben Rabi, D., Amiel, S., Nijim, F., & Dolev, T. (2009). *Bedouin children in the Negev: Characteristics, needs and patterns of service use*. Jerusalem: The Myers-JDC-Brookdale Institute (Hebrew).
Ben-Arieh, A. (2010a). Localities, social services and child abuse: The role of community characteristics in social services allocation and child abuse reporting. *Children and Youth Services Review, 32*(4), 536–543.
Ben-Arieh, A. (2010b). Public expenditure, locality characteristics and child outcomes. *Children and Youth Services Review, 32*(12), 1778–1786.
Ben-Arieh, A. (2016). *Social workers under attack: What should and could be done*. Meeting Point, 11, 21 (Hebrew). Retrieved from https://user-1723486.cld.bz/nekudat-mifgash-11
Ben-Arieh, A., & Gal, J. (1998). The paradox of child poverty in Israel: Window on the world. *European Journal of Social Work, 1*(3), 347–359.
Ben-Arieh, A., & Kimhi, M. (2007). Children's rights revolution and social services for children. In U. Aviram, J. Gal, & Y. Katan (Eds.), *Formulating social policy in Israel: Trends and issues* (pp. 309–338). Jerusalem: Taub Center for Social Policy Studies in Israel (Hebrew).
Ben-Arieh, A., Khoury-Kassabri, M., & Haj-Yahia, M. M. (2006). Generational, ethnic, and national differences in attitudes toward the rights of children in Israel and Palestine. *American Journal of Orthopsychiatry, 76*(3), 381.
Benbenishty, R., & Chen, W. (2003). Decision making by the child protection team of a medical center. *Health and Social Work, 28*(4), 284–292.
Benbenishty, R., Jedwab, M., Chen, W., Glasser, S., Slutzky, H., Siegal, G., Lavi-Sahar, Z., & Lerner-Geva, L. (2014). Predicting the decisions of hospital based child protection teams to report to child protective services, police and community welfare services. *Child Abuse & Neglect, 38*(1), 11–24.
Benbenishty, R., Davidson-Arad, B., López, M., Devaney, J., Spratt, T., Koopmans, C., Knorth, E. J., Witteman, C. L., Del Valle, J. F., & Hayes, D. (2015). Decision making in child protection: An international comparative study on maltreatment substantiation, risk assessment and interventions recommendations, and the role of professionals' child welfare attitudes. *Child Abuse & Neglect, 49*, 63–75.
Ben-David, V. (2011). Judicial bias in adjudicating the adoption of minors in Israel. *Children and Youth Services Review, 33*(1), 195–203.
Ben-David, V. (2015). Profiles of families at high risk of child maltreatment in Israeli court cases dealing with the termination of parental rights. *Child and Adolescent Social Work Journal, 32*(4), 359–373.
Ben-David, V. (2016). Court considerations in the termination of parental rights: A comprehensive analysis of Israeli court decisions. *Family Court Review, 54*(4), 591–602.
Berkovitz, M. (2007). Aspects of police investigations of child maltreatment. In D. Horowitz, Y. Ben-Yehuda, & M. Hovav (Eds.), *Abuse and neglect of children in Israel: Victims, law enforcement and justice, health, education and welfare* (pp. 209–269). Jerusalem: Ashalim (Hebrew).

Bloomberg Global Health Index. (2017, May 20). Retrieved from https://www.fromthegrapevine.com/health/these-are-2017-healthiest-countries-world#!

Bnai Zion Medical Center. (2017, May 20). *The center for children who are victims of sexual assault* (Hebrew). Retrieved from http://www.b-zion.org.il/pages/907.aspx

Boas, H., Rosenthal, A., & Davidovitch, N. (2016). Between individualism and social solidarity in vaccination policy: The case of the 2013 OPV campaign in Israel. *Israel Journal of Health Policy Research, 5*(1), 64.

Bross, D. C., Krugman, R. D., Lenherr, M. R., Rosenberg, D. A., & Schmitt, B. D. (1988). *The new child protection team handbook*. New York: Garland.

Bross, D. C., Ballo, N., & Korfmacher, J. (2000). Client evaluation of a consultation team on crimes against children. *Child Abuse & Neglect, 24*(1), 71–84.

Buchbinder, E., & Shoob, T. (2013). Essential partnership: Child welfare officers' perceptions of cooperation with Rabbis in the Ultra-Orthodox Jewish community in Israel. *Journal of Social Service Research, 39*(2), 204–217.

Budd, K. S. (2005). Assessing parenting capacity in a child welfare context. *Children and Youth Services Review, 27*(4), 429–444.

Central Bureau of Statistics (CBS). (2017a). *Central Bureau of Statistics, population of Israel* (Hebrew). Retreived from http://www.cbs.gov.il/reader/?MIval=cw_usr_view_SHTML&ID=629

Central Bureau of Statistics (CBS). (2017b). *Central Bureau of Statistics, Children, selected Data for the International Child Day, 2016* (Hebrew). Retreived from http://www.cbs.gov.il/reader/newhodaot/hodaa_template.html?hodaa=201611345

Chiesa, A., & Bross, D. (2014). *Child protection teams. Chadwick's child maltreatment*. St Louis: STM Learning.

Cohen, S. (2005). *A house with a window: Advocacy centers for children and their families*. Jerusalem: The Ministery of Social Affairs and Social Services, the Schusterman Family Foundation and Ashalim (Hebrew).

Dagan, S. W., Ben-Porat, A., & Itzhaky, H. (2016). Child protection workers dealing with child abuse: The contribution of personal, social and organizational resources to secondary traumatization. *Child Abuse & Neglect, 51*, 203–211.

David, P., & Schiff, M. (2015). Learning from bottom-up dissemination: Importing an evidence-based trauma intervention for infants and young children to Israel. *Evaluation and Program Planning, 53*, 18–24.

Davidov, J., Sigad, L. I., Lev-Wiesel, R., & Eisikovits, Z. (2017). Cross-disciplinary craftsmanship: The case of child abuse work. *Qualitative Social Work, 16*(5), 717–733.

Davidson-Arad, B., & Benbenishty, R. (2008). The role of workers' attitudes and parent and child wishes in child protection workers' assessments and recommendations regarding removal and reunification. *Children and Youth Services Review, 30*(1), 107–121.

Davidson-Arad, B., & Benbenishty, R. (2010). Contribution of child protection workers' attitudes to their risk assessments and intervention recommendations: A study in Israel. *Health & Social Care in the Community, 18*(1), 1–9.

Davidson-Arad, B., & Benbenishty, R. (2016). Child welfare attitudes, risk assessments and intervention recommendations: The role of professional expertise. *British Journal of Social Work, 46*(1), 186–203.

Dinisman, T., Zeira, A., Sulimani-Aidan, Y., & Benbenishty, R. (2013). The subjective well-being of young people aging out of care. *Children and Youth Services Review, 35*(10), 1705–1711.

Dolev, T., Benbenishty, R., & Timar, A. (2001). *Decision committees in Israel: Their organization, work processes, and outcomes: A summary report*. Jerusalem: Myers-JDC-Israel (Hebrew).

Dolev, T., Szabo-Lael, R., & Ben-Rabi, D. (2007). *Community 2000 experiment: Interim report*. Jerusalem: The Myers-JDC-Brookdale Institute (Hebrew).

Dolev, T., Szabo-Lael, R., & Ben-Rabi, D. (2008a). *Child protection officers: Roles, work methods, and challenges*. Jerusalem: The Myers-JDC-Brookdale Institute (Hebrew).

Dolev, T., Szabo-Lael, R., Schmid, H., & Bar-Nir, D. (2008b). *Policy of 'Facing the Community': Research and evaluation*. Jerusalem: The Myers-JDC-Brookdale Institute (Hebrew).
Dolev, T., Ben Rabi, D., & Zemach-Marom, T. (2009). Residential care for children 'At Risk' in Israel – Current situation and future challenges. In M. E. Courtney & D. Iwaniec (Eds.), *Residential care of children – Comparative perspectives* (pp. 72–88). London: Oxford University Press.
Doron, I. (2012). Social workers and the law in Israel. In M. Hovav, E. Lawental, & J. Katan, (Eds.), *Social work in Israel*. Raanana: Hakibbutz Hameuchad (Hebrew).
Doron, I., Rosner, Y., & Karpel, M. (2008). Law, social work and professionalism: Israeli social workers' attitudes towards the 1996 Social Workers Act. *Journal of Social Welfare & Family Law, 30*(1), 3–16.
English, D., Thompson, R., White, C. R., & Wilson, D. (2015). Why should child welfare pay more attention to emotional maltreatment? *Children and Youth Services Review, 50*, 53–63.
Enosh, G., & Bayer-Topilsky, T. (2014). Reasoning and bias: Heuristics in safety assessment and placement decisions for children at risk. *British Journal of Social Work, 45*, 1771–1787 bct213.
Enosh, G., Nouman, H., & Sharon, O. (2016). Between professionalism and traditional social norms: Social workers' parental custody recommendations. *British Journal of Social Work, 47*(7), 2032–2048.
Faber, M. (2009) *Child Abuse: Acknowledging the phenomenon, legislative progress and development of treatment and protection*. Jerusalem: The Haruv Institute (Hebrew).
Faber, M. & Slotsky, H. (2007). Between protection and treatment of at risk minors: The role of child protective service workers. In D. Horowitz, Y. Ben-Yehuda, M. Hovav (Eds.), *Abuse and neglect of children in Israel: Victims, law enforcement and justice, health, education and welfare* (pp. 951–994). Jerusalem: Ashalim (Hebrew).
Fluke, J. D., Corwin, T. W., Hollinshead, D. M., & Maher, E. J. (2016). Family preservation or child safety? Associations between child welfare workers' experience, position, and perspectives. *Children and Youth Services Review, 69*, 210–218.
Freed, B., Figelson, F., & Slotzky, H. (2010). *Emergency centers: Information on emergency centers for professionals*. Jerusalem: The Haruv Institute and Ashalim (Hebrew).
Fryer, G. E., Poland, J. E., Bross, D. C., & Krugman, R. D. (1988). The child protective service worker: A profile of needs, attitudes, and utilization of professional resources. *Child Abuse & Neglect, 12*(4), 481–490.
Fugatz, D. (2007). Minor victims of crime in the mirror of the law: Trends in legislation and law. In D. Horowitz, Y. Ben-Yehuda, M. Hovav (Eds.), *Abuse and neglect of children in Israel: Victims, law enforcement and justice, health, education and welfare* (pp. 99–151). Jerusalem: Ashalim (Hebrew).
Gal, T. (2015, May 20). *Restorative child protection*. Retrieved from https://ssrn.com/abstract=2694399 or https://doi.org/10.2139/ssrn.2694399
Gal, T., & Schilli-Jerichower, D. (2017). Mainstreaming therapeutic jurisprudence in family law: The Israeli child protection law as a case study. *Family Court Review, 55*(2), 177–194.
Gal, J., & Weiss-Gal, I. (2011). Social policy formulation and the role of professionals: The involvement of social workers in parliamentary committees in Israel. *Health & Social Care in the Community, 19*(2), 158–167.
Gilbert, N., Parton, N., & Skivenes, M. (2011). *Child protection systems: International trends and orientations*. New York: Oxford University Press.
Gold, N., Benbenishty, R., & Osmo, R. (2001). A comparative study of risk assessments and recommended interventions in Canada and Israel. *Child Abuse & Neglect, 25*(5), 607–622.
Goldstein, S. & Laor, R. (2007). Intercultural aspects of the obligation to report and locate children who are victims of abuse and neglect. In D. Horowitz, Y. Ben-Yehuda, M. Hovav (Eds.), *Abuse and neglect of children in Israel: Victims, law enforcement and justice, health, education and welfare* (pp. 858–888). Jerusalem: Ashalim (Hebrew).
Gorbatov, R., & Ben-Simhon, M. (2011). Children and young people in the social services. In Y. Sabah (Ed.), (2010). *The social services review*. Jerusalem: IMWSS, Research Planning and Qualification Division (Hebrew).

Gottfried, R., (2017). Working with trauma: Compassion fatigue and compassion satisfaction among child protection social workers. *Meeting Point, 12*, 27–29 (Hebrew).

Harel-Fisch, Y., Abdeen, Z., & Navot, M. (2016). Growing up in the Middle East: The daily lives and well-being of Israeli and Palestinian youth. *Pediatrics, Child and Adolescent Health*. New-York: Nova Science Publishers, Inc.

Hershkowitz, I., Lamb, M. E., & Horowitz, D. (2007). Victimization of children with disabilities. *American Journal of Orthopsychiatry, 77*(4), 629.

Hovav, M. (2007). Preface to the law, justice and enforcement section. In D. Horowitz, Y. Ben-Yehuda, & M. Hovav (Eds.), *Abuse and neglect of children in Israel: Victims, law enforcement and justice, health, education and welfare*. Jerusalem: Ashalim (Hebrew).

Israel Ministry of Justice; IMJ. (2003). *Minister of Justice's commission on fundamental issues concerning children and law and their implementation in legislation.* Chairperson: Rotlevi, S. Jerusalem: Israel Ministry of Justice (Hebrew).

Israel Ministry of Labor and Welfare; IMLW. (1995). *The social workers ordinance no. 8.9.* Jerusalem: Israel Ministry of Labor and Welfare (Hebrew).

Israel Ministry of Labor and Welfare; IMLW. (2002). *Minister of Labor and Welfare's commission on decision committees' authorities and working procedures with child protection workers*, Chairperson: Gilat, I.Z. Jerusalem: Israel Ministry of Labor and Welfare (Hebrew).

Israel Ministry of Welfare and Social Services; IMWSS. (2004a). *Planning, intervention, and evaluation committee: Final principles paper*. Jerusalem: Israel Ministry of Welfare and Social Services (Hebrew).

Israel Ministry of Welfare and Social Services; IMWSS. (2004b). *Planning, intervention, and evaluation committee: The implementation team's decisions*. Jerusalem (Hebrew): Israel Ministry of Welfare and Social Services.

Israel Ministry of Labor, Social Affairs and Social Services; IMLSASS. (2017a, May 20). *The Ministry's budget*. Jerusalem: Israel Ministry of Labor, Social Affairs and Social Services (Hebrew). Retreived from http://www.molsa.gov.il/About/BudgetAndDonations/Pages/local-budget.aspx

Israel Ministry of Labor, Social Affairs and Social Services; IMLSASS. (2017b, May 20). *Children and youth at risk*. Jerusalem: Israel Ministry of Labor, Social Affairs and Social Services (Hebrew). Retreived from http://www.molsa.gov.il/Populations/Youth/ChildrenAtRisk/Pages/MT01_01.aspx

Israel Ministry of Labor, Social Affairs and Social Services; IMLSASS. (2017c, May 20). *Children and youth in danger and emergency* situations. Jerusalem: Israel Ministry of Labor, Social Affairs and Social Services (Hebrew). Retreived from http://www.molsa.gov.il/Populations/Youth/ChildrenAtRisk/CommunityAssistance/YouthInDanger/Pages/MT_01_03.aspx

Israel Ministry of Labor, Social Affairs and Social Services; IMLSASS. (2017d, May 20). *The 360 degrees – national program for children and youth at risk*. Jerusalem: Israel Ministry of Labor, Social Affairs and Social Services (Hebrew). Retreived from http://www.molsa.gov.il/ProjectShmid/Pages/ProjectHome.aspx

Israel Ministry of Labor, Social Affairs and Social Services; IMLSASS. (2017e, May 20). *Families in need*. Jerusalem: Israel Ministry of Labor, Social Affairs and Social Services (Hebrew). Retreived from http://www.molsa.gov.il/Populations/Distress/DistressFamily/Pages/DistressFamily2.aspx

Israel Ministry of Welfare and Social Affairs; IMWSS. (2008). *Planning, Intervention, and Evaluation Committees tools package user guide*. Jerusalem: Israel Ministry of Welfare and Social Services (Hebrew).

Israel Ministry of Welfare and Social Services; IMWSS. (2009). *Planning, Intervention, and Evaluation Committees tools package*. Jerusalem: Israel Ministry of Welfare and Social Affairs (Hebrew).

Israel Ministry of Welfare and Social Services; IMWSS. (2010). *The commission on the reform in the local social services*, Chairperson: Sabah, Y. Jerusalem: Israel Ministry of Welfare and Social Services, Research, Planning and Qualification Division (Hebrew).

Israel Ministry of Welfare and Social Services; IMWSS. (2014a). *The commission to examine the ministry's policy in relations to children's removal to out-of-home placement and custody arrangements*, Chairperson: Silman, Y. Jerusalem: Israel Ministry of Welfare and Social Affairs (Hebrew).

Israel Ministry of Welfare and Social Services; IMWSS. (2014b). *Social services in local authorities*. Jerusalem: Israel Ministry of Welfare and Social Services (Hebrew). Retreived from http://www.molsa.gov.il/Units/SocialDepartments/Documents/20%הרווחה20%שירותי20%תדריך למנהל20%אוגדן.pdf

Israel Ministry of Welfare and Social Services; IMWSS. (2014c). *Functioning and working methods of social workers to court proceedings*. Jerusalem: Israel Ministry of Welfare Social Services (Hebrew).

Israel National Council for the Child; INCC. (2016). *The state of the child in Israel: 2016 statistical yearbook*. Jerusalem: Israel National Council for the Child (Hebrew).

Itzick, M., & Kagan, M. (2017). Intention to leave the profession: Welfare social workers compared to health care and community social workers in Israel. *Journal of Social Service Research, 43*(3), 346–357.

JDC-Ashalim. (2016). Introduction to the journal on children, youth and young people at risk and their families. Ashalim Knowledge and Learning Center, *The Field Pen*, Vol. 17, II (Hebrew).

Jones, L., Bellis, M. A., Wood, S., Hughes, K., McCoy, E., Eckley, L., et al. (2012). Prevalence and risk of violence against children with disabilities: A systematic review and meta-analysis of observational studies. *The Lancet, 380*(9845), 899–907.

Kadman, Y. (1992). The law preventing maltreatment of minors and helpless persons: A turning point in Israeli society in relation to child abuse. *Social Security, 38*, 137–146 (Hebrew).

Kadman, Y. (2010). In her death her legacy to children was life: Mandatory reporting of offenses perpetrated against children: Background, review and importance. *Family and Law, 3–4*, 337–346 (Hebrew). Retrieved from http://www.mishpat.ac.il/files/650/2867/2895/2896.pdf

Kagan, M. (2016). Public attitudes and knowledge about social workers in Israel. *Journal of Social Work, 16*(3), 322–343.

Kashty, I., Gruper, E. N., & Shlasky, S. (2008). *Residential care towards the next century: Planning and developing educational facilities* (Committee report). Tel-Aviv: Ministry of Education (Hebrew).

Kilkelly, U., & Donnelly, M. (2011). Participation in health care: The views and experiences of children and young people. *The International Journal of Children's Rights, 19*, 107–125.

Korbin, J. E., & Spilsbury, J. (1999). Cultural competence and child neglect. In H. Dubowitz (Ed.), *Neglected children: Research, practice and policy* (pp. 69–88). Newbury Park: Sage Publications.

Kosher, H., Ben-Arieh, A., & Hendelsman, Y. (2016). Social work and children's rights: Implications for practice. In *Children's rights and social work* (pp. 29–44). New York: Springer International Publishing.

Krugman, R. D. (1996). The media and public awareness of child abuse and neglect: It's time for a change. *Child Abuse & Neglect, 20*(4), 259–260.

Levin, L., Gewirtz, S., & Cribb, A. (2016). Shared decision making in Israeli social services: Social workers' perspectives on policy making and implementation. *British Journal of Social Work, 47*, bcw024.

Levin-Iger, R. & Levi, H. (2007). Sexual abuse victim report. In D. Horowitz, Y. Ben-Yehuda, M. Hovav (Eds.), *Abuse and neglect of children in Israel: Victims, law enforcement and justice, health, education and welfare* (pp. 365–376). Jerusalem: Ashalim (Hebrew).

Lev-Wiesel, R., Eisikovits, Z., First, M., Gottfried, R., & Mehlhausen, D. (2016). Prevalence of child maltreatment in Israel: A national epidemiological study. *Journal of Child & Adolescent Trauma, 11*(2), 141–150.

Makaros, A., & Weiss-Gal, I. (2014). Comparison of the social and professional ideology of caseworkers and community social workers in Israel. *British Journal of Social Work, 44*(1), 100–116.

McCafferty, P. (2017). Implementing Article 12 of the United Nations convention on the rights of the child in child protection decision-making: A critical analysis of the challenges and opportunities for social work. *Child Care in Practice, 23*(4), 327–341.

Nachmani-Rot, D. (2010). The conditions by which child protective officers receive exemption from reporting offences committed towards children to the police. *Family Law, 3–4*, 379–399 (Hebrew).

Nadan, Y. (2016). Child protection in multicultural context. In B. Schwarzer, U. Kämmerer-Rütten, A. Schleyer-Lindenmann, & Y. Wang (Eds.), *Transnational social work and social welfare: Challenges for the social work profession* (pp. 181–185). New York: Routledge.

Nadan, Y., Spilsbury, J. C., & Korbin, J. E. (2015). Culture and context in understanding child maltreatment: Contributions of intersectionality and neighborhood-based research. *Child Abuse & Neglect, 41*, 40–48.

Ofek, A. (2009). *Preparations for the reform in Social Services Departments*. Jerusalem: Israel Ministry of Welfare and Social Services, Research Planning and Qualification Division (Hebrew).

Oppenheim-Weller, S., Schwartz, E., & Ben-Arieh, A. (2017). Child involvement in treatment planning and assessment in Israel. *Child & Family Social Work, 22*(3), 1302–1312.

Osmo, R., & Benbenishty, R. (2004). Children at risk: Rationales for risk assessments and interventions. *Children and Youth Services Review, 26*, 1155–1173.

Pelton, L. H. (2015). The continuing role of material factors in child maltreatment and placement. *Child Abuse & Neglect, 41*, 30–39.

Prime Minister's Commission. (1973). *Report of the Prime Minister's Committee on Children and Youth in Distress*. Jerusalem (Hebrew).

Raz, T. (2010). Children deprived of their childhood: Child welfare in the Jewish community during the British Mandate. *Society & Welfare, 3–4*, 377–395 (Hebrew). Retrieved from http://www.molsa.gov.il/CommunityInfo/Magazine/Lists/ArticlesList/Attachments/398/30-3-4-RAZ.T.pdf

Rosen, B., Waitzberg, R., & Merkur, S. (2015). *Israel: Health system review*. Health systems in transition, 17 (6). World Health Organization, on behalf of the European Observatory on Health Systems and Policies, Copenhagen, Denmark.

Rosenfeld, J., & Kedem, A. (1999). Betwixt and between the 'Generation of the Desert' and the 'Children of the Dream: Fifty years of social work in child welfare in Israel. In F. Loewenberg (Ed.), *Meeting the challenges of a changing society: Fifty years of social work in Israel*. Jerusalem: Magnes Press (Hebrew).

Saltzman, L. Y., Solomyak, L., & Pat-Horenczyk, R. (2017). Addressing the needs of children and youth in the context of war and terrorism: The technological frontier. *Current Psychiatry Reports, 19*(6), 30.

Schmid, H. (2007). Children and youth at risk in Israel: Findings and recommendations to improve their well-being. *Children and Youth Services Review, 29*(8), 1114–1128.

Schmid, H., & Benbenishty, R. (2011). Public attitudes toward child maltreatment in Israel: Implications for policy. *Children and Youth Service Review, 33*, 1134–1141.

Schmid, H., Dolev, T., Szabo-Lael, R., & Bar-Nir, D. (2008). *Towards the Community policy: Evaluation study*. Jerusalem: The Myers-JDC-Brookdale Institute (Hebrew).

Schwartz, S. (2014). A survey of arts and health programmes in Israel. *Journal of Applied Arts & Health, 4*(3), 265–279.

Shapira, T. (2010). Mandatory reporting of offenses against minors and defenseless persons and the empowerment of the welfare officer: A retrospective view. *Family Law, 3*(4), p. 317–333 (Hebrew).

Shapiro, D. (1997). Pioneering community work in a Jewish ultra-orthodox community in Jerusalem. In H. Campfens (Ed.), *Community development around the world: Practice, theory, research, training* (pp. 231–242). Toronto: University of Toronto Press.

Shefi-psychological counseling service. (2017, May 20). *Jerusalem: Israel Ministry of Education* (Hebrew). Retrieved from http://cms.education.gov.il/educationcms/units/shefi/pirusmim/catalog/

Shmueli, B. (2010). Mandatory reporting violence against children: A comparison between Jewish and Israeli law. *Family Law, 3–4*, 279–301 (Hebrew).

Shnit, D. (1998). The law and social work practice in Israel. In F. Loewenberg (Ed.), *Meeting the challenges of a changing society: Fifty years of social work in Israel*. Jerusalem: Magnes Press.

Sikron-Vazan, L., & Ben-Rabi, D. (2016). *Research report: Early childhood centers, inter-ministerial model developed by 360 degrees – The national program for children and youth at risk – Evaluation study*. Jerusalem: Myers-JDC-Brookdale Institute, Engelberg Center for Children and Youth.

Sorek, Y., Szabo-Lael, R., & Ben-Simon, B. (2014). Foster care services in Israel: Changing process and a current status. Jerusalem: Myers-JDCBrookdale (Hebrew).

Spiro, S. E. (2001). Social work education in Israel: Trends and issues. *Social Work Education, 20*(1), 89–99.

Spiro, S. E., Sherer, M., Korin-Langer, N., & Weiss, I. (1998). The professionalization of Israeli social work. In F. M. Loewenberg (Ed.), *Meeting the challenges of a changing society: Fifty years of social work in Israel* (pp. 29–50). Jerusalem: Magnes Press.

Stafford, A., Vincent, S., Parton, N., & Smith, C. (2011). *Child protection systems in the United Kingdom: A comparative analysis*. London: Jessica Kingsley Publishers.

Stalker, K., & McArthur, K. (2012). Child abuse, child protection and disabled children: A review of recent research. *Child Abuse Review, 21*(1), 24–40.

State of Israel. (2006). *National commission on children and youth in distress: Final report*, Chairperson: Schmid, H. Jerusalem: State of Israel (Hebrew).

State of Israel. (2010). *Identification of minors at risk and the formation of safety network in the community: The inter-ministry commission report*, Chairperson: Vinter, M. Jerusalem: Israel Ministry of Social Services and Social affairs, Ministry of Health, Ministry of Education, Ministry of Industry, Trade and Labor, Ministry of Public Security and Ministry of Aliyah and Immigrant Absorption (Hebrew).

Sulimani-Aidan, Y., & Benbenishty, R. (2011). Future expectations of adolescents in residential care in Israel. *Children and Youth Services Review, 33*(7), 1134–1141.

Sulimani-Aidan, Y., & Benbenishty, R. (2013). Child maltreatment reports in Israel: The intersection between community socioeconomic characteristics and ethnicity. *American Journal of Orthopsychiatry, 83*(1), 29–36.

Szabo-Lael, R., & Zadka, H. (2015). *360 degrees – The national program for children and youth at risk: The needs of the participants and the services received*. Jerusalem: Myers-JDC-Brookdale Institute Engelberg Center for Children and Youth.

Tasher, D., Rubin, L., Grossman, Z., Grotto, I., Dahan, D., Berlowitz, Y., & Somekh, E. (2016). Child health care in Israel. *The Journal of Pediatrics, 177*, S107–S115.

Taylor, J., Stalker, K., & Stewart, A. (2016). Disabled children and the child protection system: A cause for concern. *Child Abuse Review, 25*(1), 60–73.

Tzimerman, S., Ritbo, B., Pesach, N., & Karni, M. (2010). To report or not report – That is the question: A panel discussion focusing on mandatory reporting in various public systems and among the general public. *Family Law, 3–4*, 279–301 (Hebrew).

Tzimrin, H. (1983). Building up a new service for the abused child. *Child Abuse & Neglect, 7*(1), 55–60.

Tzimrin, H. (2007). A generation of action – The contribution of ELI: The society for the protection of the child for the development of services for risk in Israel. In D. Horowitz, Y. Ben Yehuda, & M. Hovav (Ed.), *Abuse and neglect of children in Israel: Victims, law enforcement and justice, health, education and welfare* (pp. 1007–1035). Jerusalem: Ashalim (Hebrew).

United Nations. (1989). *Convention on the rights of the child*. Geneva: Office of the High Commissioner of Human Rights.

United Nations Children's Fund; UNICEF. (2016). *Fairness for children: A league table of inequality in child well-being in rich countries*. Innocenti Report Card 13, UNICEF Office of Research – Innocenti, Florence.

Vismonsky, H. (2016). Dealing with offensive online posts published against public servants. *Meeting Point Magazine*, 11, 6–11 (Hebrew). Retrieved from https://user-1723486.cld.bz/nekudat-mifgash-11

Wahle, N., Ponizovsky-Bergelson, Y., Dayan, Y., Erlichman, O., & Roer-Strier, D. (2017). On the margins of racism, immigration and war: Perspectives on risk and protection of young children of Ethiopian origin in Israel. *European Early Childhood Education Research Journal, 25*(2), 305–320.

Weiss, I., Gal, J., & Dixon, J. (Eds.). (2003). *Professional ideologies and preferences in social work: A global study* (pp. 141–155). Westport: Greenwood Publishing Group.

Weiss, I., Spiro, S., Sherer, M., & Korin-Langer, N. (2004). Social work in Israel: Professional characteristics in an international comparative perspective. *International Journal of Social Welfare, 13*(4), 287–296.

Zeira, A. (2004). New initiatives in out-of-home placements in Israel. *Child & Family Social Work, 9*(3), 305–307.

Zeira, A. (2014). Training social workers to understand and use evidence. *From evidence to outcomes in child welfare: An international reader*, 161–170.

Ruth Gottfried is a lecturer at the David Yellin Academic College of Education in Jerusalem; and is an affiliated researcher at the Haruv Institute of the Hebrew University in Jerusalem and the Emili Sagol Creative Arts Therapies Research Center (CATRC) of the University of Haifa. Following her M.A. and Ph.D. studies at the University of Haifa's Graduate School of Creative Arts Therapies, Dr. Gottfried completed two post-doctoral appointments at the Schools of Social Work of Tel Aviv and Georgia State Universities, the latter as a Haruv Institute postdoctoral research fellow. In parallel with her doctoral studies (2011–2014), Dr. Gottfried served at the University of Haifa as researcher and research coordinator for an Israeli national epidemiological study focusing on the prevalence and disclosure factors of child maltreatment in Israel. Her research focuses primarily on child maltreatment and on professional quality of life among a wide range of professionals, including those working with maltreated children and youth. Dr. Gottfried lives in Tel-Aviv and is married with two children.

Asher Ben-Arieh is a professor of social work, the director of the Haruv Institute in Jerusalem and the Haruv Chair for the study of child maltreatment at the Paul Baerwald School of Social Work and Social Welfare at the Hebrew University in Jerusalem. Prof. Ben-Arieh served for 20 years as the associate director of Israel's National Council for the Child and was the founding editor-in-chief, between the years 1990–2011, of the annual "State of the Child in Israel". Prof. Ben-Arieh is one of the leading international experts on social indicators, particularly as they relate to child well-being. He initiated and coordinated the international project "Measuring and Monitoring Children's Well-Being", was among the founding members of the International Society for Children Indicators (ISCI) and was elected to be its first co-chair. Prof. Ben-Arieh is also the founding editor-in-chief of the Child Indicators Research journal (CIR) and the Child Well Being: Indicators and Research book series. He has published extensively on children's policy, child welfare and indicators of children's well being. Currently, Prof. Ben-Arieh is one of the PI's of the multi-national, multi-million International Study of Children's Well-being (ISCWeB) research project. Prof. Ben-Arieh lives in Jerusalem and is married with three children.

Chapter 9
The Dutch Child Protection System: Historical Overview and Recent Transformations

Mónica López López, Helen Bouma, Erik J. Knorth, and Hans Grietens

9.1 Introduction

Child maltreatment is recognized as a serious concern for children in Dutch society. An important step in this recognition has been the estimation of its magnitude through prevalence studies. The first national prevalence study on maltreatment of children and youth in the Netherlands (NPM-2005) was conducted in 2005, as a replication of the National Incidence Study (NIS-3) in the United States. The prevalence of child abuse and neglect was investigated based on cases reported to the *Advice and Reporting Centre on Child Maltreatment* (in Dutch: Advies-en Meldpunt Kindermishandeling; AMK from now on) and the reports of sentinels or professional informants (Euser et al. 2010). The prevalence rate of child maltreatment in 2005, as reported by sentinels, was estimated at 30 cases per 1.000 children. Remarkably, only 12.6% of these cases had reached the AMKs. Furthermore, the results of the NPM-2005 were compared with a Dutch self-report study with 1845 adolescents. In the previous 12 months, 20% of adolescents had experienced a form of child maltreatment (Lamers-Winkelman et al. 2007). The prevalence of child maltreatment turned out to be six times higher based on the self-report study than on the reports of sentinels and AMKs (Euser et al. 2010).

In 2010, the second National Prevalence Study on Maltreatment of children and youth (NPM-2010) was conducted using three methods: sentinel reports, cases reported to the AMKs and a self-report study. The overall prevalence was revealed to be relatively stable across this five-year period; the NPM-2010 showed a prevalence rate of 33.8 children per 1000. In this study, the prevalence rates based on self-report were five times higher than the prevalence rates based on sentinel reports and reports to the AMKs (Euser et al. 2013).

M. L. López (✉) · H. Bouma · E. J. Knorth · H. Grietens
University of Groningen, Groningen, The Netherlands
e-mail: M.Lopez.Lopez@rug.nl; Helen.Bouma@rug.nl; E.J.Knorth@rug.nl; H.Grietens@rug.nl

L. Merkel-Holguin et al. (eds.), *National Systems of Child Protection*, Child Maltreatment 8, https://doi.org/10.1007/978-3-319-93348-1_9

In almost half of the cases of the NPM-studies, children experienced more than one type of child maltreatment (Euser et al. 2010, 2013). The most prevalent type of child maltreatment in 2005 was neglect (56% of the cases); sexual abuse had the lowest rate (4%; Euser et al. 2010). In 2010, the highest rates of child maltreatment concerned physical neglect (37% reported by sentinels, 10% of the cases reported to the AMKs) and emotional/educational neglect (72% reported by the sentinels, 52% of the cases reported to the AMKs). Child sexual abuse was reported the lowest by sentinels as well as to child protection services (3%; Euser et al. 2013).

Although the prevalence rate based on sentinel reports and self-report remained relatively stable between 2015 and 2010, a large increase in AMK reports was found. The number of victims reported to AMKs increased by 67% in this 5-year period. This result suggests that professionals have become more aware of child maltreatment and more likely report cases. The policy issues and social events behind this shift and other key transformations in the history of the child protection system of the Netherlands are examined in this chapter.

This chapter draws on the policy analysis developed for the research project Hestia funded by Norface Welfare State Futures. HESTIA compares policies and responses to child abuse and neglect in England, Germany and the Netherlands. The chapter begins with an historical overview of the policies and events which have shaped the current child protection system. Next, we describe in detail the present Youth Act 2015 and the scope and organisation of the child protection system. In the final section, we formulate a conclusion and outline some challenges for the future of Dutch child protection policy and practice.

9.2 Development of the Dutch Policy Framework

The Dutch child protection system has transformed over the years as a result of the development of laws, signifying the change of values regarding child-rearing, and rights and responsibilities of parents. Dutch child protection policy has been influenced by international laws, including the United Nations Convention on the Rights of the Child (UNCRC) and the European Convention on Human Rights (ECHR). Since 2015, the Youth Act forms the current legal and policy framework of the Dutch youth care system, including the child protection provisions. Below we offer a brief overview of the historical development of the Dutch child protection policy, starting in 1899.

9.2.1 First Steps Towards a Child Protection System (1899–1960)

In the Netherlands, the twentieth century was marked as the century of the child; every child had the right of an unconcerned childhood, good child rearing, affection and education (Dekker 2018; Van der Bij et al. 2006). In 1899, the Dutch Federation of Child Protection was established in order to coordinate youth agencies (Baartman 2005; Jeugdzorg Nederland 2013).

In the early 1900s, the first Children's Acts were passed, which gave a new view on parenting; child-rearing became an obligation and a responsibility, and the government was entitled to intervene in child-rearing when parents did not meet their responsibilities. The first step towards this new understanding of parenting was the Act on Compulsory Education, which took effect in 1901. The new responsibilities of the Dutch government regarding child protection were established in the Children's Acts, which took effect on 1 December 1905 (Jeugdzorg Nederland 2013).

The aim of this new judicial framework was twofold: to protect children when their wellbeing and development was threatened, as well as to protect society against the risk of children becoming criminals (Baartman 2005). Therefore, this framework included three parts: the Civil Child Act regarding the parental authority and the possible guardianship; the Criminal Child Act concerning the punishment of children who committed a crime; and the Child Principles Act, which included the establishment of agencies to implement the first two acts (Jeugdzorg Nederland 2013; Van der Bij et al. 2006).

Within this new legislation, the government was enabled to take over parental authority and intervene in private family life. The government could overrule parental authority using two different measures: *ontheffing* or *ontzetting* from parental authority. *Ontzetting* was seen as the most severe measure, as it was based on a finding of culpable behaviour by the parents, such as abusing children. *Ontheffing* was based on the incapacity of parents. For an *ontheffing* as well as for an *ontzetting*, a guardian was appointed and the child could be placed in a residential care facility or a foster family. Parents could get their parental authority back when the grounds on which the measure was based no longer applied. Besides these two measures to overrule parental authority, a more temporary measure became available: the suspension of the execution of parental authority (Delfos and Doek 1982).

Together with the Children's Acts, the Guardianship Board (in Dutch: Voogdijraad) was established with the function of investigating potential child maltreatment cases reported by citizens and advising the court about child protection decisions. The Guardianship Board constituted a link between the Ministry of Justice and the private, segregated institutions, which executed the guardianship in cases of a child protection measure (Delfos and Doek 1982; Raad voor de Kinderbescherming n.d.; Van der Bij et al. 2006).

The Dutch child protection system was compartmentalised in Catholic and Protestant institutions, in which the guardians worked mainly on a voluntary basis, supported by a few paid workers (Delfos and Doek 1983; Raad voor de Kinderbescherming n.d.). Although the child protection system was mainly financed by the Dutch government since the validation of the Children's Acts, coordination and control by the government was limited; child protection was operated by the institutions, and the placements of children were not only decided on the basis of their problems, but also on the basis of religious grounds (Dekker et al. 2012).

In addition to the possibility of overruling parental authority, the *supervision order* was developed in 1922 for less severe cases. In those cases, the parents' authority was restricted and partly taken over by a family guardian. Children could stay with their parents or be placed in care (Dekker et al. 2012). With the legislation of this new child protection measure, the juvenile court was established to enforce and execute these supervision orders, as well as other child protection measures (Delfos and Doek 1982).

During the Second World War, the Guardianship Board became disorganised and its image became tarnished. All the Jewish judges and workers of the Board were discharged, as well as those workers who did not meet the political ideas of national-socialism (Van der Bij et al. 2006). After the Second World War, several changes were introduced due to changing views on child-rearing. The Children's Acts were revised, quality requirements for agencies executing supervision orders were formulated, and the rights of parents were emphasized in policy. Furthermore, the Foster Children's Act was enacted in 1953, and the rights of biological parents were introduced (Van der Bij et al. 2006). The structure of the Guardianship Board was transformed into the current *Child Care and Protection Board* (in Dutch: Raad voor de Kinderbescherming, RvdK) in 1956, introducing a shift to professionalization and relying more on paid workers and less on volunteers (Van der Bij et al. 2006).

Besides these policy advances, hardly any attention had been paid to the issue of child maltreatment until the 1960s. Dutch society was aware that physical abuse was occurring, but this was often seen as a crime by parents who were unable to raise their children due to living in an 'asocial class'. They were punished by Criminal Law and came under the attention of the *Child Care and Protection Board* to prevent criminal behaviour of children (Jeugdzorg Nederland 2013). Neglect and criminal behaviour were seen as two sides of the same coin (Baartman 2005), and the emphasis was put on the child as a perpetrator instead of the child as a victim (Dekker et al. 2012; Jeugdzorg Nederland 2013). A neglected child was a future criminal, and society had to be protected from these children (Jeugdzorg Nederland 2013).

9.2.2 Increasing Attention to Child Abuse and System De-compartmentalisation (1960–1990)

During the 1960s, physical child abuse became more prominent and the attention to child maltreatment increased in the Netherlands due to international and national influences. The article *The Battered Child Syndrome* by the American pediatrician Henry Kempe on physical abuse of very young children led to increased attention to child maltreatment in the Netherlands (Doek 2013; Jeugdzorg Nederland 2013). However, this attention focused on young children who were suffering serious injuries harmed by their parents or caregivers and the subject 'neglect' was left behind (Jeugdzorg Nederland 2013).

Furthermore, the first figures on child maltreatment in the Netherlands were published in 1967. The number of children's deaths due to child maltreatment in the Netherlands was estimated at 120 children per year based on newspapers. The number of hospitalised children due to child maltreatment was 1200, and the total figure for child maltreatment was estimated at 12,000 children in that same year. These estimations stimulated the advance of research on prevalence (Doek 2013; Jeugdzorg Nederland 2013).

In 1969, the Dutch government established a research committee to develop a strategy to combat child maltreatment (Jeugdzorg Nederland 2013). As a result, in 1970 the Association against Child Maltreatment was established and in 1972 four pediatricians started working at the Agency Confidential Doctors (in Dutch: Bureau Vertrouwens Arts; BVA) (Jeugdzorg Nederland 2013). Doctors and other persons could report to this agency their concerns about the safety of children. In the first year, the confidential doctors received 432 reports (Jeugdzorg Nederland 2013).

During the mid-1960s, the compartmentalised system started to change due to the empowerment revolution and the de-compartmentalisation movement (Dekker et al. 2012). The 'empowerment revolution' led to certain criticism of forced child protection measures. The main principle was that family support had to be voluntary and without breaking the ties between parents and children. This led to a decrease in involuntary child protection measures (overruling parental authority and the supervision order), and a decline in the number of out-of-home placements (Dekker et al. 2012; Van der Bij et al. 2006). When an out-of-home placement was necessary, family foster care was preferred above residential care, which led to the closing of many institutions during the 1970s.

In addition, the understanding of the causes of child maltreatment changed in the 1970s towards a view on maltreating families as parents facing difficulties in raising their children due to psychological or psychiatric problems or to behavioural problems of children. Children who were placed in care were increasingly seen as victims of negative pedagogical circumstances instead of the cause of problems. The focus of child protection policy was not related to a specific social class, nor to the re-education of children from 'asocial families'. Furthermore, children were getting more involved in decision-making, and informing children about decisions concerning their life became increasingly important (Dekker et al. 2012).

During the period 1965–1990, sexual morals changed, and the sexual abuse of minors started receiving more attention. Since 1985, the subject of sexual abuse of children has become a more prominent topic on the Dutch political agenda (Commissie Samson 2012; Deetman et al. 2011).

9.2.3 The Act on Youth Services (1989–2005)

Due to the rising aversion towards enforced child protection measures and the high costs of institutional care, alternative forms of care were developed in the late 80s. Foster care was still preferred above institutional care, and day care and support for independent living became new forms of care. These were the first steps towards the Act on Youth Services, which was implemented in 1989 (Dekker et al. 2012). This Act aimed to respond to the fragmented care panorama by transferring the responsibility of youth care from the state to the provinces. This was established in the 'zo-zo-zo-beleid': care had to be provided as ('zo') close to home as possible and to be as ('zo') unobtrusive and as ('zo') short as possible. Furthermore, this Act established the Inspectorate of Youth Services and Youth Protection in order to supervise the quality of care and the execution of the Act on Youth Services (Van der Bij et al. 2006).

In 1994, the Working Group Reporting Centre on Child Maltreatment was established to organise one central and recognisable access point for reports of child maltreatment. This working group developed the AMKs to investigate suspected child maltreatment cases, which progressively replaced the BVAs (Van Burik and De Savornin Lohman 1997).

During the 1990s, youth care became a 'free market system' offering care, which led to changes in the structure of the child protection system. In 1996, the Child Care and Protection Boards were organised in one national Board with local units (Dekker et al. 2012). In 1994, the Act on Youth Services was adapted: municipalities were able to create a *Youth Care Agency* (In Dutch: Bureau Jeugdzorg, BJz). These agencies became an important key institution in the child protection system, aiming to combat the segmentation in youth care by arranging one entry point, which could lead families more quickly to better youth care facilities. The AMKs were included in these Youth Care Agencies (Dekker et al. 2012; Jeugdzorg Nederland 2013; Van der Bij et al. 2006).

In 1988, the Council for Youth Policy disapproved every form of violence towards children (Baartman 2005, 2007). Due to rising awareness for children's rights and changing ideas about child-rearing, Dutch society became progressively more reticent regarding violence towards children, and the basis of child-rearing became a relationship between parents and children in which the child feels safe and secure (Baartman 2007).

During the 2000s, the Dutch child protection policy received criticism due to media reporting on scandals of child maltreatment. Whereas the criticism during the 1960s and 1970s was focused on too early and too intrusive intervention, the criticism of the 2000s focused on too delayed and too limited intervention in risky child-rearing situations (Dekker et al. 2012). An important milestone was the *case of Savanna*, a child known by the child protection services who died after maltreatment inflicted by her mother (Jeugdzorg Nederland 2013; Knijn and Van Nijnatten 2011). The media-attention to this case initiated a public debate on the protection of children with a focus on why professionals had not intervened in time, and why none of the involved institutions had taken responsibility. In the case of Savanna, the caseworker was held responsible and a legal procedure for involuntary manslaughter was initiated. Although the caseworker was not declared guilty, social workers in child welfare were impacted by this process, resulting in more conservative child protection decisions and an increase of out-of-home placements (the so-called 'Savanna-effect'; see Dekker et al. 2012).

Due to this criticism, the call for a responsive and preventive approach increased. In 2005, the programme 'Better Protected' was set up by the Ministry of Justice to improve the child protection system in reducing the duration of protection cases by more organised cooperation, a better exchange of information, improvement of the execution of child protection measures, and revision of the child protection acts (Dekker et al. 2012; Ministry of Justice and Directorate of Legal Youth Policy 2005).

9.2.4 The Decentralisation (2005–2015)

The Act on Youth Care, implemented in 2005, included a new definition of child maltreatment and also described the role of the different agencies involved in child maltreatment prevention and intervention. The Act on Youth Care 2005 required the provinces and three metropolitan regions to offer youth care, coordinated by Youth Care Agencies. These agencies had to function as the access point for care. Furthermore, these agencies had to arrange an AMK with the task of advising people with concerns about child maltreatment and to investigate reported cases (Dekker et al. 2012; Jeugdzorg Nederland 2013).

In addition, the Social Support Act took effect in 2007. That Act described the responsibilities of municipalities for the prevention of child maltreatment, the approach to domestic violence (including children witnessing domestic violence), and the role of women shelters for children who witnessed domestic violence (Kinderombudsman 2014). By the end of 2011, each municipality needed to have a *Youth and Family Centre* (Centrum voor Jeugd en Gezin, CJG) aiming to offer a coherent support response for child-rearing, to organise child welfare at the level of the municipality, and to bring basic care closer and more accessible to families. The first Youth and Family Centres were established in 2008. Since January 2012, each Dutch municipality must have at least one CJG (Jeugdzorg Nederland 2013).

Since 2007, every form of violence in child-rearing has been prohibited by article 247 of Civil Law (Burgerlijk Wetboek, book 1, article 247), including the 'pedagogical slap'. This resulted in an increased conviction that every form of violence towards children is fundamentally wrong (Baartman 2007; Musschenga 2005).

The Action Plan 2012–2016 focused on the prevention of child maltreatment with a more integrated approach and the incorporation of the *Signs of Safety* approach (Turnell and Edwards 1999) in the overall chain of child protection. Signs of Safety aims to set up an enforceable and controllable plan in cooperation with parents regarding the safety of their own children. Besides stimulating the use of Signs of Safety, the role of municipalities became an important issue in the Action Plan (Ministry of Health, Welfare and Sport, and Ministry of Security and Justice 2011).

In relation to the increasing awareness of children's rights, the Netherlands developed the institute of the *Child Ombudsman* in 2011, commissioned to advise the government, increase the awareness of children's rights and to investigate complaints. The Child Ombudsman established a Children's Right Monitor to measure the progress of the Netherlands concerning children's rights.

9.3 The Youth Act 2015

In January 2015, the Youth Act replaced the Act on Youth Care 2005. This new Act introduced a decentralisation of the youth care administrative and financial responsibilities from the provinces to the municipalities. The underlying idea was that simplifying the structure would lead to a more efficient, coherent and cost-effective system (Bosscher 2012).

The Youth Act 2015 provides an overall framework for services; however, municipalities have the authority to arrange the actual implementation of child protection services (Simons et al. 2015). Besides the responsibility for preventive support, child-rearing and family support and youth health, the municipalities became responsible for the following services: (a) intensive ambulatory support, intensive specialised pedagogical home support, day intervention, residential care and foster care; (b) youth mental health care, care for youth with mental disabilities, personal care, dyslexia care and short stay care; (c) services for young people in closed care; and (d) enforced measures regarding child protection and youth rehabilitation.

This transition had several consequences for policy on child maltreatment. Municipalities became responsible for the overall chain of child protection: to prevent, to detect, and to intervene with child maltreatment, and to offer support and care to children and families. The AMK and the *Support Centre for Domestic Violence* (in Dutch: Steunpunt Huiselijk Geweld, SHG) were combined into the AMHK (in Dutch: *Advies en Meldpunt Huiselijk Geweld en Kindermishandeling*; from now on AMHK), aiming to arrange a recognisable and accessible point for all cases of suspended domestic violence and child maltreatment (Memorie van Toelichting Jeugdwet 2013, chapter 4.5). Furthermore, whereas in the past the Youth Care Agencies had to provide the child protection measures, under the new legislation this has to be provided by certified agencies.

9.3.1 *Key Principles Underlying the Youth Act 2015*

Article 2.1 of the Youth Act 2015 presents the basic principles of youth care: (1) early prevention and identification of problems in child-rearing and up-growing, psychological problems and disorders; (2) de-medicalisation and normalisation by strengthening the child-rearing environment; (3) improvement of the child-rearing capabilities of parents and the social environment; (4) using, recovering and strengthening the problem-solving abilities of youth, parents and their social environment; (5) promoting the safety of the child-rearing environment; (6) offering integral support for families according to the principle ‘one family, one plan, one director’ to realise better cooperation around families; and (7) arranging and executing family group plans and arranging support according to these plans.

Participation and de-medicalization are important aspects contained in the second principle. The self-reliance of citizens has to be facilitated and the social network acquires an important role in offering support. This is based on the ideas of the 'pedagogic civil society' (Memorie van Toelichting Jeugdwet 2013, chapter 1.3). In a pedagogic civil society, citizens share responsibility in the upbringing of children; the environment provides families practical support with everyday child-rearing problems. This contributes to the well-being, the reduction of stress and a higher quality of child rearing. Regarding child maltreatment, child protection is seen as a public responsibility (De Winter 2013). The Memorandum mentions the need of a positive youth policy, which is based on the capabilities of youth and in which parents and children are being heard and have a voice in the development of services for youth (Memorie van Toelichting Jeugdwet 2013, chapter 1.3). The idea of normalisation and de-medicalisation requires a cultural change regarding the behaviour of professionals, parents and agencies; improving their own strengths is the key issue in supporting families (Stoltenborgh et al. 2013, chapter 3.3).

An important key point of the Youth Act 2015, as represented in the basic principles, is the focus on the own strength and problem-solving abilities of youth and their family, aiming to prevent problems and to minimise the need of specialised services. The needs of clients function as the starting point of care; care is provided when families are unable to manage problems (Stoltenborgh et al. 2013, chapter 1.3).

The basic principle regarding the safety of the child is very important in the context of child protection. Following on the UNCRC, the government and the municipalities gain an important role in providing safety for children when parents are unable to secure this (Stoltenborgh et al. 2013, chapter 3.5). The Youth Act 2015 focuses on the safety by prevention of child maltreatment and domestic violence. According to this basic principle, improving the safety of children is a key issue in the Action Plan 2012–2016 (Ministry of Health, Welfare and Sport, and Ministry of Security and Justice 2011).

Another basic principle of the Youth Act 2015 is the offering of an integral approach following the principle 'one family, one plan, one director'. Underlying is the belief that parents bear responsibility for the upbringing of their child. If they are not able to bring up their child by themselves, one of the professionals involved will support them, which makes this professional the director of the care process (Memorie van Toelichting Jeugdwet 2013, chapter 3.4).

9.4 Scope of the Child Protection System

The current Youth Act 2015 did not introduce a new definition of child maltreatment, but used the definition of the Act on Youth Care 2005. Various types of child maltreatment were included in this definition: *violent or threatening behaviour of physical, psychological or sexual nature* (Jeugdwet 2014, article 1.1).

Although the definition of child maltreatment given in the Youth Act 2015 includes different types of child maltreatment, the types are not explicitly described in the Dutch legislation. The Dutch government distinguishes the following types of child maltreatment on their official website: physical abuse, physical neglect, psychological or emotional abuse, psychological or emotional neglect (including witnessing domestic violence) and sexual abuse (Rijksoverheid n.d.). Some institutions, articles and reports mention additional forms and more specific forms of child maltreatment, for instance female genital mutilation and sex trafficking (see e.g., Nationaal Rapporteur Mensenhandel en Seksueel Geweld tegen Kinderen 2014). The main types of child maltreatment found in governmental documents are described in Table 9.1.

9.5 Organisation and Process of the Child Protection System

The Dutch child protection system is part of the broader youth care system, which recently changed under the Youth Act 2015. In cases of child maltreatment, the municipalities are responsible for identifying, investigating, treating and monitoring cases of child maltreatment. The Act Compulsory Reporting Code Domestic Violence and Child Maltreatment aims to improve the identification of child maltreatment. After reporting, the AMHK plays an important role in investigating maltreatment and referring children to voluntary care. The Child Care and Protection Board and Juvenile Court become involved in investigating and deciding whether involuntary, compulsory child protection measures are necessary, which fall under Civil Law. Moreover, within Criminal Law, the police and Public Prosecution Service can be involved in prosecution of perpetrators.

9.5.1 Reporting Code Domestic Violence and Child Maltreatment

Although there is no mandatory reporting in the Netherlands, the Act Compulsory Reporting Code Domestic Violence and Child Maltreatment obliges professionals working in health care, education, day care, social support, youth care, and justice (e.g. residential care and the Central Agency for the reception of asylum seekers) to implement a reporting code in their organisations. The Dutch government offers a conceptual model with five basic steps: (1) clarify the signals; (2) consult a colleague and, if necessary, consult the AMHK or an expert on injury interpretation; (3) talk with the client; (4) assess violence or child maltreatment; and (5) decide: provide support or report to the AMHK. This Act is not only applicable for professionals working with children, but also it formulates the 'child check' for professionals working with adult clients. This implies that professionals have to examine whether their clients have children and whether the physical or mental well-being of their clients could be a risk for the safety or development of the children.

Table 9.1 Principal forms of child maltreatment contemplated in the Dutch child protection policy

Type of maltreatment	Description
Physical abuse	Includes every form of physical violence against a child (Rijksoverheid, n.d.). The guide 'De maat van kindermishandeling' (in English: The standard of child maltreatment) developed by Baeten and Willems (2007) defines physical abuse as hurting by parents due to another reason than an accident, except physical interventions due to cultural traditions like circumcision of boys and earrings. Particular forms of physical abuse are the shaken-baby syndrome, the Munchausen-by-proxy syndrome/pediatric condition falsification and the circumcision of girls (De Baat et al. 2011; Jeugdzorg Nederland 2013; Netherlands Youth Institute n.d.). Another form of physical abuse is fetal maltreatment, which includes pregnant women exposing the fetus to health risks due to (excessive) use of nicotine, alcohol or drugs by the mother (Jeugdzorg Nederland 2013).
Physical neglect	This refers to cases in which parents or other caretakers do not meet the physical needs of their child for a long period; and where the care standards needed according to children's rights in relation to their age and development is lacking (De Baat et al. 2011; Jeugdzorg Nederland 2013; Netherlands Youth Institute n.d.; Rijksoverheid n.d.). Baeten and Willems (2007) define four areas of possible physical neglect: nourishment, clothes, housing and the visiting of a doctor, dentist or psychologist. Furthermore, they add criteria for families living in poverty; in these cases, physical neglect is defined as when parents are unable or unwilling to use social services. In addition, in the guidelines for municipalities, prenatal neglect is mentioned as a form of child maltreatment (Ministry of Health, Welfare and Sport et al. 2011).
Psychological or emotional abuse	This is an umbrella term covering various types of emotional abuse and emotional, normative and pedagogical neglect (Baeten and Willems 2007). Emotional or psychological neglect is the lack of positive attention for a long period; parents or other caregivers ignore basic needs of their child, such as love, warmth, a sense of security and support (De Baat et al. 2011; Jeugdzorg Nederland 2013; Netherlands Youth Institute n.d.). Psychological abuse is seen as an active and more overt form of maltreatment whereas psychological neglect is seen as a more passive and covert form (Jeugdzorg Nederland 2013).
Sexual abuse	It includes every form of sexual contact forced by an adult to a child or by an older child to a younger child. Children who become victim of sexual abuse are not able to resist the perpetrator, because they are physically and relationally dependent and lack power. Further, perpetrators are physically stronger and tend to use physical or psychological violence (De Baat et al. 2011; Jeugdzorg Nederland 2013; Netherlands Youth Institute n.d.; Rijksoverheid n.d.).

(continued)

Table 9.1 (continued)

Type of maltreatment	Description
Witnessing domestic violence	It has recently been recognized as a type of child maltreatment in the Netherlands. In certain documents, it is mentioned as a separate category, while in others it is characterized as emotional abuse or neglect. Domestic violence is defined in the Social Support Act as physical, psychological or sexual violence or the threatening with such violence, by a caregiver or a person living under the same roof as the child. The guideline for AMHKs refers to violence by (ex-)partners, family members and family friends and states that 'domestic' does not refer to the place, but to the relation between the perpetrator and the victim. Domestic violence can take several forms: physical, psychological or sexual abuse, for instance violence between (ex-)partners, honour-related violence, forced marriages, child maltreatment, violence against or neglect of elderly people or violence towards parents (Baeten 2014). The guidelines of the police describe that children witnessing domestic violence are treated as victims of domestic violence (Pattje 2015). Besides conflicts between parents, witnessing maltreatment of siblings is mentioned as a type of child maltreatment (Jeugdzorg Nederland 2013). Furthermore, the Taskforce Child Maltreatment and Sexual Abuse considers the impact of a 'messy divorce' as a form of child maltreatment (Taskforce Kindermishandeling en Seksueel Misbruik n.d.).
Educational neglect	It is mentioned as a type of child maltreatment in several studies and in the guidelines for municipalities (Euser et al. 2010; Ministry of Health, Welfare and Sport et al. 2014; Stoltenborgh et al. 2013). Stoltenborgh et al. (2013) define educational neglect as (p. 346): 'the failure to provide the care and supervision that are necessary to secure a child's education. It includes for example failing to enrol a child of mandatory school age in school, permitting chronic absence from school and failing to attend to special educational needs'. Baeten and Willems (2007) mention normative and educational maltreatment together as one type of child maltreatment. They define this type as when parents' or caregivers' behaviour shows that they are not willing to concern the socialisation of their child on a minimal level (normative maltreatment), including the provision of appropriate education (educational maltreatment).

9.5.2 AMHK

The Youth Act 2015 led to the combination of the AMK and the SHG into the AMHK. This integration into one service makes it clearer for citizens and professionals where they can ask for advice and report cases of family violence (Memorie van Toelichting Jeugdwet 2013, chapter 4.5).

In cases of suspicions regarding child maltreatment, everyone can contact the AMHK to ask for advice or to report a case. When someone *asks for advice*, the AMHK only advises the caller and does not have contact with the family. Only when someone *reports a case* to the AMHK, the AMHK registers personal details of the family reported. After a report, the AMHK can decide to refer the case to social care services already involved with the family, to arrange new social care services or to start an investigation. An investigation aims to substantiate the child maltreatment report and decide on next steps. In case children or families need support or specialized care, the AMHK refers them to other agencies, as this is not their responsibility. The AMHK can only decide on and refer to voluntary supports. When an enforced child protection measure is necessary, the AMHK refers the case to the Child Care and Protection Board.

9.5.3 Child Care and Protection Board

The Child Care and Protection Board is organised on a national level and falls within the Ministry of Safety and Justice. Performing child protection investigations is only one of the tasks of the Child Care and Protection Board; other investigations focus on custody, juvenile justice and adoption (Raad voor de Kinderbescherming 2015a).

Whereas each citizen can report concerns to the AMHK, this is not the case for the Child Care and Protection Board; only the AMHK, certified agencies and municipalities authorised for this are allowed to request the Board to investigate a case. Only in exceptional cases of immediate danger, citizens can contact the Board (Jeugdwet 2014, article 3.1; Raad voor de Kinderbescherming 2015a). Furthermore, the Child Care and Protection Board itself can decide to start a child protection investigation for cases in which they are involved in other types of investigations. Besides requesting to investigate, the parties mentioned above can discuss a case with the Advice Team of the Child Care and Protection Board, which exists since 2015. Involving the Board in an earlier stage as an advisor aims to prevent the necessity of compulsory child protection measures (Raad voor de Kinderbescherming 2015b).

In child protection investigations, the Child Care and Protection Board scrutinises the (physical) safety and development of the child by examining the family situation through conversations with the child, parents and other persons involved in the family (e.g. teachers, social workers). Based on this investigation, the Board decides whether a compulsory child protection measure is necessary. When the Board considers that a child protection measure is necessary, the case is referred to the juvenile court. However, when a measure is not needed, the Board refers the family to the local child welfare team of the municipality, without any action needed from the juvenile court. The local team of the municipality can refer families to social care services.

In addition to this advising and investigating role, the Child Care and Protection Board has an assessing and supervising role. Certified agencies, performing the child protection measures, can ask the juvenile court to extend or end those measures. The Child Care and Protection Board has the duty to assess those requests prior to submission to the Court (Raad voor de Kinderbescherming 2015b).

9.5.4 *Juvenile Court*

The Juvenile Court is the only institution that can enforce compulsory child protection measures. For this purpose, the Juvenile Court uses the investigation report and the advice formulated by the Child Care and Protection Board. Yet, the Juvenile Court is not obliged to follow this advice. The Juvenile Court can enforce several child protection measures: a (temporary) supervision order with or without an out-of-home placement, and the suspension or ending of the parental authority.

In the case of a **supervision order**, the authority of the parents is restricted and partly taken over by an official family guardian from a certified agency; the parents remain responsible for the care of their child, but they are obliged to follow the advice of the guardian. In addition, an out-of-home placement is possible during a supervision order (Memorie van Toelichting Jeugdwet 2013, chapter 5.2). The Juvenile Court can enforce a supervision order when a minor's development is threatened, when the required support to take away this threat is not accepted sufficiently, and when it is expected that the (authorized) parents are able to accept the full responsibility of child-rearing again in a longer term (Burgerlijk Wetboek, book 1, article 255). The maximum length of a supervision order is one year. However, until the child is 18 years old, this can be prolonged by the Court every year (Burgerlijk Wetboek, book 1, article 258 and 260).

In cases of real and immediate danger and where there are substantial grounds for a supervision order, a **temporary supervision order** and a temporary out-of-home placement can be enforced. This measure makes immediate action possible and can last at most three months (Burgerlijk Wetboek, boek 1, article 257).

Besides enforcing a supervision order, the Juvenile Court can **end parental authority**. This can be done when parents make improper use of their authority or when the development of the child is seriously threatened and parents cannot be responsible for raising and caring for their child (Burgerlijk Wetboek, book 1, article 266). When this measure is enforced, a guardian is appointed and the child is placed out-of-home (Memorie van Toelichting Jeugdwet 2013, chapter 5.2).

Besides a definitive overruling of parental authority, it is possible to **suspend the parental authority**, partially or totally, for a certain period of time, no longer than three months. This measure is used, for instance, when the parent does not give permission for the child to receive necessary health treatment, as is the case for some orthodox religious groups in the Netherlands.

9.5.5 *Certified Agencies*

The enforced child protection measures have to be performed by certified agencies (Jeugdwet 2014, article 3.2). Their main aim is to improve the quality of the execution of child protection measures. The requirements for certifying agencies have been defined in 2015 with the implementation of the Youth Act. Those requirements refer to expertise, methods, interventions, organisation, processes and cooperation with other agencies. In practice, many of the 'old' Youth Care Agencies became certified and have been performing the child protection measures since 2015. Within those agencies, a guardian is appointed to (partly) take over the parental authority.

9.5.6 *Responses Towards Perpetrators: Police and the Public Prosecution Service*

The police and Public Prosecution Service can be involved in cases of child maltreatment in several ways. Guidelines have been developed regarding cooperation between the AMHK and the police, aiming to improve children's safety (Pattje 2015; Topberaad Jeugd 2014). The AMHK always requests information from the police about the persons involved in a report (Pattje 2015). The police can also get involved during the triage and investigation for the safety of the child; frequently in cases of severe child maltreatment (like physical abuse or neglect, sexual abuse, honour related violence, circumcision of girls, and forced marriages). Another reason to involve the police could be when the AMHK has serious suspicions about the criminal behaviour of one of the persons involved (Baeten 2014).

Moreover, the police can report cases to the AMHK when they encounter situations in which children are living in alarming circumstances. This could include directly threatening events in which the child is a victim of child maltreatment, children witnessing domestic violence, children who have run away, or cases of prostitution. Furthermore, the police has a method for detecting risky child-rearing situations for children younger than 12 years old (ProKid; see Topberaad Jeugd 2014). Using this method, the police reports cases of witnessing domestic violence or criminal behaviour of children younger than 12 years old (Pattje 2015).

Besides the police, the Public Prosecution Service has a role in the chain of child protection. First, they can ask the Juvenile Court to enforce a child protection measure; for example in addition to a punishment regarding juvenile rehabilitation or when parents are detained (Topberaad Jeugd 2014). Furthermore, the Public Prosecution Service is involved in the criminal justice aspect of child maltreatment. They search for a way in which Criminal Law can contribute to long lasting improvements and a safer life for the child. In considering the use of criminal law, they cooperate with several agencies, such as the Child Care and Protection Board. In determining the sanction, the protection of the child forms the basic principle. Furthermore, support for the family and possible other civil decisions are considered (see website Public Prosecution Service: www.om.nl/algemeen/english).

9.6 Conclusion and Challenges for the Future

The Dutch child protection system is built on solid ground and has a long history. Although the system has undergone several major transformations during the last three decades, for many years there has been a clear focus on serving the best interests of children, with the Convention of the Rights of Children playing a key role. Great efforts are made to prevent child maltreatment or to intervene at an early stage. International frameworks and recent research findings guide these efforts. Large-scale prevalence studies have shown the epidemic scope of child maltreatment in the Netherlands. Both the high prevalence rates of child maltreatment and reviews of serious and fatal cases have led to significant refinements in procedures for identifying different forms of child maltreatment and for reporting.

The Dutch child protection system can be characterized as a family-oriented system (Gilbert 1997). Out-of-home placement of a child is considered a last-resort measure, which is often preceded by intensive family support in order to keep the child in the home. Out-of-home placement in many cases has a temporary character. Family placement, in particular placement in family foster care, is – especially for young children – preferred above placement in residential settings.

The implementation of the new Youth Act in 2015 was a major change. Decentralisation of responsibilities and money streams makes the municipalities responsible for the provision and the quality of care for vulnerable children and families. This policy brings new challenges, in particular to the local teams in the municipalities and their partners in the child welfare field. At this moment, no large-scale evaluation of the system has been conducted and therefore little is known about the impact of these recent reforms on children and families or the systems that serve them. Preparing the transition, procedures to improve screening and early identification of child maltreatment have been developed, but the composition of local teams and their expertise strongly varies. In the near future, it will become clear whether the Dutch society has evolved into a truly pedagogical civil society and whether vulnerable children and families benefit from the recent transformation of the system. A first evaluation of the Youth Act 2015 shows that real innovations in the field, in accordance with the principal aims of the law, are still in the pipeline (Friele et al. 2018).

References

Baartman, H. (2005). Preventieve opvoedingsondersteuning: Een must?! [Preventive parenting support: A must?!]. In H. Baartman, R. Bullens, & J. Willems (Eds.), *Kindermishandeling: De politiek een zorg* [Child maltreatment: A concern of politics] (pp. 158–176). Amsterdam: SWP Publishers.

Baartman, H. (2007). Kindermishandeling. Over het trekken van grenzen en maten van zorg [Child maltreatment. About thresholds and measures of care]. In P. Baeten, & J. Willems (Eds.), *De maat van kindermishandeling. Meldcode en criteria van kindermishandeling* [The standard of child maltreatment. Reporting code and criteria of child maltreatment] (2nd ed., pp. 9–13). Amsterdam: SWP Publishers.

Baeten, P. (2014). *VNG-model handelingsprotocol voor het Advies- en Meldpunt Huiselijk geweld en Kindermishandeling 'Veilig Thuis'* [VNG-model action protocol for Advice and Reporting Centre on Domestic Violence and Child Maltreatment 'Safe at Home']. The Hague: VNG.

Baeten, P., & Willems, J. (Eds.) (2007). *De maat van kindermishandeling. Meldcode en criteria van kindermishandeling* [The standard of child maltreatment. Reporting code and criteria of child maltreatment] (2nd ed.). Amsterdam: SWP Publishers.

Bosscher, N. (2012). *The decentralisation and transformation of the Dutch youth care system.* Utrecht: Netherlands Youth Institute.

Commissie Samson. (2012). *Omringd door zorg, toch niet veilig. Seksueel misbruik van door de overheid uit huis geplaatste kinderen, 1945 tot heden* [Surrounded by care, still not safe. Sexual abuse of out-of-home placed children looked after by the state, 1945 until present]. Amsterdam: Boom.

De Baat, M., Van der Linden, P., Kooijman, K., & Vink, C. (2011). *Combating child abuse and neglect in the Netherlands.* Utrecht: Netherlands Youth Institute.

Deetman, W., Draijer, N., Kalbfleisch, P., Merckelbach, H., Monteiro, M., & De Vries, G. (2011). *Seksueel misbruik van minderjarigen in de Rooms-Katholieke kerk. Deel 1: het onderzoek* [Sexual abuse of minors in the Roman Catholic Church. Part 1: the study]. Amsterdam: Balans.

Dekker, J. J. H. (2018). Demystification of the century of the child: The conflict between romanticism and disenchantment in (residential) youth care from the 1830s to 2000. In E. J. Knorth et al. (Eds.), *Professionalization and participation in child and youth care: Challenging understandings in theory and practice* (pp. 27–48). London/New York: Routledge – Taylor & Francis Group (Series: Routledge Revivals).

Dekker, J. J. H., Amsing, M., Van der Bij, I., Dekker, M., Grietens, H. W. E., Harder, A. T., ... Timmerman, M. C. (2012). *Jeugdzorg in Nederland, 1945–2010. Resultaten van deelonderzoek 1 van de Commissie Samson: Historische schets van de institutionele ontwikkeling van de jeugdsector vanuit het perspectief van het kind en de hem/haar verleende zorg* [Child and youth care in the Netherlands, 1945–2010. Outcomes of sub-study 1 by the Samson Committee: Historical outline of the institutional developments in the youth sector, looking at the child and the care provided to him/her]. Groningen: University of Groningen.

Delfos, G., & Doek, J. E. (1982). *Maatregelen van kinderbescherming* [Measures of child care and protection]. Zwolle: Tjeenk Willink.

Delfos, G., & Doek, J. E. (1983). *Organen van kinderbescherming* [Institutions of child care and protection]. Zwolle,: Tjeenk Willink.

De Winter, M. (2013). Door allerlei perverse prikkels worden problemen te makkelijk omgezet in diagnoses [Because of several perverse incentives problems are being transformed into diagnoses too easily]. In K. Bakker, H. Kooijman, & J. Prakken (Eds.), *Om het kind. Visies op een ander jeugdstelsel* [On behalf of the child. Views on another youth care system] (pp. 8–15). Nijkerk: Callenbach.

Doek, J. E. (2013). Henry Kempe's legacy: National and international impact. In R. D. Krugman, & J. E. Korbin (Eds.), *C. Henry Kempe: A 50 year legacy to the field of child abuse and neglect* (pp. 221–229). Dordrecht: Springer.

Euser, E. M., Van IJzendoorn, M. H., Prinzie, P., & Bakermans-Kranenburg, M. (2010). Prevalence of child maltreatment in the Netherlands. *Child Maltreatment, 15*(1), 5–17. https://doi.org/10.1177/1077559509345904.

Euser, S., Alink, L. R. A., Pannebakker, F., Vogels, T., Bakermans-Kranenburg, M., & Van IJzendoorn, M. H. (2013). The prevalence of child maltreatment in the Netherlands across a 5-year period. *Child Abuse & Neglect, 37*(10), 841–851. https://doi.org/10.1016/j.chiabu.2013.07.004.

Friele, R. D., Bruning, M. R., Bastiaanssen, I. L. W., De Boer, R., Bucx, A. J. E. H., De Groot, J. F., Pehlivan, T., Rutjes, L., Sondeijker, F., Van Yperen, T. A., & Hageraats, R. (2018). *Eerste evaluatie Jeugdwet: Na de transitie nu de transformatie* [First evaluation Youth Act: After the transition it's time for the transformation]. The Hague: ZonMw.

Gilbert, N. (Ed.). (1997). *Combating child abuse: International perspectives and trends.* New York: Oxford University Press.

Jeugdzorg Nederland. (2013). *De kleine gids kindermishandeling. Achtergronden, signaleren en de meldcode* [The small guide child maltreatment. Backgrounds, signalling and the reporting code]. Alphen aan den Rijn: Kluwer.

Kinderombudsman. (2014). *Preventie van kindermishandeling in gemeenten: Van papier naar werkelijkheid* [Prevention of child mistreatment in municipalities: From paper to reality]. The Hague: Kinderombudsman.

Knijn, T., & Van Nijnatten, C. (2011). Child welfare in the Netherlands: Between privacy and protection. In N. Gilbert, N. Parton, & M. Skivenes (Eds.), *Child protection systems: International trends and orientations* (pp. 223–240). New York: Oxford University Press.

Lamers-Winkelman, F., Slot, N. W., Bijl, B., & Vijlbrief, A. C. (2007). *Resultaten van een landelijk onderzoek naar de omvang van kindermishandeling onder leerlingen van het voortgezet onderwijs* [Outcomes of a national survey regarding the scale of child abuse with students in secondary education]. Amsterdam/Duivendrecht: WODC, Ministry of Justice.

Ministry of Health, Welfare and Sport, & Ministry of Security and Justice. (2011). *Children safe. Action plan tackling child maltreatment 2012–2016*. The Hague: Author.

Ministry of Health, Welfare and Sport, Ministry of Security and Justice, & Association of Netherlands Municipalities. (2014). *Digitale handreiking aanpak kindermishandeling* [Digital guidelines on the approach of child maltreatment]. The Hague: Author.

Ministry of Justice, & Directorate of Legal Youth Policy. (2005). *Beter beschermd. Programma voor een effectieve en efficiënte jeugdbescherming* [Better protected. A program on effective and efficient child protection]. The Hague: Author.

Musschenga, B. (2005). Het gebruik van lijfstraffen in de opvoeding: Tolereren of niet? [The application of corporal punishment while raising children: Something to tolerate or not?]. In H. Baartman, R. Bullens, & J. Willems (Eds.), *Kindermishandeling: De politiek een zorg* [Child maltreatment: A concern of politics] (pp. 116–134). Amsterdam: SWP Publishers.

Nationaal Rapporteur Mensenhandel en Seksueel Geweld tegen Kinderen. (2014). *Op goede grond. De aanpak van seksueel geweld tegen kinderen* [On solid grounds. Approaching sexual violence against children]. The Hague: Author.

Netherlands Youth Institute. (n.d.). *Dossier kindermishandeling* [Dossier child maltreatment]. Retrieved from: http://www.nji.nl/Kindermishandeling

Pattje, W. (2015). *Model voor samenwerkingsafspraken tussen Veilig Thuis, Politie en OM* [Model for cooperation arrangments between 'Safe at Home', the Police and the Public Prosecution Service]. The Hague: Vereniging van Nederlandse Gemeenten.

Public Prosecution Service. (n.d.). *The Public Prosecution Service at a glance*. Retrieved from: www.om.nl/algemeen/english

Raad voor de Kinderbescherming. (2015a). *Het kwaliteitskader van de Raad voor de Kinderbescherming* [The quality frame of the Child Care and Protection Board]. The Hague: Author.

Raad voor de Kinderbescherming. (2015b). *Protocol beschermingszaken* [Protocol on child protection cases]. The Hague: Author.

Raad voor de Kinderbescherming. (n.d.). *Geschiedenis* [History]. Retrieved from: http://www.kinderbescherming.nl/over_de_raad/geschiedenis/

Rijksoverheid. (n.d.). *Kindermishandeling* [Child maltreatment]. Retrieved from: http://www.rijksoverheid.nl/onderwerpen/kindermishandeling

Simons, M., Meertens, R., & Tielen, N. (2015). *De kleine gids Jeugdwet* [The small guide Youth Act]. Alphen aan den Rijn: Wolters Kluwer.

Stoltenborgh, M., Bakermans-Kranenburg, M., & Van IJzendoorn, M. H. (2013). The neglect of child neglect: A meta-analytic review of the prevalence of neglect. *Social Psychiatry and Psychiatric Epidemiology, 48*(3), 345–355. https://doi.org/10.1007/s00127-012-0549-y.

Taskforce Kindermishandeling en Seksueel Misbruik. (n.d.). *Vechtscheidingen: Bij een strijd tussen de ouders verliest het kind* [Messy divorces: While parents are fighting the child is the loser]. Retrieved from: http://www.taskforcekinderenveilig.nl/themas/373/vechtscheidingen-bij-een-strijd-tussen-de-ouders-verliest-het-kind.html

Topberaad Jeugd. (2014). *Procesmodel jeugdbeschermingsketen 2015* (No. 0.8) [Process model for the child protection chain 2015 (no. 0.8)]. Utrecht: Author.

Turnell, A., & Edwards, S. (1999). *Signs of safety: A solution and safety oriented approach to child protection casework*. New York/London: W.W. Norton & Company.

Van Burik, A., & De Savornin Lohman, P. (1997). *Evaluatie modelontwikkeling Advies- en Meldpunten Kindermishandeling. Eindrapport* [Evaluation model development Advice and Reporting Centre on Child Maltreatment. Final report]. Amsterdam: DSP.

Van der Bij, I., Willemse, T., Dane, J., & Lechner, D. (2006). *Honderd jaar kinderbescherming. Uitgave ter gelegenheid van het jubileum van de Raad voor de Kinderbescherming en de Kinderwetten (1905–2005)* [Hunderd years of child protection. Edition attendant on the jubilee of the Child Protection Board and the Children's Acts (1905–2005)]. Amsterdam: SWP Publishers.

Law and Policy

Burgerlijk Wetboek Boek 1. Geraadpleegd op 15 juni 2015, van http://www.wetboek-online.nl/wet/BW1.html

ECHR, 2002. Geraadpleegd op 15 februari 2015, van http://www.echr.coe.int/Documents/Convention_ENG.pdf

Instellingsbesluit Taskforce Kindermishandeling en seksueel misbruik (2012, 31 August). Geraadpleegd op 15 maart 2015 van http://wetten.overheid.nl/BWBR0031974/

Jeugdwet 2015. (2014, 1 maart). Geraadpleegd op 20 januari 2015, van http://wetten.overheid.nl/BWBR0034925

Memorie van toelichting Jeugdwet 2015. (2013, juli). Geraadpleegd op 20 januari 2015, van http://www.rijksoverheid.nl/documenten-en-publicaties/kamerstukken/2013/07/01/memorie-van-toelichting-bij-de-jeugdwet.html

Memorie van Toelichting Wet herziening maatregelen kinderbescherming. (2009, 30 juli). Geraadpleegd op 15 juni 2015 van https://zoek.officielebekendmakingen.nl/kst-32015-3.html

Wet herziening maatregelen kinderbescherming, 2015. (2014, 12 maart). Geraadpleegd op 15 juni 2015 van https://zoek.officielebekendmakingen.nl/stb-2014-130.html

Wet Herziening Maatregel OTS (2015, 26 April). Geraadpleegd op 15 Juni 2015 van https://zoek.officielebekendmakingen.nl/stb-1995-255.html

Mónica López López obtained her PhD in Psychology at the University of Oviedo, Spain. She is an Associate Professor at the Faculty of Behavioural and Social Sciences of the University of Groningen, the Netherlands. Mónica seeks the way of improving child protection systems through research on decision-making, with a special interest in assessments and decisions of out-of-home placement and reunification, decisions of matching children with foster families, and participation of children and families in decision-making. In her research, she focuses on the voice of the service users, children and families, as a powerful instrument to improve welfare services. Since 2015, she has worked on Hestia, a European funded project comparing policies and practices of child protection in England, Germany and the Netherlands. Mónica is a board member of the European Scientific Association on Residential and Family Care for Children and Adolescents (EUSARF).

Helen Bouma obtained her Master Degree at the Faculty of Behavioral and Social Sciences of the University of Groningen in 2013. She has worked with refugee children, in research as well as in the practice field. In 2015, she joined the research project Hestia. In Hestia, she has conducted a policy analysis of the Dutch child protection system and a study of the experiences of parents involved with it. Her PhD study focuses on children's participation in the child protection system.

In addition, Helen coordinates project Hebe, aiming to gain knowledge about the experiences of children with the child protection system and to develop new methods for involving children in research. Helen's goal is to give children in care a voice and to show the value of including children's views in research and evaluation of policy and practice. She works in close connection with the practice field in the Netherlands by cooperating with policy makers and child protection agencies on assessing and embedding child participation in child protection policy, guidelines and practice.

Erik J. Knorth obtained his PhD in Psychology at Leiden University, the Netherlands. He is professor emeritus at the University of Groningen (Department of Special Needs Education and Youth Care). His research is focused on client-, service- and professional decision-making characteristics that impact treatment outcomes for children and young persons with serious emotional and behavioural problems, including those (at risk of) being placed out of home. From 1998 until 2016 he served the European Scientific Association on Residential and Family Care for Children and Adolescents (EUSARF) as its vice-president. Erik is editor-in-chief of the 'International Journal of Child and Family Welfare'. He published widely in the field on a range of topics.

Hans Grietens obtained a master's degree in clinical child and developmental psychology at the University of Leuven (Belgium) and a PhD in social sciences at the University of Groningen (Netherlands). Since 2010, he is Full Professor in the Faculty of Behavioral and Social Sciences of the University of Groningen. He is conducting research on child welfare issues, with foster care and child maltreatment being his core subjects. He is studying decision-making processes in the foster care system, in especially matching and reunification, experiences and needs of foster children, interventions for foster families, and short- and long-term outcomes of foster placement. In his research on child maltreatment he is focusing on policies towards abuse and neglect, participation of children in child protection investigations, parenting foster children with complex trauma and historical abuse of children in the foster care system. He has a particular interest in studying voices of vulnerable children and in qualitative research methods. He is president of the European Scientific Association on Residential and Family Care for Children and Adolescents (EUSARF).

Chapter 10
Child Protection System in South Korea

Bong Joo Lee

10.1 The Child Protection System in Context

10.1.1 Background

The national child protection system to intervene in child abuse and neglect cases in South Korea was first instituted in 2000. The recent inception reflects that child maltreatment was not considered a social problem that required public intervention before 2000. Child maltreatment had been regarded largely as a private family matter. Parents are considered to have a full power to use whatever child rearing practices they see fit even though they might be harmful to the children.

Many traditional child rearing practices are deeply rooted in Confucianism (Lee 2009). Confucianism places a strong emphasis on family cohesion and autonomy. It values authoritarian, patriarchal, and hierarchical child rearing practices. Children are expected to be respectful and obedient to their parents. In such a cultural tradition, children were largely regarded as belongings of their parents, rather than as individual human beings with rights.

The core value of Confucianism revolves around the family. Thus, a matter such as a child abuse allegation had been strictly regarded as a family matter, leaving no room for intervention from the society. 'Saving face' is a very important concept with regard to keeping family matters within the family. This cultural tradition explains why Korean families generally have a tendency not to seek help outside of the family, from social service agencies. Because of this cultural tradition, neighbors suspecting child abuse are still very reluctant to report it, fearing that they are violating the suspected family's dignity. Family members prefer solving the 'family problem' by themselves instead of seeking help outside of the family.

B. J. Lee (✉)
Department of Social Welfare, Seoul National University, Seoul, South Korea
e-mail: bongjlee@snu.ac.kr

L. Merkel-Holguin et al. (eds.), *National Systems of Child Protection*,
Child Maltreatment 8, https://doi.org/10.1007/978-3-319-93348-1_10

This cultural context has been a challenge to the newly formed national child protection system. Changes in South Korean's attitudes toward and awareness of child maltreatment have been slow. It is recognized that many child abuse and neglect cases are not reported to the child protection system. For example, in recent years, there have been multiple child deaths due to repeated abuse and neglect that had not been reported to the child protection system.

10.1.2 Brief History of Child Protection System

The demand for large-scale modern type of child welfare services to take care of children began in Korea during the Korean War (1950–1953). Prior to that time, the state's involvement in protecting children was minimal, with available services mostly provided to orphans by religious-affiliated voluntary organizations.

The passage of the Child Welfare Law in 1961 marked a turning point in the history of Korean child welfare policy development as child welfare programs began to be supported financially by the government and shaped by national laws and regulations. The landmark legislation for the first time spelled out the definition of a child needing protection by society and the means to provide different types of services according to their specified needs. However, while the law specified several types of child welfare service programs, the main one continued to be orphanages for children who could not be looked after in their homes due to extreme poverty, parents' death, or abandonment by their parents.

The revised Child Welfare Law in 1981 broadened the scope of the government's child welfare policy from focusing only on children in need of "protection" to promoting the well-being of all Korean children. It was also time when Korea was experiencing a rapid economic growth through industrialization. The per capita gross national income reached $4000 during the mid-1980s for the first time. During this time, the Korean society finally escaped from the absolute destitution it had suffered since the beginning of the country's modernization. As such, the revised 1981 law reflected the state's confidence to take up responsibility for protecting children based on economic development.

The legislation, in principle, shifted the focus of child welfare policy from providing services to selected groups of children at risk to promoting family and child well-being and prevention. However, careful examination of the law reveals that it stopped short of implementing any actual programs or policies directed at accomplishing the declared policy goal (Kim 1998). Rather, the revised law's main emphasis was still to provide necessary substitute care for children who could not be cared by their own families, and the main vehicle for providing such care was residential facilities (Lee 2009).

The revision of the Child Welfare Law in 2000 was a particularly important piece of legislation in that it specified abuse and neglect as a condition when a child needed protection that requires government intervention. The law defined what constitutes child abuse and neglect, mandated reporting systems including establishment of a 24-hour hotline, instituted regional Child Protection Centers, and provided a legal basis for government intervention in cases of suspected child abuse and neglect (Lee 2009). This resulted in a total of 17 Child Protection Centers being established in 2000. The number of Centers increased to 61 by 2017.

The 2000 revision of the Child Welfare Law was a historic development, where for the first time in its history protecting children from abuse and neglect has become the state's responsibility in South Korea. Before the legislation, child rearing practices were considered purely an individual family matter. The state was not supposed to intervene in the family matter especially in the relationship between parents and children. While the revision was a major development, its implementation has been difficult and limitations of the law are noteworthy.

Despite the fact that the Law had clauses requiring mandatory reporting, it failed to specify the procedures and legal authority for intervention, especially when an out-of-home placement is required. As a result, there have been very few out-of-home placements, even for those reported and substantiated cases of abuse and neglect (Chang 2003). The revision was also ambiguous about resources and guidelines necessary to enable the newly established Child Protection Centers to deal more effectively with the abused and neglected children and their families. The revision also lacked mandatory services for parents.

In order to resolve some of the problems encountered in implementing the 2000 revision of the law, another major revision of the Law was done in 2014. The 2014 revision of the Law included mandatory service requirement for abuse/neglect perpetrators, better coordination between Child Protection Centers and the police, and strengthened the criminal punishment for child maltreatment.

In recent years, there have been several child death cases that received much public attention in the media. These cases highlighted the need for strengthening child protection system. One of the responses to these tragic child death cases was to increase the punishment to the level of a criminal case. As a result, the Special Law on Punishment of Child Abuse and Neglect Crimes was enacted in 2014.

The Law toughened the punishment levels for severe abuse and neglect acts. The Law also made it easier to remove children from parental custody in case of severe abuse and neglect findings. It also strengthened mandatory reporting requirement. Most importantly, it mandated emergency protective custody for suspected abuse and neglect cases (Lee et al. 2015). With the passage of the Law, the police are required to respond to *all* child abuse and neglect reports along with the Child Protection Center workers.

10.1.3 Roles of Government, NGO, and Legal Sector

Most of child protection services were provided by NGOs before the 2000 legislation. However, the services were sporadic and did not have a legal mandate. One of the most significant developments in NGOs' activities was the establishment of the Korean Association of Child Abuse Prevention in 1989. The Association's main activity was focused on public relations to increase the awareness of child abuse and neglect as a social problem in Korean society (Kim 2003). However, because the Association did not provide any direct child protection services, their reach was limited.

Good Neighbors, an NGO in South Korea, opened a 'child abuse counseling center' in Sung Nam area (which is a suburb of Seoul, the capital of South Korea) in 1996. The center was one of the first direct child protection service resources developed in the country. The center received reports of child maltreatment and began providing child protection services. Good Neighbors increased the number of its centers to 17 by 2000, covering all the major regions of the country (Lee et al. 2015).

The revision of the Child Welfare Law in 2000 was influenced by the efforts of the NGOs, which strongly demanded changes in how Korean society dealt with child abuse and neglect. The revision of the law was in response to growing public concern about abuse and neglect of children. Before the legislation, there was no law mandating the reporting of suspected child abuse and neglect. Selected services were voluntarily provided to abused children and their families by private agencies and advocacy groups.

Most Child Protection Centers are operated by not-for-profit voluntary organizations, underwritten by central and local governmental funding. The Centers receive and investigate the child abuse/neglect reports, and also provide family preservation and reunification services. Those children who are determined to be at imminent risk of harm are placed into shelters, group homes, residential care settings and foster care (including kinship) homes.

It is interesting to note that actual operation of the Child Protection Centers was delegated to private agencies from the beginning in South Korea. Most other child welfare services are also provided by voluntary agencies, while most or all of funding sources for the services are from central or local governments.

10.2 The Child Protection System in Action

10.2.1 Orientation of Systems

The national child protection system is supervised by the South Korean central government, but administered locally. The Child Protection Centers (CPC) are the core of the national child protection system. Each center covers a designated geographic area. Reports of suspected child maltreatment are directed to a designated local CPC. When the CPC substantiates a maltreatment report following investigation, it can arrange protection services including taking protective custody of the child, providing family preservation services, referring cases for counselling and mental health services, placing children in foster care, and/or providing family preservation services.

The majority of child maltreatment reports come from local schools, private social service agencies, hospitals, and public social service authorities. This is likely because although anyone can report suspected child maltreatment, the law classifies school teachers, medical professionals, private child welfare service workers, and public social service personnel as mandated reporters.

The basic orientation of the child protection system can be described as retributive by focusing on punishing the perpetrators of abuse and neglect, in most cases, the parents of child victims. The laws and regulations are clear about the penalties and punishments for the perpetrators, but do not offer sufficient level of services related to family preservation and/or reunification.

The retributive approach has even been strengthened with introduction of the Special Law on Punishment of Child Abuse and Neglect Crimes in 2014. This Law toughened the punishment levels for severe abuse and neglect acts. Because child maltreatment incidence is first approached as a 'crime,' the role of the police has been strengthened in the investigation process. With the passage of the Law, the police are required to respond to all child abuse and neglect reports along with the CPC workers. The 24-hour hotline call number was integrated to the crime reporting police call number, which is 112 in South Korea. That means all child maltreatment reports are first handled by the police 112 call center workers.

10.2.2 Current Flow of CPS Cases

Figure 10.1 shows the flow of CPS cases from the reporting to child placement, if required. When a report is made to the 24-hour hotline police call center, a CPS worker along with the police undertakes investigation, typically involving a home visit, to determine whether child maltreatment occurred. If through the investigation it is determined that the risk of harm to the child is imminent, a protective custody of the child can be taken and the child can be placed in an emergency setting for 72 h without a Court order. Whether a protective custody is taken or not, a formal decision is made by CPC based on the evidence from the investigation.

If it is determined that there is enough evidence to suggest actual harm was done to the child, the case becomes a substantiated child maltreatment case. If the harm is minor or evidence is not sufficient, the case is referred to the community service agencies as an early intervention case for further monitoring and service. The community service agencies include public child welfare centers and private community welfare centers. They provide monitoring and family supporting services, and, if needed, further referrals to specialized services such as mental health and family counselling.

When the case is substantiated, a determination of out-of-home placement is required. When a placement is needed, the CPC asks the Court to issue the child protection order to separate the child from the parents. When the court issues such an order, the child is now placed in foster care, relative care, residential care, or group homes. When a placement is not warranted, the child can stay with the parents

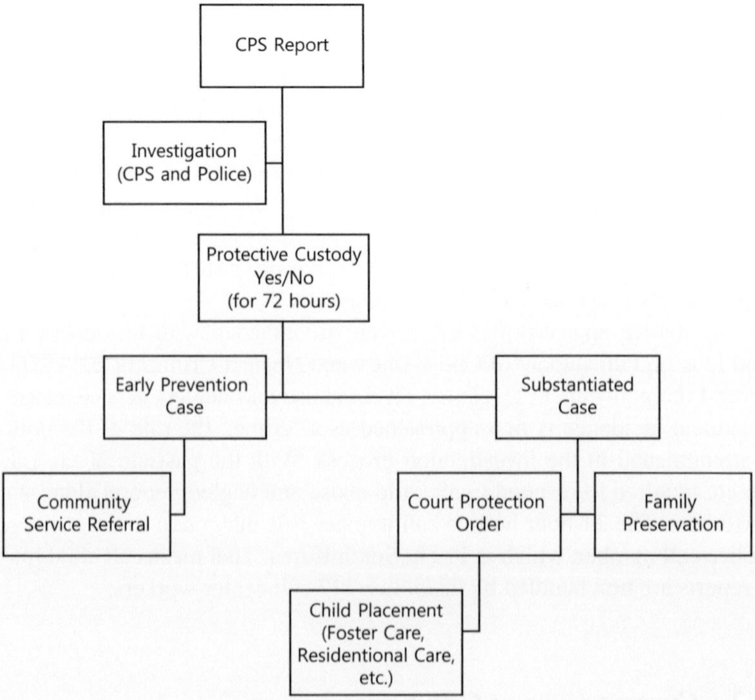

Fig. 10.1 Diagram of CPS Case Processing in South Korea

while the family receives family preservation services. When it is determined after a monitoring period that the risk of child maltreatment is minimal, the case is closed.

10.2.3 Prevalence and Characteristics of the Reported CPS Cases

The national child protection center maintains a central database to keep track of all CPS reports. In 2015, 19,203 cases of child maltreatment were reported to the national CPS system and 11,715 of them were substantiated. These figures represent a substantiated child maltreatment report rate of 1.32 per 1000 children aged 0–17 in South Korea (Ministry of Health and Human Services 2016).

As shown in Fig. 10.2, the number of child maltreatment reports has been increasing continuously from 2001 when the data collection began. During the 15 years from 2001 to 2015, the number of substantiated maltreatment cases increased more than 400% from 2105 to 11,715 cases.

For the more recent period, it is interesting to find that the number of CPS cases has increased dramatically since 2014 when the new legislation (Special Law on Punishment of Child Abuse and Neglect Crimes) was enacted. From 2013 to 2014,

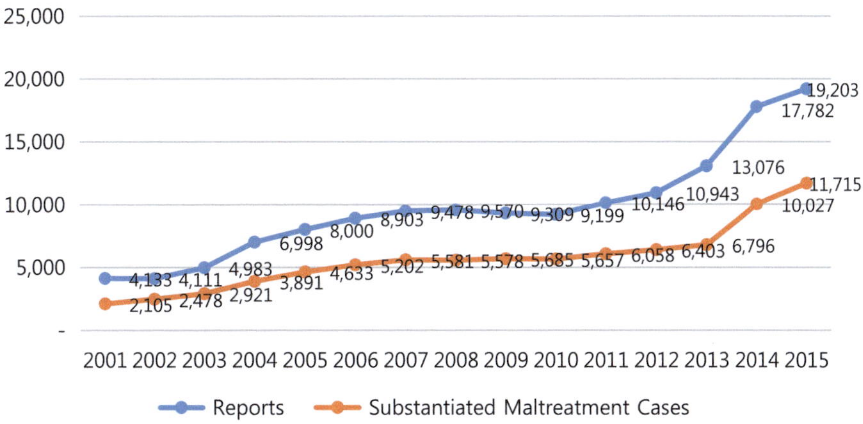

Source: Ministry of Health and Human Services, 2016

Fig. 10.2 Trends of CPS reports: 2001–2015. (Source: Ministry of Health and Human Services 2016)

the number of substantiated child maltreatment cases increased almost 50% from 6796 to 10,027. From 2014 to 2015, while less, there was still a 17% increase.

With the increasing number of reported child maltreatment cases, the key question is how much of the increase is due to the actual increase of child maltreatment or to the changes in reporting behaviors. As the national child protection system is strengthened, people's awareness of child maltreatment increased, which probably resulted in the greater likelihood of reporting. Even without changes in the actual population-level child maltreatment incidence rate, changes in reporting behavior alone can result in increased number of 'reported' cases.

While it is difficult to tease out exactly how much of the increase in the number of reported CPS cases is due to reporting behavior or population-level maltreatment incidence rate changes, it is safe to assume not all of the increase is not caused by the changes in population-level maltreatment incidence rate in such a short period of time. As a matter of fact, the large increase we observed from 2014 provides some evidence to support the reporting behavior change explanation.

While reports and substantiated cases of child maltreatment have been increasing in recent years, there is still a concern that many cases of child abuse and neglect are going unreported. A key barrier has been the strong emphasis on family cohesion and autonomy in Korean society (Lee 2007). Because of this cultural tradition, those suspecting child abuse are still very reluctant to report it, fearing that they would be violating the suspected family's dignity. We can assume that the members of the suspected family themselves prefer to resolve any problems within the family rather than seeking help elsewhere.

A recent study of the incidence of child maltreatment based on a nationally representative sample of 5051 families with children provides a clue to the discrepancy between incidents and reports in Korea. The study reported an estimated child

Fig. 10.3 The status of the reporters: 2015. (Source: Ministry of Health and Human Services 2016)

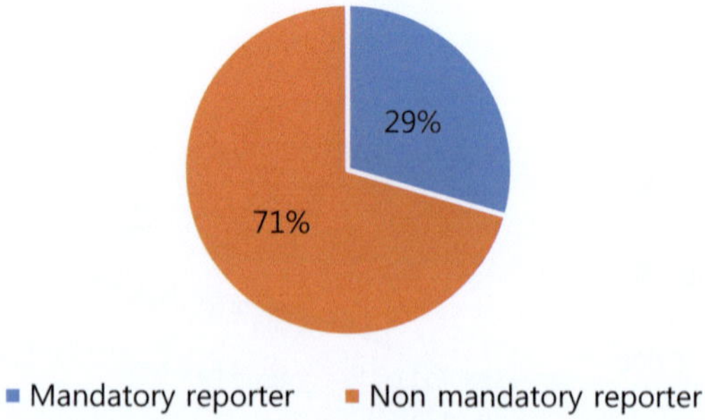

Source: Ministry of Health and Human Services, 2016

Table 10.1 Age distribution of substantiated cases: 2015

<1	344	2.9%
1–3	1312	11.2%
4–6	1683	14.4%
7–9	2123	18.1%
10–12	2289	19.5%
13–15	2600	22.2%
16–17	1364	11.6%
Total	11,715	100%

Source: Ministry of Health and Human Services (2016)

maltreatment rate of 25.3% among the child population of 0–18 year olds, using the severe child abuse/neglect categories of the Parent–Child Conflict Tactics Scales (CTSPC) (Ahn et al. 2017). Simply comparing this population-level incidence child maltreatment rate to that of reported cases reveal that approximately only one out of 190 maltreatment incidents is reported to CPS.

Of the 16,651 child maltreatment reports in 2015, about 29% were made by mandatory reporters. The remaining 71% were from the non-mandatory reporters (see Fig. 10.3). One might expect a higher rate of reporting from mandatory reporters, especially since there has been a strong effort to increase child abuse and neglect awareness among the mandatory reporters.

Table 10.1 shows the age distribution of the substantiated cases in 2015. The age category of 13-15 year old was the most prevalent with 22.2% of the cases, followed by the 10-12 year old category with 19.5%. It is interesting to note that the number of child maltreatment cases increases as the age increases except for the 16-17 year old category.

The relationship between perpetrators and child victims in substantiated child maltreatment cases is shown in Fig. 10.4. The vast majority of the perpetrators (about 80%) were the parents of the maltreated children. Caretakers who take care of other people's children for a part of the day, including day care center workers, school teachers, and child welfare center workers, account for 12% of perpetrators. Strangers were only 3% of the total substantiated cases in 2015.

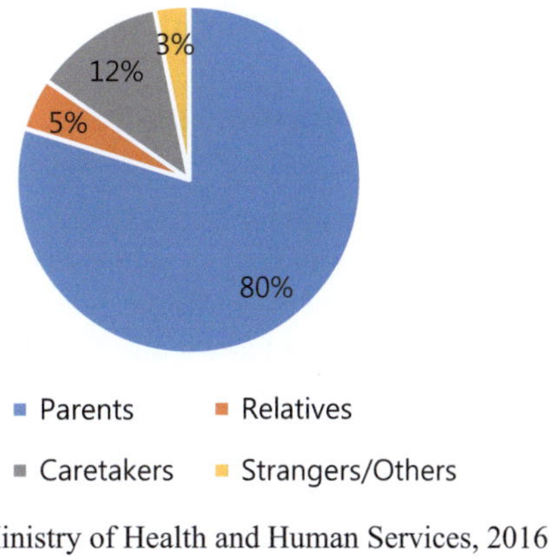

Fig. 10.4 Perpetrator relationship: 2015. (Source: Ministry of Health and Human Services 2016)

Table 10.2 Allegation types of substantiated child maltreatment cases: 2015

Physical abuse	6661	38%
Emotional abuse	7197	41%
Sexual abuse	629	4%
Neglect	3175	18%
Total	17,662	100%

Source: Ministry of Health and Human Services (2016)
Note: Multiple allegations are included in the figures shown in the table

Table 10.3 Initial placement of substantiated cases

Own family	8588	73.3%
Short-term shelters	1790	15.3%
Residential care	234	2.0%
Kinship Foster Care	968	8.3%
Hospital	107	0.9%
Non-relative Foster Care	11	0.1%
Death	17	0.1%
Total	11,715	100.0%

Source: Ministry of Health and Human Services (2016)

As shown in Table 10.2, of the substantiated child maltreatment cases in 2015, the most frequent allegation type was emotional abuse (41%), followed by physical abuse (38%), neglect (18%) and sexual abuse (4%).

Of those 11,715 substantiated abuse and/or neglect cases, the vast majority of children (about 73%) were protected in their own families, with 27% being placed in foster care settings. Of these, about 15% were placed in temporary short-term shelters, 8% in kinship care homes, 2% in residential care settings, 1% in hospitals, and less than 1% (11 children) were placed in family foster care homes with non-relatives (Table 10.3).

10.3 Policy Challenges

10.3.1 Emerging Concerns

A primary concern for South Korea's child protection system has been the low level of child abuse and neglect awareness. It has been a slow process of dismantling the cultural barrier of authoritarian and hierarchical child rearing practices. While there has been a growing knowledge and awareness of child maltreatment in recent years, it is still in its infancy. A strong cultural tradition of treating parenting style as a 'family matter' has clearly been a barrier to the implementation of child protection systems, policies and laws. Confucianism's tradition of 'saving face' by keeping family matters within the family has also been a significant barrier.

One of the consequences of the lack of child maltreatment awareness has been the low level of reporting. As shown in the previous section, even the reporting rate of the mandatory reporters has been lower than expected. The reported child maltreatment rate is believed to be far lower than the estimated population-level child maltreatment incidence rate.

While Korea's child protection system is managed and supported by the central and local governments, the actual delivery of services is contracted out to the NGOs. Because the system is built on privatization of child protection service functions, public accountability of the services has been weak. Child protection service activities generally require intervening in parents' custodial right of children, which requires public accountability and authority. At times, lack of public authority makes it difficult to enforce protective services.

Insufficient public resources for the child protection system has been an enduring issue since the inception of the national system, limiting the reach and accessibility of child protection services. The current estimate is that each Child Protection Center covers about 160,000 children aged 0–17. In terms of the number of CPC workers, the ratio is one worker to 18,000 children. The caseload of the CPC workers has been very high, with an average of about 56 cases per worker (Lee et al. 2015). The over-burdened system has been struggling to deliver service quality and accessibility. The situation has even worsened since 2014 when the number of reports began to increase rapidly, while the budget for the child protection system has not kept up.

While the Court's involvement and cooperation have improved since legislation of the Special Law on Punishment of Child Abuse and Neglect Crimes in 2014, the Court system is still underdeveloped from the standpoint of being professionally capable of dealing with child protection cases. The Court, in general, still values parental rights more than children's rights. A strong emphasis on parental rights has been a barrier for CPS interventions.

The lack of an early intervention system has emerged as a salient issue in recent years. The child protection system of South Korea is built upon the mandatory reporting scheme. The child protection system's primary working model is to 'investigate' only after reporting of suspected child maltreatment cases. One of the limitations of such a report-based system is the difficulty to reach out to prevent child maltreatment before receiving a report. The over-burdened child protection system has had difficulty in developing an effective community based early intervention system.

The broad meaning of child protection system includes child protection services, kinship care, family foster care, residential care, and adoption services. A major problem for South Korea's child protection system has been a lack of systematic coordination among these 'sub-systems.' There are government and NGO agencies working in each service area, but they are often working in isolation. For example, a decision to place a child in out-of-home settings is made mostly by which service 'gate' the child has entered, not by considering what is best for child's interest. Without a meaningful coordination among the related agencies, it has been very difficult to institute individual service planning and/or permanency planning for each child.

10.3.2 Future Needs and Directions

Since inception of the national child protection system in 2000, it can be argued that there has been significant progress in protecting children from abuse and neglect. However, there are clearly areas that need further development to better protect the vulnerable children from abuse and neglect in South Korea.

Public accountability of the child protection system needs to be strengthened. With all of the child protection service functions being privatized to NGOs, it is difficult to secure the public accountability and authority of the child protection system. One way of improving public accountability of the system is to separate the investigation and service functions and have the public sector assume the investigation role. One of the limitations with the current system has been the privatization of all functions of child protection including the investigation. The investigation function requires a higher level of public authority and accountability, because it has to intervene to limit or deprive the parents' custodial rights when needed. NGO workers who have to perform the investigation roles report they often feel that they don't have the necessary authority particularly with difficult cases (Lee et al. 2015).

Role conflicts experienced by child protection workers doing investigation and then providing services have been another issue. During the investigation process, the workers might have to confront the parents to gather and examine the evidence of child maltreatment. However, during the service provision process, the same worker has to develop a partnership with the parents to work together for making positive changes. The child protection workers who have to perform these two somewhat incompatible roles often confess uncomfortable feelings (Lee et al. 2015). While separating the investigation and service provision roles might reduce such role conflicts in the field of child protection services that solution is not without controversy and potential conflict, as it results in multiple workers for the same family.

Strengthening service components of the child protection system is another important future direction. The essential services of family preservation and reunification are not fully developed in South Korea's child protection system. With the lack of resources, the over-burdened system cannot develop these professional services. The retributive orientation of the system tends to emphasize judicial interventions, neglecting service components.

However, this is the time to strengthen the restorative approach of the system. The vast majority of the perpetrators are parents of the child victims. The goal of the system should not end at 'punishing' the parents and separating their children from them. The ultimate goal of the system is to make the family a safe place for children and when necessary, reuniting children with parents. In order to pursue this goal, the service components of the system have to be strengthened.

At present South Korea's child protection system is too inflexible. Every child maltreatment report, regardless of severity of the case, has to go through the same process. Change toward a more flexible system is necessary in order to offer services that can be tailored to the needs of the family. High risk cases require the strict traditional judicial process. Low risk cases, with police approval, can go to service track for prevention services. Many states in the U.S., which has the similar report-based child protection system, have recently adopted 'differential response system' approach (National Quality Improvement Center on Differential Response in Child Protective Services 2011). The differential response system is an effort to make the system more flexible, while strengthening the restorative approach and meeting families' service needs. In order to make South Korean child protection system more service friendly, adopting some components of the differential response system should be considered as a future direction.

A system or an agency cannot protect children from abuse and neglect alone. It needs help from other systems and/or agencies at the community level and from families. Service network and coordination are the key components of the child protection system. The Child Protection Centers, while working as a hub for protecting children from abuse and neglect, need to strengthen the service network with other child and family service resources at the community level. Developing effective service integration and coordination approaches is a key for improving child protection system in South Korea.

Finally, the early intervention system needs to be improved in order to better protect children from abuse and neglect. Prevention is better than treatment. The report-based child protection system often can result in weaker early prevention services because its main mode of operation is responding after the report is made. The focus should be reducing the risk of abuse and neglect by promoting awareness of child abuse and neglect at the community level. Screening and detection of children and families at risk are also important early intervention strategies. By building stronger service network with other community agencies, early intervention and prevention strategies should be a priority for child protection system in South Korea.

References

Ahn, J., Lee, B. J., Kahng, S. K., Kim, H. L., Hwang, O. K., Lee, E. J., Shin, H. R., Yoo, M. S., Lee, S. Y., Cho, Y., Yoo, Y. S., Kwak, Y. J., Shin, Y. M., Lim, J. Y., Cho, Y. J., Park, S. Y., & Yoo, J. (2017). Estimating the prevalence rate of child physical and psychological maltreatment in South Korea. *Child Indicators Research, 10*(1), 187–203.

Chang, W. (2003, May 21). *Analysis of current situation of child protective services and their challenges.* A discussion paper presented at the public discussion for improving the CPS system. Seoul.

Kim, H. (1998). The review and proposal of the institutional child care program in the revision of the Child Welfare Law. *Study of Korean Child Welfare, 7*, 95–125.

Kim, H. M. (2003). Future tasks of Korean child abuse prevention policy. *Children and Rights, 7*(3), 1–28.

Lee, B. J. (2007). Adoption in Korea: Current status and future prospects. *International Journal of Social Welfare, 16*, 75–83.

Lee, B. J. (2009). Residential care in Korea: Past, present, and future. In M. Courtney & D. Iwaniec (Eds.), *Residential care of children: Comparative perspectives*. New York: Oxford University Press.

Lee, B. J., Kim, G. H., & Ahn, J. (2015). *A study of ways to improve child protection system for better prevention and protection from child abuse: Focusing on functions and roles of child protection agency*. Seoul: Good Neighbors.

Ministry of Health and Human Services. (2016). *2015 national child maltreatment report*. Seoul: Ministry of Health and Human Services.

National Quality Improvement Center on Differential Response in Child Protective Services. (2011). *Differential response in child protective services: a literature review*. US DHHS, ACF, ACYF.

Bong Joo Lee is Professor of Social Welfare at Seoul National University. His research focuses on child welfare, child poverty, early intervention, and social service reform issues. He is Editor-in-Chief of Child Indicators Research, an international journal on child indicators.

Chapter 11
Structure and Challenges of Child Protection in Switzerland

Andreas Jud and René Knüsel

11.1 Introduction[1]

In Switzerland, the child protection and child welfare system are structured according to the political principles of federalism and subsidiarity which include the goals of organizing service systems on the cantonal[2] level and providing services at the lowest political level (cf. Jud et al. 2013). Subsequently, there are 26 cantonal variations of organizing mandated and voluntary support for children in need. This contribution outlines the pillars of this complex framework, describes data (or the lack thereof) on reported incidents of child maltreatment in Switzerland, addresses ongoing developments and some of the challenges the system faces.

[1] This manuscript includes translated and adapted parts of a manuscript that has previously been published in German (Jud and Hauri 2016).

[2] The 26 cantons are Switzerland's provincial jurisdictions.

A. Jud (✉)
Child and Adolescent Psychiatry/Psychotherapy, University of Ulm, Ulm, Germany

School of Social Work, Lucerne University of Applied Sciences and Arts, Lucerne, Switzerland
e-mail: andreas.jud@uniklinik-ulm.de; andreas.jud@hslu.ch

R. Knüsel
Observatory on Child Maltreatment, University of Lausanne, Lausanne, Switzerland
e-mail: rene.knusel@unil.ch

L. Merkel-Holguin et al. (eds.), *National Systems of Child Protection*, Child Maltreatment 8, https://doi.org/10.1007/978-3-319-93348-1_11

11.1.1 *Legislative Framework for Child Protection in Switzerland*

Switzerland signed and ratified the United Nations' Convention on the Rights of the Child (UN CRC); it guides and frames federal and cantonal legislation on children. At the federal level, the Swiss Civil Code (SCivC)[3] provides the Child Protection Authorities (CPAs) with the means to support children and protect them from harm (Art. 307 to 312 SCivC), if necessary against the parent's will. The SCivC refers to the child's wellbeing[4] and its endangerment (e.g. Art. 307 SCivC). It however lacks definitions on the situations or events that may constitute an endangerment of the child's wellbeing. While the SCivC does not contain the terms child maltreatment, child abuse, and child neglect, it has been argued that the articles on child protection orders aim at interventions in the context of child maltreatment (e.g. Jud 2013): They are only intended for situations of child endangerment where parents are unable or unwilling to remedy (cf. Rosch and Hauri 2016, p. 415). This rationale covers parental failure of adequately providing for a child's needs or supervision but obviously also includes (potential) harm directly inflicted by the parents.

The cantons are responsible to implement a structure of authorities and services to counter endangerments to children's wellbeing. Yet, only a minority of cantons provides a specialized and unified legislative framework on children and youth (e.g. Schnurr 2011). Some services and authorities are cantonally administered, some regionally or locally with a large variance in size and caseload. The public child protection sector is detailed in the section, Public Child Protection.

Violent offenses against children are penalized in the Swiss Criminal Code (SCrimC). While Article 187 SCrimC defines criminally liable sexual acts with children and Art. 219 SCrimC refers to criminally liable neglectful behavior (but does not define it), no other single article defines criminally liable behavior that is physically or psychologically violent against children.[5] As in public child protection, the structure of criminal authorities and police forces is a responsibility of the cantons with a similar variety of organizations and units. Law enforcement connected to protecting children from harm is discussed in the section, Prosecuting child maltreatment offenses.

[3]The Federal Council provides on its webpage English translations of Swiss law while reminding readers that English translation are only for information purposes and have no legal force (see https://www.admin.ch/gov/en/start/federal-law/classified-compilation.html).

[4]The German term "Kindeswohl" literally translates to child wellbeing. However, the French version of the SCivC is worded differently: It refers to "le développement de l'enfant" that literally translates to child development. The different notions attached to the wording likely influence child protection in the different parts of the country (cf. subsection, Managing diversity on a small scale). The use of the term child wellbeing – instead of the best interests of the child – has been criticized by the UN Committee on the rights of the child (2015).

[5]The SCrimC lists physically and psychologically violent acts independent of the victim's age and development (Art. 111ff., Art. 122ff., and Art. 180ff. SCrimC).

11.1.2 Managing Diversity on a Small Scale

Public child protection and law enforcement are only two pillars in supporting and protecting children in need and from harm. Organizations in the educational, health and social sector apply their professional mandate (cf. Trocmé et al. 2016) to triage children and provide help on a voluntary basis. The section, Child Protection in the educational, health and social sector, discusses these organizations and focuses on agencies that specialize in supporting victimized children. The variety of services or organization in this sector is even larger than for public child protection and is driven by historically different developments of infrastructure in different areas of the country.

The diversity of services and authorities arising from 26 cantonal and sub-cantonal variations of organizing child protection and child welfare is amplified by Switzerland's cultural and linguistic variety. The country covers an area with three different major languages – German, French, and Italian. Most cantons are monolingual, some however bilingual and one canton even trilingual. Different languages not only imply different labels of organizations but are also associated with different concepts of the state. Structures in the French-speaking part of Switzerland, for example, tend to be stronger hierarchically organized than in the German-speaking part (e.g. Ladner 2016).

Readers should keep in mind that this diversity takes place on a relatively small scale. A total of approximately 8.5 million inhabitants populated Switzerland in 2016 (Federal Statistical Office 2017), yet the smallest canton only included around 15,500 inhabitants (Federal Statistical Office 2016a). The mean population size of Switzerland's 2324 municipalities is at only 3510 inhabitants per municipality in 2015 (Federal Statistical Office 2016b).

Overall, the sectors of public child protection, law enforcement and agencies specialized in voluntary support for victimized children combine a total of over 650 agencies.[6] The number is changing at least on an annual basis as new agencies are founded while others cease to exist or are merged. Focusing on the three aforementioned sectors will provide a helpful overview on child protection in Switzerland. Of course, such an overview does not include all organizations that are linked to the child protection system(s) of Switzerland by directly supporting victims and/or as sentinels to CPAs.

[6] An overview on agencies in these sectors for each canton can be found at http://www.optimus-study.org/fileadmin/user_upload/documents/2013/Newsletter/Cartographie_2013.pdf. The list is also linked to geographical map at https://www.google.com/maps/d/viewer?mid=1JkF6qA4ow441fRoeW1bcxaXCFgM&ll=46.8006166113862%2C8.2114529000004&z=8

11.2 Public Child Protection

11.2.1 Legal Basis for Interventions

Growing up in a family environment, in an atmosphere of happiness, love and understanding is considered quintessential for the best interest of the child (Preamble UN CRC). Art. 296 SCivC designates the parents responsible for the upbringing and wellbeing of their children. If the parents fail their duty, the SCivC mandates that the state protects children who are endangered regarding their physical, mental, intellectual or social development (cf. Rosch and Hauri 2016, p. 415), independent of the fact whether the endangerment has arisen from the parents fault or lack of competence to adequately protect their child from (potential) harm (cf. Rosch and Hauri 2016, p. 411).

Once a state intervention is deemed necessary, it has to follow the principle of proportionality: The intervention should be appropriate to successfully support and protect the child; if several interventions would support and protect the child adequately, the least invasive has to be chosen (cf. Rosch and Hauri 2016, p. 411f). Family law includes several child protection orders that range from directives[7] and admonitions (Art. 307 SCivC) to the revocation of the parents' right to decide on place of residence (Art. 310 SCivC),[8] and finally to the withdrawal of parental responsibility (Art. 311 and Art. 312 SCivC). By far the most prevalent order is, however, the appointment of "a child deputy whose function is to help the parents look after the child by providing advice and practical support" (Art. 308 SCivC). Around 80% of child protection orders in place 2015 were deputyships (Konferenz für Kindes- und Erwachsenenschutz (KOKES) 2016).[9] Usually, a deputyship also accompanies the placement of a child in out-of-home care by revocation of the parents' right to decide on place of residence. Advice and practical support through a deputyship is provided on a mid- to long-term basis (cf. sub-section, Processing a report).

11.2.2 Child Protection Authorities and Mandated Services

There are three roles for organizations in Swiss public child protection: (a) Organizations that provide a risk assessment, (b) the child protection authority that enacts the order by usually appointing (c) a deputyship to a field worker at a child and youth service. Table 11.1 summarizes the three different roles.

[7] A directive may, for example, call the parents to visit a pediatrician with their child.

[8] This child protection order consequently includes the child's placement in out-of-home care.

[9] Terminations of the parental responsibility, on the other hand, make up less than 1% of orders in place 2015 (Konferenz für Kindes- und Erwachsenenschutz (KOKES) 2016).

Table 11.1 Roles in Swiss public child protection

(a) Risk assessment	Specialized or general social services provide a risk assessment for reported incidents of an endangerment of child wellbeing. They recommend the appropriate services or child protection orders.
(b) Decision on child protection orders	The Child Protection Authorities (CPAs) are responsible for enacting child protection orders. In most cases, they issue a general and unspecified mandate to a social worker appointing him/her a deputy to the child. In more severe cases, the authorities can place the child in out-of-home care or finally withdraw parental custody.
(c) Mandated services	As deputies to the child, field workers in child and youth services provide advice and practical support to child and its family.

The CPAs are the organizations that decide on child protection orders. Some of these authorities are constituted as courts; others take the form of administrative authorities (Konferenz der Kantone für Kindes- und Erwachsenenschutz (KOKES) 2017). Courts prevail in the French-speaking part of Switzerland, administrative authorities in the German-speaking part. The recent revision of the national legislative framework for child and adult protection aimed at increasing professionalization in public child protection; the national legislative requirements had a huge impact on the structure of authorities responsible for child protection orders: Their number has been reduced dramatically from previously 1415 Tutelary Authorities before 2013 to now 142 CPAs (Konferenz der Kantone für Kindes- und Erwachsenenschutz (KOKES) 2017). An evident goal of reducing the number of authorities was to guarantee a catchment area of around 50,000 inhabitants (cf. Konferenz der kantonalen Vormundschaftsbehörden (VBK) 2008). While authorities constituted of lay members have been common before the legislative change, all members of a CPA are now employed. The traditional lay authorities, especially, the ones in small rural municipalities (cf. sub-section, Managing diversity on a small scale), had several disadvantages: Not only might they have lacked professional knowledge on child maltreatment and the development of children, the small catchment area was also prone to biases and lack of experience in handling reported cases. So the need for professionalization has been the one major driver of updating the legislation on public child protection in Switzerland. It was intended that a CPA now should gather knowledge from different disciplines and backgrounds, particularly integrating members from social work, psychology or pedagogy beside law professionals (cf. Konferenz der kantonalen Vormundschaftsbehörden (VBK) 2008). Yet, not all cantons have implemented these standards: Some CPA have a catchment area well below 50,000 inhabitants (Konferenz der Kantone für Kindes- und Erwachsenenschutz (KOKES) 2017), other CPAs are not constituted interdisciplinary but purely out of law professionals (Rieder et al. 2016).

A decision on a child protection order is preceded by a risk assessment. It may be provided by a field worker in a general social service or a service specialized on risk assessment for CPAs. The risk assessment proceedings comprise several weeks and include meetings with the child and its family in the field worker's office and home visitations. At the end of risk assessment, the field worker will compile his findings in a report for the CPA accompanied by recommendations on interventions to take (or if none is necessary). Once a deputy to the child has been installed by the CPA, the mandate is primarily transferred to a professional field worker, usually with a social work background and affiliated at a general social service or an organization specialized on deputyships. If both roles are combined within a general social service, the frontline worker for risk assessment may also be the future deputy.

11.2.3 Processing a Report

Since the reform of Child and Adult Protection Law, implemented in 2013, the SCivC mandates professionals "acting in an official capacity" to report to CPAs when a "person needs assistance" (Art. 443 SCivC). Notwithstanding this requirement, the decision to report still depends on the professional's discretion: He/she must decide whether the situation is sufficiently serious to be reported and whether it can be adequately addressed by subsidiary services within a reasonable timeframe (Rosch 2012). Professionals bound by a professional secret (e.g. physicians or psychologists) have to trade off the duty to report against the duty to keep the professional secret. Cantonal laws may go beyond the federal law and name more groups or even the public as mandated reporters. Currently, the Federal Parliament debates whether to extend the mandatory reporting of alleged child maltreatment from professionals "acting in an official capacity" to all professionals working with children.[10]

Reports on alleged situations of endangerment of child wellbeing are addressed to the CPA responsible for the place of the child's residence. If a report is considered serious, a risk assessment on behalf of the CPA will take place. Based on this risk assessment, the CPA will decide whether or not to enact a child protection order. Mandates of deputyships are transferred to a field worker in a specialized or general social service. He/she has to usually report biannually on the progress of the child and whether the problems surrounding the child have been tackled in close collaboration with the parents or not; consequently, he/she recommends to the CPA whether the mandate should still be in place or terminated. The CPA subsequently decides on the termination of the mandate. However, once installed, deputyships usually last several years until the child reaches the age of majority at 18 years and the mandate ends automatically (cf. Voll 2008, p. 127 f.). A lack of regular termination before the age of majority also affects cases where the child's situation has improved and it may not necessarily need support any more (cf. Jud et al. 2011). In a decision under uncertainty, keeping a case within the system may appear to the decision-maker as the less risky thing do: If the situation should worsen again, the child is still monitored. Furthermore, the termination of a mandate is associated with negative

[10] See the federal parliament's webpage on the progress of the debate (https://www.parlament.ch/de/ratsbetrieb/suche-curia-vista/geschaeft?AffairId=20150033).

incentives related to workload: Terminating the mandate means extra work for the deputy and ultimately his/her terminated deputyship will be replaced by a newly enacted one that brings along even more work (cf. Voll 2008, pp. 128–130). This is a challenge in a system where deputies often are responsible for 100 cases per 100% employment (cf. Jud and Fegert 2014), and relatively easy cases will allow the field workers to spend more time on the most difficult cases.

11.2.4 Challenges

The constantly high workload for frontline workers in public child protection is a huge source of frustration for professionals. Other challenges involve increasing the degree of standardization and comparability of risk assessment across regions and cantons. Currently, procedures for risk assessment in an individual organization are usually idiosyncratic, standardized tools are hardly ever used. This embodies the danger of handling cases with similar problems and contexts differently, not guaranteeing equality before the law. To bridge this gap, schools of social work have developed tools and approaches for an improved quality in risk assessment (e.g. Biesel et al. 2017; Hauri et al. 2016). Further issues in professionalization of public child protection in Switzerland are achieving interdisciplinarity for decision-making on child protection orders (sub-section, Child protection authorities and mandated services).

For the subjects of Swiss public child protection, the degree of children's participation in decision-making proceedings has been criticized by the Committee on the Rights of the Child (UN Committee on the Rights of the Child 2015). Even infants and toddlers have ways to articulate their wishes, interests, and feelings. Members of CPAs lack training in adequately including the very young. Language barriers are, however, not an issue with school-aged children. Still, studies show a relatively high age-threshold for participation in the decision-making process in Switzerland (Mitrovic et al. 2017): In a survey among professionals in CPAs, only 74% of respondents would have involved a 6-year old, healthy child in a vignette on a decision on out-of-home care. To counter the lack of children's participation, the newly developed professional approaches to risk assessment in Swiss child protection include parts that promote the participation of children (e.g. Biesel et al. 2017, p. 23, 175 f.; Hauri et al. 2016, p. 624 f.).

While the substantial structural and professional changes by the 2013 newly installed national legislation on child and adult protection has been "critically acclaimed" by experts and frontline workers in child protection as a milestone of increasing professionalization in serving the best interest of the child, there has been public resistance. Conservative and right-wing politicians primarily in the German-speaking part of Switzerland seek to overturn the legislative changes and return to a model of lay member authorities for municipalities.[11] Negative media coverage has

[11] A committee is preparing a federal popular initiative that may lead to a national vote on the topic, see http://stopp-der-kesb-willkuer.ch/Volksinitiative/

led to a vilification of authorities and a denial of the authorities' common sense – a topic that is also common in discourses on other national child protection systems (e.g. Ayre 2001). A response to negative media coverage and the marred image of CPAs has been the installation of an ombudsperson for people involved in the processes of establishing a child protection order.[12] The installation of the ombudsperson will be evaluated. Not uncommon for Switzerland, this ombudsperson is not financed by the state, but by a private initiative.

11.3 Prosecuting Child Maltreatment Offenses

The legislative basis for criminally liable violence against children has been introduced in the sub-section, Legislative framework for child protection in Switzerland. Agencies responsible for holding perpetrators criminally liable have to investigate and substantiate an allegation. As they are focused on the perpetrator, the Victims of Crimes Act (VCA) requires penal authorities to forward the contact information of victims of criminal offences to agencies providing aid. These agencies then have the obligation to contact the victim and offer help and counseling free of charge. As their services are provided on a voluntary basis, details on victim aid agencies are discussed below (cf. sub-section Victim aid agencies).

11.3.1 Penal Agencies

In severe cases of child maltreatment, prosecution and conviction of the perpetrator(s) can be a part of protecting the child from further harm. This goal is accompanied by the societal or individual need for dispensing justice and convicting felonies. Penal authorities handling cases of criminally liable child maltreatment include the police forces, the criminal courts and the agencies of prosecution, with specialized juvenile courts and juvenile prosecution organizations to enforce juvenile criminal law (see Table 11.2 for an overview).

Processes and tasks in prosecuting violence against children are distributed on different agencies and organizations. First in time is the police. Officers investigate potential crimes and have to take all means necessary to avoid an obscuration of the violent acts. For an adequate interaction with victimized children, several of the cantonally organized police corps have specialized child protection units. Investigating offenses is not the only police task associated with protecting children from further harm. The police are also bound to intervene in cases of imminent danger to life and health of a child. In several cantons, police forces have, for example, the right to temporarily enact an eviction order against violent spouses (e.g. Art. 43 ff. Polizeigesetz SG). This intervention not only prevents children from witness-

[12] See http://kescha.ch/ for details.

Table 11.2 Penal agencies in Switzerland

Police	Responsible for investigating perpetrators of criminally liable violence against children and protecting children from further harm through preventive tasks. Some cantons and large cities have police units specialized against child maltreatment.
Agencies of (juvenile) prosecution	Although part of the investigation in criminal cases lies with the police, public prosecutor's offices have the jurisdiction over the case and have to decide whether there is enough evidence to bring charges. Young offenders between the ages of 10–18 years are subject to juvenile criminal law that prioritizes protection and education over punishment. Apart from the age of the offender, juvenile prosecution agencies fulfill the same functions as other agencies of prosecution.
Criminal courts	The judges at criminal courts are responsible for sentencing offenders.
Victim aid agencies	Victims of crimes have a legal right to voluntarily get support free-of-charge. Note that although these agencies are associated with the SCrimC, through the voluntariness of their support they are discussed in sub-section, victim aid agencies.

ing violence, but reduces the likelihood for direct violence against children (e.g. Chang et al. 2008). Unlike for prosecution, the preventive police tasks are subject to discretion.

Although the police are responsible for an essential part of the investigation in criminal cases, the public prosecutor's offices have jurisdiction over the case and have to decide whether there is enough evidence to bring charges or if the case must be closed for lack of evidence. The public prosecutor's offices are not only responsible for investigating onerous but also exonerating evidence about the (potential) perpetrator. Once the public prosecutor has brought charges, a criminal court will be responsible for deciding on a conviction and the severity of the sentence. During a criminal proceeding, victims might be confronted with yet more professionals and functions, including criminal defense lawyers, forensic experts etc.

11.3.2 Reporting Child Maltreatment Offenses

To avoid disruptions of supporting relationships between an allegedly victimized child and a professional, there is no mandatory reporting legislation for professionals towards penal authorities. On the other hand, also professionals in a legally privileged client-professional relationship are allowed to report crimes against children, e.g. a sexual act with a minor, severe physical violence or gross neglect. Legislation on the cantonal level might be more strict and include mandatory reporting of sexual offenses against children (e.g. Einführungsgesetz zur Schweizerischen Straf- und Jugendstrafprozessordnung St. Gallen, 962.1). Once reported, penal authorities have to prosecute crimes against children ex officio (Art. 7 Swiss Criminal Procedure Code (SCPC)).

Sexual victimization of children is considered an especially horrendous crime by Swiss society. In a 2008 federal popular initiative citizens voted for an annulment of the time limit to prosecute sexual or pornography offenses involving prepubescent children (Art. 123b Swiss Federal Constitution).

11.3.3 Challenges

To convict perpetrators of sexual abuse or other forms of violence against children, adequate proof is needed. This regularly includes getting painful details on the crimes through interrogating the child. To avoid secondary traumatization, victimized children are generally not confronted with the perpetrator and interrogated once with a person specialized on child development present (Art. 154(4) SCPC). Interrogations with victimized children are videotaped for use in court (Art. 154(4) SCPC). Child-friendly and standardized methods of interrogation have been developed and improved. They are, however, not applied nationwide.

Police officers are regularly called to interfere in situations of intimate partner violence. While the possibility to enact a temporary eviction order equips the police with a tool to deal with the immediate fallout of the situation encountered, a follow-up for children as direct or indirect victims of domestic violence is not secured. Although Art. 443 SCivC mandates police officers to report children in need of support to the CPA, and many police corps routinely send the rapport to CPAs if children have been present at interventions on domestic violence, this procedure is not yet universal.

11.4 Child Protection in the Educational, Health, and Social Sector

Various organizations offer help and support to children and families with difficulties. Some public and private bodies have established specialized agencies supporting children affected by sexual abuse, maltreatment or neglect. To guarantee a better overview on the highly complex network of organizations in and around the Swiss child protection system(s), the next sub-sections focus on these agencies specialized on supporting victimized children. To complete the picture; however, it also briefly addresses sentinels in the educational, health and social sector.

For school-aged children, schools are usually the one environment in which children spend most of their time, beside their families. Teachers might be highly trusted caregivers in a child's life. The proximity to children is one of the factors that make professionals in schools and school services important sentinels for alleged child maltreatment or other forms of endangerment to child wellbeing. In recent years, school social work, usually provided locally in schools, have become highly prevalent. Studies have found that about 80% of schools have access to school social work in Switzerland (e.g. Jud 2012). School social workers provide a range of preventive tasks, psychosocial counseling and other interventions. Through their school-based offices, the threshold for pupils to get support is low. In Switzerland, schools psychologists and agencies for school psychology are also highly prevalent. Contrary to school social workers, they are usually located at a regional level and primarily responsible for problems related to school performance.

The health and mental health sector assemble a variety of professionals (pediatricians, psychiatrists and psychotherapists, gynecologists, physicians, nurses, etc.) that are both sentinels of alleged child maltreatment and a source of support and care. An important opportunity for screening in pediatric practice are the 15 recommended check-ups at the ages of 1 week, 1 month, 2 months, 4 months, 6 months, 9 months, 1 year, 1,5 years, 2 years, 3 years, 4 years, 6 years, 10 years, 12 years and 14 years (Ambühl et al. 2011). The checklists for these check-ups include indicators for potential child maltreatment; however, only check-ups for preschoolers are paid through the mandatory health insurance (Baumann 2010). Through their follow-up care after birth, midwives are another important sentinel for (risk for future) child maltreatment. Up to 16 visits until 56 days after birth are paid through health insurances (cf. Art. 29 Swiss Federal Act on Health Insurance). So the midwives are able to observe the baby, its mother and the premises independent of the family's socio-economic status.

The state is not only responsible for public child protection; in the child welfare sector it also provides voluntary support free-of-charge for children and families who seek it. This orientation, prevalent in continental Europe, has been labeled child and family services-oriented by Gilbert (1997, 2012). Triggers for seeking voluntary support through child welfare services might range from toddlers' psychomotor development to school performance and conflicts with adolescents. While providing support, child welfare workers sometimes identify situations of child maltreatment, with a risk assessment and potentially a child protection order and deputyship to follow. Frequently, general social services provide both voluntary support for children and families in need, risk assessment in cases of alleged child maltreatment and mandated services on the basis of a child protection order. This means that a child and its family might receive the full complement of services from the same organization. The social sector also contains a multitude of sentinels of alleged child maltreatment, including professionals in out-of-home care, church social welfare and others. While this introductory overview discussed professionals with a more generalist approach within their sector, the following sections will discuss agencies in the health and social sector specialized in protecting and supporting victimized children.

11.4.1 Interdisciplinary Child Protection Teams

Soon after Henry Kempe, pioneer of medical child protection, founded one of the first multidisciplinary child protection teams (CPT) in Denver, its first equivalent was established in 1969 at the University Children's Hospital Zurich (Lips 2013).

Since then, CPTs have been established in a majority of Swiss children's hospitals. The teams bring together professionals of different disciplines, for example, pediatricians, psychiatrists, psychologists, pediatric surgeons, social workers, and nurses. Together, the CPT evaluates the risk of child maltreatment in internally[13] referred cases. The members of the clinical CPT will substantiate the maltreatment, judge its severity, decide on when to confront the parents with the allegation, determine the services needed and decide if a report to the CPA or a criminal complaint will be made. See the section on National administrative datasets for the caseload of clinical CPTs in Switzerland.

Besides the clinical CPTs, many cantons have established regional or cantonal child protection teams (cf. Krüger and Niehaus 2010). Unlike the clinical CPTs, they support professionals in the field that are confronted with situations of alleged child maltreatment and try to help them find the best solution to support the victimized child. While their interdisciplinary assembly does usually not contain pediatric surgeons or nurses, it will often include legal professionals and police officers.

11.4.2 Private Foundations and Hotlines

Private foundations handle a sizeable caseload of alleged situations of child sexual victimization in Switzerland. These foundations are usually located in urban centers and provide help often both on the internet, via telephone or locally by psychosocial counseling or psychotherapeutic care.

Unlike in neighboring Germany (e.g. Jud and Fegert 2015), Switzerland does not have a national hotline on child sexual abuse or other forms of child maltreatment. The well-established national hotline of the Pro Juventute foundation covers all types of situations that younger citizens might be troubled by or concerned with from breaking-ups, to pocket money and smoking pot. Through their support of youth, they sometimes encounter situations of child maltreatment. In this case, they will triage the situation and try to connect the calling child with local offers of support and protection.

11.4.3 Victim Aid Agencies

As introduced previously (see Table 11.2), victims of crimes are entitled to support free-of-charge (Art. 9(1) VCA). Private or semi-private agencies as described in the two previous sections might be recognized as victim aid agencies and will be able to fund a part of the victim's support through federal money. If such agencies are absent in a community, cantons are obliged to install a public victim aid agency.

[13] Some CPTs like the one at University Children's Hospital in Zurich also evaluate externally referred cases.

The VCA defines a victim as a person who has experienced a violation of his/her psychological, physical or sexual integrity through a crime (Art. 1(1) VCA). The definition applies independent of the fact whether a perpetrator has been investigated or not, whether a perpetrator has been found guilty or not and whether a perpetrator has been acting intentionally or negligently (Art. 1(3) VCA). Crimes that qualify as breaching a child's integrity are:

- offenses against life and health (homicide, bodily harm, assault, etc.),
- offenses against individual liberty (coercion, deprivation of liberty, etc.), and
- sexual crimes (e.g. Art. 187 SCrimC).

The VCA, however, encompasses not only victims of violence but also victims of traffic offenses. Support provided based on the VCA may include psychosocial counseling on a short-, mid- or long-term basis, legal counseling as well as financial support (Art. 2 VCA). If necessary, the victim is referred to psychiatric or psychotherapeutic care. Financial support may be provided as financial emergency aid but may also cover loss of income as a consequence of victimization. Finally, the victim aid agencies can provide financial compensation in the sense of a symbolic recognition for the harm suffered (Art. 22 f. VCA).

Not only are victims entitled to receive supportive services but these services are also available to victims' relatives such as parents. Furthermore, adult survivors of crimes in their childhood are also entitled to receive support. Importantly, services are, however, only provided if the victim wishes to receive them (Art. 2 VCA).

11.4.4 Challenges

Challenges in the educational, health and social sector are plentiful; this section only addresses a few relevant to violence against children. While the number of regional, non-clinical CPTs had at first increased largely in the 1990s and early years of the new millennium, their numbers have now decreased. In the canton of Zurich, Switzerland's most populous canton, the majority of the regional CPTs handle only relatively few cases. The administrators therefore are considering changing the structure and dissolving the regional CPTs (Isabella Feusi, head of child welfare in the canton of Zurich, personal communication, August 24, 2016). Some clinical CPTs, on the other hand, have large caseloads but struggle with improving their risk assessment. While standardized approaches have often been lacking so far, some CPTs are now trying to establish reliable ways of assessing risk by applying operationalized measures of maltreatment severity.

Private foundations focusing on supporting maltreated children struggle with accessibility for victims as they are primarily located in urban centers of larger cantons. Rural communities in small cantons do not have the same opportunity to access this support. Furthermore, the private foundations often focus solely on child sexual abuse. This is clearly an important task, however, the more prevalent forms of child maltreatment, especially child neglect, do not get the same attention.

11.5 On the Incidence of Child Maltreatment in Switzerland

A major issue in Swiss child protection is the lack of solid nationally representative data on the size of the problem and on how many maltreated children get access to support and protection in different sectors. Switzerland lacks uniform and therefore comparable data on the institutionally identified and supported victims of child maltreatment. Without uniform data, we do not know how well our system works and if some of the most vulnerable, for example, children with disabilities, are identified and served. This gap has been criticized repeatedly in the Committee on the Rights of the Child's response to Switzerland's state reports (UN Committee on the Rights of the Child 2002, 2015). In the absence of a uniform national data collection program, there are some administrative data sets described below.

11.5.1 National Administrative Data Sets

For over two decades, the national Association of Child and Adult Protection Authorities annually collected and published the numbers of newly enacted and ongoing child protection orders (e.g. Konferenz der Kantone für Kindes- und Erwachsenenschutz (KOKES) 2011, 2014). In the 1990s and early 2000s only aggregated data were collected, often in an incomplete or inaccurate way (Estermann 2013). Therefore Estermann (2013) concluded a massive underestimation of the actual number of child protection orders until 2003 and assumes random fluctuations in later years. Together with new child and adult protection legislation, data collection has been adapted in 2013 to also include the reasons for enacting a child protection order – e.g. types of child maltreatment. Unfortunately, the categories of reasons for a child protection order lack a definition and many authorities are reluctant to document them, especially authorities in the French-speaking part of Switzerland. So far, no results concerning the incidence of child maltreatment by the type of child protection orders have been published.

In 2010, the Federal Office of Statistics (Bundesamt für Statistik (BFS) 2010) introduced the annual report of Police Criminal Statistics, a uniform data collection program on registered offenses throughout Switzerland. Out of the 7329 sexual offenses in 2016 (Bundesamt für Statistik (BFS) 2017b), 17% (n = 1230) were sexual acts with children (Art. 187 SCrimC), and 359 of these sexual crimes took place in the context of domestic violence (Bundesamt für Statistik (BFS) 2017b). Besides data on the frequency of offenses, the Federal Office of Statistics (Bundesamt für Statistik (BFS) 2011) also counts the frequency of counseling by victim aid organizations. The variables cover the type of offense, demographics of the victim and variables related to counselling. In 2016 (Bundesamt für Statistik (BFS) 2017a), 4271 counseling sessions have been provided on the basis of Art 187 SCrimC, sexual acts with children. For other types of violence, publications do not include information on child victims. Both data sets – the Police Criminal Statistics and the

Victim Aid Statistics – are restricted to offenses, and, therefore, generally to severe forms of child maltreatment. Further limits include that both data sets record cases and not individuals.

Clinical CPTs at hospitals are another source for nationwide data on child maltreatment (e.g. Wopmann 2016, 2017). They annually collect a few variables related to their caseload of allegedly maltreated children. An advantage compared to other data sets is their collection of data on the type of maltreatment. However, there are also some caveats: The data set is restricted to one specific type of agency and not all clinical CPTs participate.

11.5.2 Optimus Study Switzerland

The Optimus Study Switzerland has been a response to the lack of shared data on the prevelance of violence against children. It now contains three cycles. The first cycle aimed both at the prevalence of child sexual victimization through a population survey (Mohler-Kuo et al. 2014) and estimating the reported incidence of child sexual victimization via an agency survey (Maier et al. 2013). For the latter, a total of 2354 child protection agencies and sentinels were identified in 2010. Out of these, a stratified random sample of 1267 agencies was drawn and contacted. The 350 participating agencies (27.6%) collected a total of 911 newly reported cases of child sexual victimization for a period of 6 months (March 2010–August 2010). Weighted estimates indicate that 2.68 children per 1000 children in the population are reported to agencies based on an alleged incident of child sexual abuse (Maier et al. 2013). Comparable to findings in the population survey, the number of female victims and peer perpetrators was greater (Averdijk et al. 2012; Maier et al. 2013; Mohler-Kuo et al. 2014).

The first Optimus Study cycle had major limitations. First, for a child protection system, a focus on child sexual victimization is an isolated view. The different agencies and organizations not only intervene when sexual violence has been allegedly perpetrated but also when other forms of violence or neglect are present. Multiple victimization is not the exception but rather the rule (e.g. Dong et al. 2004; Romano et al. 2011). Furthermore, the first cycle's agency survey struggled with low participation rates, especially in the French and Italian parts of Switzerland (cf. Maier et al. 2013). The research consortium's lack of familiarity with certain sectors and local contexts (particularly the French and Italian parts of Switzerland) and consequently lacking trust between researchers and practice contributed to low participation. Furthermore, agencies' and frontline workers' time constraints were also a limiting factor. A financial incentive for completing a lengthy questionnaire for each case did not outweigh the time constraints. A second cycle was initiated aimed at knowledge mobilization in the field, and focused on building mutual trust between researchers and practice. The newly built research team was both rooted in the German- and French-speaking parts of Switzerland, members were familiar with different sectors and used well-known experts from different disciplines and regions as facilitators for entering into contact with providers. Frontline workers, administrators and policy-makers should not view an agency survey and a potential future national surveillance of agency response to child maltreatment as a bureaucratic nuisance, but a tool to improve the network of services for the best interests of children. Stakeholders in Swiss child protection were invited to participate in the process of developing a shared definition and operationalization of different types of child maltreatment. They also supported the study team in developing a questionnaire for a second wave of data collection.

The practice-validated questionnaire was one pillar of establishing high participation in Optimus Study's third cycle and second wave of data collection. Its study design contained more pillars: It focused on all the different forms child victimization. Moreover, workload for participation was kept at a minimum: Agencies were asked to upload excerpts of their administrative data to the study data set. Through a mapping process, the various sets of administrative data were standardized and transferred to match the study variables' operationalization. If necessary, agencies were then able to complete missing data from their case files. The study team also upheld the mutual exchange between research and practice initiated in cycle 2; invitations to participate were accompanied by several support letters from stakeholders at the national and regional level. The different factors led to an excellent rate of participation: Data are available from 83% of the contacted agencies. They are being analyzed as this chapter is being published. Hopefully, this survey will mark a milestone on Switzerland's way to national surveillance data in child protection.

11.6 Strengths, Limitations and Challenges

This section adds to and summarizes the strengths, limitations and challenges that apply to the totality of agencies and professionals that comprise Switzerland's child protection system. Switzerland has an extensive network of agencies and professionals involved in tackling children's problems and protecting them from violence (cf. sub-section, Managing a diversity on a small scale). The advantage of a well-established system of available services comes with a caveat: Children and their caregivers may experience many professionals who they may perceive as interfering in their life. To illustrate, in a file analysis of 164 cases with a deputyship, a median of 15 professionals was involved per case, a maximum of 68 professionals (Jud 2008, p. 52). Coordination of the roles of different professionals, their functions and affiliation is a critical endeavor when a child and its family have simultaneously to struggle with the consequences of violence. It is difficult for professionals to coordinate services in a way that children and their families will benefit from instead of being overburdened (cf. Sanders et al. 2013). While agencies in child protection and child welfare readily apply the label of case manager to their frontline workers, their function may not correspond entirely to the methodical approach of case management (e.g. Löcherbach and Mennemann 2009).

Another major issue in Swiss child protection, and a precondition for reliable and shared data on child maltreatment across sectors, is the lack of shared definitions on types of child maltreatment or endangerments to child wellbeing. Many organizations and teams lack explicit definitions of child maltreatment and apply definitions they perceive as implicitly shared by co-workers and members of their team. The Optimus Study implied and advocated an exchange between public child protection, the penal sector and specialized agencies in the health and social sector (cf. sub-section, Optimus Study Switzerland). Continuing and upscaling this exchange will promote discourse on shared definitions of different types of child victimization. A combined symposium for practitioners from different sectors and backgrounds might mark a further step in producing and disseminating child protection knowledge outside of disciplinary silos.

A vast majority of professionals in the different sectors has an adequate degree for their function. An analysis of Zurich's general social service employees showed, for example, that almost 98% of frontline workers had a degree in social work (Jud and Fegert 2014). Some sentinels of alleged situations of child maltreatment, however, only rarely attend programs of continuing education on child maltreatment or child protection (for principals, see Jud and Gartenhauser, 2015). Although almost every professional in Swiss child protection or child welfare has an academic degree, this does not necessarily trickle down to applying evidence-informed decisions. While evidence-informed risk assessment is on the rise, presently there is only limited understanding regarding the use of evidence-informed interventions in the Swiss child protection system (or contexts similar to the Swiss child protection system) is available (e.g. Jud and Gartenhauser 2014).

Finally, we aim at highlighting the challenge of including children and families in the proceedings that are interfering in their lives. While listening to the perspectives of children and families is primarily an ethical requirement for agencies in child protection, future research might provide evidence on a positive impact of participatory approaches on a children's developmental outcome. Furthermore, a recent study dismisses the fear of certain groups that hearing children might be highly stressful for them (Karle and Gathmann 2016). Improving the participation of children in proceedings affecting their lives also includes the development of adequate methods to hear younger children and children with disabilities. Generally, listening to the perspectives of children and families in the child protection system embodies the opportunity to learn from them on how to improve policies, procedures and processes.

11.7 Conclusion

While Switzerland invests a sizeable amount of resources in child protection and child welfare, there is still potential to allocate further resources to a vulnerable group of citizens if we bear in mind that Switzerland is one of the wealthiest economies in the world.[14] The Committee on the Rights of the Child (UN Committee on the Rights of the Child 2015) recommends that Switzerland establish a budgeting process which adequately takes into account children's needs at the federal and cantonal levels. This includes development of a tracking system of allocations and monitoring of the efficacy, adequacy, and equitability of the distribution of resources.

A final note shall be reserved for advocating the abolishment of corporal punishment. It was briefly abolished in Switzerland between 1874 and 1897, however, corporal punishment remained legal thereafter. To date, Switzerland still does not ban corporal punishment; it is still not considered as physical violence if it does not exceed the level generally accepted by society (cf. UN Committee on the Rights of the Child 2015). While law prohibits adults from hitting other adults and animals for punishment, parents are still allowed to chastise their offspring. Ethical reasons, a decline of corporal punishment after implementation of a ban (Zolotor and Puzia 2010), and negative outcomes of punitive parenting practices (Tang and Davis-Kean 2015) support a call for a legal ban of corporal punishment – now and for all.

References

Ambühl, D., Bächler, A., Baumann, T., Jenni, O., Leuchter Ha-Vinh, R., Lips, U., Pizzagalli, C., Pellaud, N., & Zollinger, B. (2011). *Checklisten für die Vorsorgeuntersuchungen nach den Empfehlungen der Schweizerischen Gesellschaft für Pädiatrie* (4th rev. ed.). Fribourg: Swiss Society of Paediatrics.

Averdijk, M., Müller-Johnson, K., & Eisner, M. (2012). *Sexual victimization of children and adolescents in Switzerland: Final report for the UBS optimus Foundation*. Zürich: UBS Optimus Foundation.

Ayre, P. (2001). Child protection and the media: Lessons from the last three decades. *British Journal of Social Work, 31*, 887–901.

Baumann, T. (2010). Neue Checklisten der SGP für die Vorsorgeuntersuchungen. *Paediatrica, 21*(3), 39–40.

Biesel, K., Fellmann, L., Müller, B., Schär, C., & Schnurr, S. (2017). *Prozessmanual: Dialogisch-systemische Kindeswohlabklärung*. Bern: Haupt.

Bundesamt für Statistik (BFS). (2010). *Polizeiliche Kriminalstatistik (PKS): Jahresbericht 2009*. Neuchâtel: BFS.

Bundesamt für Statistik (BFS). (2011). *Polizeiliche Kriminalstatistik (PKS): Jahresbericht 2010*. Neuchâtel: BFS.

Bundesamt für Statistik (BFS). (2017a). *Opferberatungen nach Straftat 2000–2016*. Neuchâtel: BFS.

Bundesamt für Statistik (BFS). (2017b). *Polizeiliche Kriminalstatistik (PKS): Jahresbericht 2016*. Neuchâtel: BFS.

Chang, J. J., Theodore, A. D., Martin, S. L., & Runyan, D. K. (2008). Psychological abuse between parents: Associations with child maltreatment from a population-based sample. *Child Abuse & Neglect, 32*(8), 819–829.

[14] As for example seen in total central government debt in reference to the GDP (see, http://stats.oecd.org/index.aspx?DataSetCode=PDB_LV) or other OECD statistics.

Dong, M., Anda, R. F., Felitti, V. J., Dube, S. R., Williamson, D. F., Thompson, T. J., Loo, C. M., & Giles, W. H. (2004). The interrelatedness of multiple forms of childhood abuse, neglect, and household dysfunction. *Child Abuse & Neglect, 28*(7), 771–784.

Estermann, J. (2013). Reanalyse der Fallzahlen im Erwachsenenschutzrecht. *Zeitschrift für Kindes- und Erwachsenenschutz, 68*(2), 71–78.

Federal Statistical Office. (2016a). *Permanent resident population in private households by canton and household size*. Retrieved July 24, 2017, from https://www.bfs.admin.ch/bfs/en/home/statistics/population.assetdetail.1362812.html

Federal Statistical Office. (2016b). *Permanent resident population in private households by commune and household size*. Retrieved July 24, 2017, from https://www.bfs.admin.ch/bfs/en/home/statistics/population.assetdetail.1362772.html

Federal Statistical Office. (2017). *Permanent resident population, 2016*. Retrieved July 24, 2017, from https://www.bfs.admin.ch/bfs/en/home/statistics/population.html

Gilbert, N. (1997). *Combatting child abuse: International perspectives and trends*. New York: Oxford University Press.

Gilbert, N. (2012). A comparative study of child welfare systems: Abstract orientations and concrete results. *Children and Youth Services Review, 34*(3), 532–536. https://doi.org/10.1016/j.childyouth.2011.10.014.

Hauri, A., Jud, A., Lätsch, D., & Rosch, D. (2016). Anhang I: Das Berner und Luzerner Abklärungsinstrument zum Kindesschutz. In D. Rosch, C. Fountoulakis, & C. Heck (Eds.), *Handbuch Kindes- und Erwachsenenschutz: Recht und Methodik für Fachleute* (pp. 590–627). Bern: Haupt.

Jud, A. (2008). Kindesschutzmassnahmen und beteiligte Professionelle. In P. Voll, A. Jud, E. Mey, C. Häfeli, & M. Stettler (Eds.), *Zivilrechtlicher Kindesschutz: Akteure, Prozesse, Strukturen* (pp. 51–64). Luzern: Interact.

Jud, A. (2012). Zwischen Schule und Kindesschutz: Zur Rolle der Schulsozialarbeit bei Gefährdungsmeldungen durch Schulen. *Sozial Aktuell, 44*(4), 30–31.

Jud, A. (2013). Überlegungen zur Definition und Erfassung von Gefährdungssituationen im Kindesschutz. In D. Rosch & D. Wider (Eds.), *Zwischen Schutz und Selbstbestimmung* (pp. 49–65). Bern: Stämpfli.

Jud, A., & Fegert, J. M. (2014). Vom Umgang mit Risiken und Fehlern: Evaluation der Leistungserbringung in der KJH der Stadt Zürich. *Jugendamt, 87*(7–8), 358–362.

Jud, A., & Fegert, J. M. (2015). Kinderschutz und Vernetzung im Bereich Prävention von und Intervention bei sexuellem Kindesmissbrauch. In J. M. Fegert, U. Hoffmann, E. König, J. Niehues, & H. Liebhardt (Eds.), *Sexueller Missbrauch von Kindern und Jugendlichen* (pp. 63–73). Berlin: Springer.

Jud, A., & Gartenhauser, R. (2014). Literatur-Review zur Wirksamkeit eingesetzter Methoden in der Kinder- und Jugendhilfe. In A. Jud, J. M. Fegert, & M. Schlup (Eds.), *Kinder- und Jugendhilfe im Trend – Veränderungen im Umfeld der Kinder- und Jugendhilfe am Beispiel der Stadt Zürich* (pp. 109–120). Luzern: Interact.

Jud, A., & Gartenhauser, R. (2015). The impact of socio-economic status and caregiver cooperation on school professionals' reports to child protection services in Switzerland. *European Journal of Social Work, 18*(3), 340–353. https://doi.org/10.1080/13691457.2014.933093.

Jud, A., & Hauri, A. (2016). Akteure und Institutionen im Schweizer Kinderschutz und den Frühen Hilfen. In J. M. Fegert & U. Ziegenhain (Eds.), *Frühe Hilfen und frühe Interventionen im Kinderschutz [E-Learning-Kurs]*. Ulm: Universitätsklinikum Ulm.

Jud, A., Perrig-Chiello, P., & Voll, P. (2011). Less effort in worsening child protection cases? The time-course of intensity of services. *Children and Youth Services Review, 33*, 2027–2033.

Jud, A., Fluke, J., Alink, L. R., Allan, K., Fallon, B., Kindler, H., Lee, B. J., Mansell, J., & van Puyenbroek, H. (2013). On the nature and scope of reported child maltreatment in high-income countries: Opportunities for improving the evidence base. *Paediatrics and International Child Health, 33*(4), 207–215. https://doi.org/10.1179/2046905513Y.0000000092.

Karle, M., & Gathmann, S. (2016). The state of the art of child hearings in Germany. Results of a nationwide representative study in German courts. *Family Court Review, 54*(2), 167–185. https://doi.org/10.1111/fcre.12212.

Konferenz der kantonalen Vormundschaftsbehörden (VBK). (2008). Kindes- und Erwachsenenschutzbehörde als Fachbehörde (Analyse und Modellvorschläge). *Zeitschrift für Vormundschaftswesen, 63*(2), 63–128.

Konferenz der Kantone für Kindes- und Erwachsenenschutz (KOKES). (2014). Schweizerische Statistik Kindesschutzmassnahmen: Jahresvergleich 2003–2012. *Zeitschrift für Kindes- und Erwachsenenschutz, 69*(1), 92.

Konferenz der Kantone für Kindes- und Erwachsenenschutz (KOKES). (2017). KESB: Organisation in den Kantonen (Stand: 1.1.2017). *Zeitschrift für Kindes- und Erwachsenenschutz, 72*(1), 5.

Konferenz für Kindes- und Erwachsenenschutz (KOKES). (2011). Schweizerische Statistik der Massnahmen im Kindes- und Erwachsenenschutz 2010 (alle Kantone). *Zeitschrift für Kindes- und Erwachsenenschutz, 66*(5), 414–421.

Konferenz für Kindes- und Erwachsenenschutz (KOKES). (2016). KOKES-Statistik 2015: Anzahl Personen mit Schutzmassnahmen. *Zeitschrift für Kindes- und Erwachsenenschutz, 71*(4), 313–315.

Krüger, P., & Niehaus, S. (2010). Länderbericht deutschsprachige Schweiz. In E. Dawid, J. Elz, & B. Haller (Eds.), *Kooperation von öffentlicher Jugendhilfe und Strafjustiz bei Sexualdelikten gegen Kinder* (pp. 138–220). Wiesbaden: KrimZ.

Ladner, A. (2016). Administrative reforms in Swiss municipalities over the last twenty years – The end of new public management? *Lex Localis - Journal of Local Self-Government, 14*(2), 185–207.

Lips, U. (2013). Kinderschutz und Medizin. In D. Rosch & D. Wider (Eds.), *Zwischen Schutz und Selbstbestimmung* (pp. 105–118). Bern: Stämpfli.

Löcherbach, P., Mennemann, H., & Hermsen, T. (2009). *Case Management in der Jugendhilfe*. München: Reinhardt.

Maier, T., Mohler-Kuo, M., Landolt, M. A., Schnyder, U., & Jud, A. (2013). The tip of the iceberg. Incidence of disclosed cases of child sexual abuse in Switzerland: Results from a nationwide agency survey. *International Journal of Public Health, 58*, 875–883. https://doi.org/10.1007/s00038-013-0498-6.

Mitrovic, T., Jud, A., & Rosch, D. (2017). Praxis der KESB zum Einbezug von verwandten und nicht verwandten Personen bei Kindesplatzierungen: Ergebnisse einer schweizweiten Online-Befragung. *Zeitschrift für Kindes- und Erwachsenenschutz, 72*(3), 173–191.

Mohler-Kuo, M., Landolt, M. A., Maier, T., Meidert, U., Schönbucher, V., & Schnyder, U. (2014). Child sexual abuse revisited: A population-based cross-sectional study among Swiss adolescents. *The Journal of Adolescent Health, 54*(3), 304–311 e301. https://doi.org/10.1016/j.jadohealth.2013.08.020.

Rieder, S., Bieri, O., Schwenkel, C., Hertig, V., & Amberg, H. (2016). *Evaluation Kindes- und Erwachsenenschutzrecht*. Luzern: Interface.

Romano, E., Bell, T., & Billette, J. M. (2011). Prevalence and correlates of multiple victimization in a nation-wide adolescent sample. *Child Abuse & Neglect, 35*(7), 468–479. https://doi.org/10.1016/j.chiabu.2011.03.005.

Rosch, D. (2012). Melderechte, Melde- und Mitwirkungspflichten, Amtshilfe: Die Zusammenarbeit mit der neuen Kindes- und Erwachsenenschutzbehörde. *Die Praxis des Familienrechts, 13*(4), 1020–1051.

Rosch, D., & Hauri, A. (2016). Zivilrechtlicher Kindesschutz. In D. Rosch, C. Fountoulakis, & C. Heck (Eds.), *Handbuch Kindes- und Erwachsenenschutz* (pp. 410–449). Bern: Haupt.

Sanders, J., Munford, R., Liebenberg, L., & Ungar, M. (2013). Multiple service use: The impact of consistency in service quality for vulnerable youth. *Child Abuse & Neglect, 38*(4), 687–697. https://doi.org/10.1016/j.chiabu.2013.10.024.

Schnurr, S. (2011). *Grundleistungen in Kinder- und Jugendhilfe*. Basel: Institut Kinder- und Jugendhilfe, Fachhochschule Nordwestschweiz.

Tang, S., & Davis-Kean, P. E. (2015). The association of punitive parenting practices and adolescent achievement. *Journal of Family Psychology, 29*(6), 873–883. https://doi.org/10.1037/fam0000137.

Trocmé, N., Akesson, B., & Jud, A. (2016). Responding to child maltreatment: A framework for mapping child protection agencies. *Child Indicators Research, 9*, 1029–1041. https://doi.org/10.1007/s12187-015-9362-y.

UN Committee on the Rights of the Child. (2002). *Concluding observations of the committee on the rights of the child: Switzerland.* New York: United Nations.

UN Committee on the Rights of the Child. (2015). *Concluding observations on the combined second to fourth periodic reports of Switzerland.* New York: United Nations.

Voll, P. (2008). Durchführung und Aufhebung von Massnahmen. In P. Voll, A. Jud, E. Mey, C. Häfeli, & M. Stettler (Eds.), *Zivilrechtlicher Kindesschutz: Akteure, Prozesse, Strukturen* (pp. 111–131). Luzern: Interact.

Wopmann, M. (2016). *Gleichbleibend hohe Anzahl von Fällen von Kindsmisshandlung an schweizerischen Kinderkliniken.* Baden: Schweizerische Gesellschaft für Pädiatrie, Fachgruppe Kinderschutz der schweizerischen Kinderkliniken.

Wopmann, M. (2017). *Erneute Zunahme der Fälle von Kindsmisshandlungen an Schweizerischen Kinderkliniken.* Baden: Schweizerische Gesellschaft für Pädiatrie, Fachgruppe Kinderschutz der schweizerischen Kinderkliniken.

Zolotor, A. J., & Puzia, M. E. (2010). Bans against corporal punishment: A systematic review of the Laws, changes in attitudes and behaviours. *Child Abuse Review, 19*(4), 229–247.

Andreas Jud, Ph.D., has a chair on child maltreatment epidemiology and trends at the University of Ulm, Germany, and is staff at Lucerne University of Applied Sciences and Arts, School of Social Work. He contributes for more than a decade to the growing empirical knowledge base on agency response to child maltreatment and heads several research projects on decision-making in child protection, e.g. on reporting alleged child maltreatment, standardized assessment, enacting child protection orders, etc. Moreover, he serves as an Associate Editor of "Child Abuse & Neglect", the leading academic journal in its field. An SNSF-sponsored scholarship at Montreal's McGill University launched his international career with conceptual and empirical output on different child protection systems. Both nationally and internationally, he is strongly advocating for an improved epidemiological data collection on legal, health and social services responses to child maltreatment.

René Knüsel, Ph.D., is the Director of the Observatory on Child Maltreatment at the University of Lausanne since 2009, where he teaches Social Policy and Social Problems. He became interested in issues surrounding child abuse when he taught social work courses at the University of Fribourg. Since then, he has been working in Lausanne and regularly organizes continuing education courses for various professionals and other stakeholders. In his research, he is particularly interested in how different professionals (such as doctors, nurses, and early childhood educators) approach the subject of child abuse and has published several articles on this subject. In the last years, he has been working to create conditions for the regular production of qualitative and quantitative data on child maltreatment in Switzerland.

MIX
Papier aus verantwortungsvollen Quellen
Paper from responsible sources
FSC® C105338
FSC
www.fsc.org

If you have any concerns about our products,
you can contact us on
ProductSafety@springernature.com

In case Publisher is established outside the EU,
the EU authorized representative is:
Springer Nature Customer Service Center GmbH
Europaplatz 3, 69115 Heidelberg, Germany

Printed by Libri Plureos GmbH
in Hamburg, Germany